Call Me American

CALL ME AMERICAN

A MEMOIR

Abdi Nor Iftin

WITH MAX ALEXANDER

ALFRED A. KNOPF NEW YORK 2018

THIS IS A BORZOI BOOK

PUBLISHED BY ALFRED A. KNOPF

Published in the United States by Alfred A. Knopf,
a division of Penguin Random House LLC, New York,
and distributed in Canada by Random House of Canada,
a division of Penguin Random House Canada Limited, Toronto.

www.aaknopf.com

In Chapters 15 and 16 some names of individuals
have been changed to protect their privacy.

Library of Congress Cataloguing-in-Publication Data
Names: Iftin, Abdi Nor, author. | Alexander, Max, 1957– Author.
Title: Call me American : a memoir /
by Abdi Nor Iftin with Max Alexander.
Description: First edition. | New York : Alfred A. Knopf, 2018. |
"This is a Borzoi Book."
Identifiers: LCCN 2017043213 | ISBN 9781524732196 (hardcover) |
ISBN 9781524732202 (ebook)
Subjects: LCSH: Iftin, Abdi Nor. | Somali Americans—Maine—Biography. |
Immigrants—Maine—Biography. | Muslims—Maine—Biography.
Classification: LCC CT275.I43 A3 2018 | DDC 305.893/540741—dc23
LC record available at https://lccn.loc.gov/2017043213

Jacket design by Kelly Blair
Text design by Soonyoung Kwon

Manufactured in the United States of America
First Edition

This book is for my proud nomad mother, who saved me. Mom, you nursed my bloody feet after I had walked for miles with you without shoes; you gave me hope with your stories of brave life in the bush; and when I rested my head on a graveyard full of kids of my age, you would not let me join them. Your strength kept me alive in the city of the dead. Now I am safe in America. So long as we both live, I will return that strength and support to you.

A mule that grazes with horses thinks it is a horse.

—SOMALI PROVERB

CONTENTS

Call Me American

1

Under the Neem Tree

I was born under a neem tree, probably in 1985. Neem trees grow everywhere in Somalia, with fragrant blossoms like lilacs and medicinal bitter sap that prevents sores. People everywhere in Somalia brush their teeth with those twigs. Their green fruit turns yellow and juicy, a great treat for the birds. The trees have small leaves, but the limbs spread wide and give shelter from the sun—a good place to have a baby. A good place to be born.

I was born into a culture where birthdays are not celebrated, or even recorded. This became a problem for me when I left Somalia and entered the world of documents and paperwork. My first birthday record was in Kenya at a refugee registration center. The officers there did not bother to ask me when I was born, because they know Somalis have no idea; the flood of Somali refugees coming into Kenya are always surprised by the question. The officers simply wrote down my birthday as January 1, 1985. To them, every Somali is born on New Year's Day. Arriving in America was different. Here the officials didn't want to make up "January 1." I had to come up with a birth date and stick with it for the rest of my life. It's a strange thing to choose your own birthday. Some people are born lucky, others born unlucky, but nobody gets to choose when he was born, or where. But there I was. I decided I should choose a date around the middle of the year, which would be equally close to whatever was my real birthday. And I wanted a number that was easy to remember. So I chose June 20, 1985.

My parents don't know the day of my birth, but my mom remembers it was very hot. The blazing sun had turned the streets of Mogadishu ash white and the rooms of our small block house into bread ovens. Mom was on her back under the shade of the neem tree, resting on a *jiimbaar,* a bed made of cow leather stretched over sticks. Our neighbor Maryan cooled Mom's head with a fan woven from straw, and cleaned the blood. The women of the neighborhood filled the house, curious to see if the baby would be a boy or a girl. They brought fragrant resins and incense like myrrh and *uunsi.* For me they brought *xildiid,* the root of a plant that is mixed with water to bathe and protect the baby. *Xildiid* is one of hundreds of therapeutic plants that grow in Somalia. You can smell the sweet flowers and pungent leaves on the trees and the low bushes that grow everywhere.

Somalia was once called the Land of the Perfumes; before the wars began, my country exported fragrant and medicinal plants all over the world. My mom remembers *somagale,* a seasonal plant that sprouts from the ground in the rainy season. She would uproot the plants, crush them, and apply the paste to any bleeding wounds. *Awrodhaye* was another plant she used to stop bleeding and prevent infections. Mom still believes in those traditional plants that cure everything. She believes knowledge of them has helped her survive anywhere. My mom worried I would not be as strong as her because people in the city don't know much about the plants and how to survive off the land. Today she asks me on her phone if any of those plants can be found in America. I have not seen them here, but I tell her I have learned other ways to survive.

While my mom was giving birth, the neighborhood women sat on the edges of the *jiimbaar* talking and laughing, happy to welcome a new baby. Somali culture dictated that my dad had to stay away from the house; he would stay at his friend Siciid's place for forty days, the amount of time a woman is supposed to remain chaste after labor. During that time she is called not by her name but rather *Umul,* which means "maternal."

The moment I appeared, Maryan ran down the street to break the good news to my dad that a boy was born (boys are much more appreciated than girls in Somalia). As the women who surrounded Mom ululated in joy, other female neighbors joined the party. My dad took a day off from work and partied with his friends, buying them qat leaves, a stimulant like strong coffee chewed by men in Arabia and the Horn of Africa. Qat is illegal in the U.S. and in much of Europe. He visited us, as a guest in his own house, at least twice during the day. Mom was still sleeping under the neem tree, near clay bowls and glass jars full of porridge and orange juice and the bottled soft drink Vimto, her favorite. Out of respect to my dad she covered her hair while he was there, looking down as she answered his questions. They would never kiss or hug in public. He stood tall and aloof from her bed, examining me, his second son, lying next to Mom.

The women perfumed the rooms of the house and swept the yard bent over, using a short broom. They came in and out. That same evening, Maryan walked in with ten men, all of them respected local sheikhs. They wore beaded necklaces, the longest string on the leader, and each sheikh kept, in his front pocket, a neem twig for brushing his teeth and a comb and small mirror for grooming his beard after meals. They circled the *jiimbaar* in the yard where I was lying next to Mom. Some women were cooking a big pot of camel meat; others were mixing a jar of camel milk with sugar and ice cubes from the store.

Camel meat and sweet milk together are called *duco,* a blessing for the newborn. For an hour the sheikhs blessed me, verse after verse, very loud, which makes the blessing greater. Afterward, they all sat on a mat on the ground, washed their hands in a dish of water, and feasted on the camel meat and milk. They must have been very hungry because my mom says by the time they were gone, the serving plate was nothing but bones. This blessing and feast meant I would grow better, be healthy and obedient to my parents. For my mom they left a bowlful of the blessed water called *tahliil.* The sheikhs bless the water by spitting in it; their spit contains prayers. Mom splashed the water on her body every day. She also splashed some on all corners of our house and drank some to prevent curses. Before I left Somalia for Kenya in 2011, two sheikhs had to spit in the water for me so I would stay safe in my travels. That was Mom's idea.

Soon after I was born, Mom went back to doing her housework, with me tied to her back so that she was there for me whenever I cried out for milk. She watched me crawl out of the shade of that same neem tree into the scorching heat of the sun, and she was there when I took my first steps on the hot dusty ground. At bedtime she told me Somali folktales and sang lullabies like "Huwaaya Huwaa": "Mommy is not here, she tiptoed away. She may be with the camel herders. Soon she will return with butter and camel milk." Mom and her stories were my universe.

My dad was working and didn't do much child care, which is normal in Somalia, except to pull out my loose baby teeth or when he did my circumcision. My older brother, Hassan, and I got circumcised on the same day, at the ages of four and three. Hassan was first. "Look at the airplane!" Dad said. Hassan looked up in the sky at the plane, and the sharp Topaz razor came down on his foreskin. Hassan did not even cry; he was always the bravest boy I ever met. When it was my turn, I realized what was coming and I cried, rolling on the ground. Everyone in the neighborhood came to watch the commotion. Two men held me tight to the ground as Dad used the other side of the razor on me. In a moment my foreskin was gone. "Now you are a man," Dad said.

Of course we were not men, we were still children, and we never strayed far from our mom. Mom likes to call herself the brave daughter of her brave parents. Her name is Madinah Ibrahim Moalim. She was named Madinah after the holy city in Saudi Arabia. Her parents loved that city; they loved Madinah like I love America. It was their biggest dream to see the place where the Prophet Muhammad is buried, but unfortunately they never got to see it. Mom stole the dream from them and always talked about Madinah and Mecca as the best places to be on Earth. It costs three thousand dollars to go to Saudi Arabia to perform the hajj, and my mom wants to do it before she dies. Growing up with a huge number of Somali exiles returning from Saudi Arabia, I never understood why my mom and her parents dreamed of living in a place where Somalis are unwelcome. It would be many years before I realized that Somalis are pretty much unwelcome everywhere, and dreams are all we have.

I may not know the day I was born, but at least I know where. Mom was born in the bush and has no idea where because her parents were always moving with the goats and camels. It must have been a little before Somalia got independence from the Italians in 1960. She never saw an Italian or British colonialist but remembers her parents talking about people with no skin that they had seen driving back and forth. Mom spent her toddler days on the hump of a camel, being fed with her mom's breast milk and camel milk. She says it does not matter how old she is, but she knows she is as old as her camel Daraanle, who was also born the day she was. With hundreds of camels, my mom's parents had a newborn animal almost every day. They didn't know how to count with numbers, but they named and marked every camel, goat, and cow and could keep track of them by their names. At the end of the day, when all the animals returned to their corral of thorn branches, my grandmother would count all the goats by their names, while my grandfather did the same with the cows and camels. In total they had almost five hundred animals. They provided the family with milk, meat, and transportation, but there were far more animals than they needed for food. Somali herdspeople have no permanent home, no belongings besides clothes, some jewelry, and cooking utensils. Their wealth is the size of their herd. They have no insurance payments, no loans, no future plans, nothing to worry about except lions and hyenas. To them there are only two days: the day you are born, and the day you die. Everything in between is herding animals.

My grandparents on both sides were proud pastoralists. They herded their animals across the rangeland of Bay region in south-central Somalia, always moving to find water. They had never heard of Mogadishu or even Somalia, much less Nairobi or New York. Their grazing land was all they knew. Bay lies between the Jubba and the Shabelle Rivers, which nourish the soil. It has more livestock than anywhere else in Somalia and is famous for its gorgeous Isha Baidoa waterfall and the smooth, patterned clay landscape around Diinsoor and Ufuroow villages. Nomads of Bay region enjoy two rainy seasons over the year: *Dayr,* with light rains, begins in mid-October; *Gu* brings heavy rains in mid-April. Before it rains, as the clouds build, the animals can smell the coming rain and they dance in anticipation. The people see the excitement of the animals, and they raise their hands to thank God: *"Alhamdulilah!"*

The rains mean plentiful water, so the nomads can finally settle down for a few months and build their makeshift huts from sticks carried on the backs of camels. At night the animals stay close to the hut in their corral, and the families sit around a fire near them. They dance with songs for the animals—clapping, stomping their feet on the ground, spinning and shaking their heads, and singing, *"Hoo hoobiyoo haa!"* "You know my camel by its mark, you know me by my mark!" There is laughter and fresh water and jubilation. A good time for patriotic stories, folktales, poems, and delicious meals of corn and meat. In his time, Iftin, my grandfather, would tell his own brave stories. He would talk about the day he met a pride of lions face-to-face near his house and chased them away for a mile. Eventually, the rains stop, the water dries up, and the nomads pack up their stick huts and thorny corrals on the camelbacks and move on.

My parents as well as grandparents could name their own great-great-great-grandparents; they could spend a whole night naming them and telling the stories they have passed down. All these ancestral names carry pride; every single one of them was a brave man or woman, someone who owned many livestock and was well known in the area and probably killed a lion. Brave sons and daughters of brave parents. My parents never talked about their lives without talking about the lives of their parents and ancestors because to Somali nomads there is no individual life, only the life of your family. And like their ancestors, my parents followed the Muslim rules. Women have to respect their husbands. Men have power over everything. My parents never questioned these rules or how they came about.

My mom, Madinah, was a very beautiful nomad girl, tall

and slim, with dark hair, a long neck, long legs, and beautiful eyes. One summer day at a watering hole somewhere in Bay region, probably near Buurhakaba with its huge hills, my dad, Nur Iftin, and his herd encountered my mom and hers. She remembers it was raining lightly.

Herdspeople between the two rivers are respectful of each other's cattle, which is not always the case in other parts of Somalia. Also they were both proud members of the Rahanweyn clan. So when they met, it was friendly. My dad says he could not take his eyes off my mom. He had never seen such a beautiful woman, but most important he liked how shy she was, which in Somalia is a sign of interest. Mom was barefoot, wearing her long *guntiino* dress, which goes over only one shoulder, a necklace of black wooden beads, and metal bands around her upper arms. The scars on her neck and arms said without words how brave she was fighting wild animals.

Dad was in his *macawis,* a knee-length cloth wrapped tightly around his waist. He wore his nomad sandals made of animal leather. His camels mixed with Mom's goats around the watering hole. He approached her, and he bragged about his wealth, the animals, which is the only pickup line in the nomadic culture.

My mom liked him at first sight. Not many men were even taller than my tall mom, but he towered over her. He had a scar on his forehead that showed he had also wrestled wild animals. His high Afro hairstyle crowned his head and wide shoulders. His feet, whitened with the dust, showed that he had walked miles and was still not tired. As he stood there, he introduced Mom to his favorite camels, naming them as they grazed. They also had names for the wild animals that threatened their herds. They talked about Fareey, a local lion who had been terrorizing the herds. Fareey was named for his missing toe, which made his footprints in the clay distinct. Fareey and his pride were smart and killed many animals, including some belonging to my parents' families, after dark. My dad swore that he would find Fareey and his pride and kill them all to protect my mom's goats. He never did find that lion, but it was a way to show my mom that he could care for her.

After their first brief meeting, my parents searched for each other for a couple months, like the guy in *The Gods Must Be Crazy* who is looking for his two lost boys. When they finally met at another watering hole, my dad believed his prayers had been answered. Now Nur Iftin could not hide his love for Madinah and said he wanted to marry her. She did not say yes or no, but grinned and looked down coyly. In Somalia, that means yes. She was around seventeen, he was in his twenties. Dad arranged a meeting with her parents, and one day both families met in a place near Baidoa, the biggest city in the region, where the agreement was negotiated: fifty camels as a dowry that my dad's parents paid to my mom's parents.

The wedding happened in a town called Hudur, about sixty miles from Baidoa. This was the rainy season, so the animals were fat, and there was so much meat and milk at the wedding. Guests invited to the wedding were relatives and their own parents. Mom was in a mud hut all day with what they called the expert women, who told her stories about what would happen on the wedding night, and how she would want to be obedient to her husband, and how everything he says she must accept. It was a rented hut; they had to deposit goats to stay there. Neither of them had ever seen a banknote or a coin. At the same time my dad was in a neighbor's hut with the men teaching him about the first days of marriage.

On the evening of the wedding, six men walked with Dad to the hut where Mom was waiting nervously. Inside the hut were carved wooden ornaments called *xeedho,* which are decorations to celebrate the wedding, brilliantly patterned clay vessels known as *dhiil* containing milk, butter, and meat, and a soft cow leather for them to sleep on. After seven days, when their honeymoon officially ended, my dad was dressed in traditional clothes, a white cotton sheet that was wrapped around his waist as a skirt, another piece over his shoulders as a shawl, and seated outside the hut. Then two men held a *dhiil* full of camel milk and poured it all over him. This signified my dad was now a husband. The evening ended with Dad riding one of the camels as a celebration escorted by some men singing and dancing, but my mom stayed inside the hut, too shy to come out and see people after the wedding bed.

My parents spent most of their early marriage walking through the bush with their herds, remembering places by the trees. They walked miles every day into no-man's territory. No one stopped them or asked who they were. It was a peaceful time. To my parents, heaven was beyond the shiny stars they saw at night, and hell was under their feet. When my mom's bare feet burned in the baking sun, she remembered God's words that on Earth are samples of hellfire. They believed Earth was flat and that it was Allah's land, they were only guests. It rains when Allah wills, it turns dry when Allah wills. Animals and humans die when Allah wills. *"Inshallah!"*

In some ways the nomadic life is more like life in America than the way Somalis live in cities. In the bush Somali men and women work together, talk freely with each other, and even play games together. To survive on the land, a husband and wife must work as a team to make sure their animals are grazed well and that they all get back home by dusk. My dad had introduced my mom to several games like high jump, sprint running, and chasing dik-diks, the little antelopes not much bigger than a cat. Mom loved all those games. They would hold sticks five feet high, then take turns jumping over them. Mom learned to jump and land without stumbling. She said Dad never beat her at this game. Mom was shy and respectful to her husband, but when it came to games and fun, she was a fierce competitor. They sprinted together across the bush, leaping over thornbushes while chasing the fast dik-diks.

Bay region is famous in Somalia for growing corn, beans, rice, sesame, papayas, mangoes, and the tree that produces frankincense resin. Most of that resin is bought by the Catholic church in Rome, but my parents knew nothing of Rome or Christianity. To them the most amazing place in the world was the Isha Baidoa waterfall. It was like their vacationland. *Isha* means "eye," and the water flows from a crack high in the rock that looks like an eye. My mom still believes that eye belongs to an angel. During their nomadic travels they stopped twice a year to shower under the water falling from the angel's eye.

The city of Baidoa is called Baidoa the Paradise for both the nearby waterfall and the fertile red soil. The farms of corn and *masago,* a type of grain, grow right inside the city, among the mud houses and the mango and banana trees. In the center of town is the huge Afar Irdoodka market, where people come from all across the country to buy and sell food, medicinal herbs, and supplies. Everywhere in that city, donkeys loaded with supplies are moving toward the market.

The Rahanweyn tribe live in Baidoa and on all the land between and surrounding the Jubba and Shabelle Rivers. The word "Rahanweyn" translates into "large number." There are so many of them, spread across the bush. To most of the other Somali tribes the Rahanweyn are looked down on because they are mostly nomads and poor and have nothing to do with politics. Also, the dialect the Rahanweyn speak, called Maay, is dismissed as the speech of beggars and the lower class because it is not comprehensible to most other Somalis. It is different in sentence structure and is complex to outsiders. So for centuries the Rahanweyn lived their own life, on land belonging to no one.

My parents' courtship and wedding happened sometime in the 1970s. Soon after the wedding, in 1977, a terrible drought hit Somalia. The rains of *Dayr* and *Gu* never came. The corn withered. The red clay land around Baidoa turned parched and bare, its wide cracks littered with skeletons of the animals. Those that survived were thin and dying. The nomads knew it was God's choice but could not understand why he would do this, because they were not sinful people. They decided Allah wanted the animals for himself and was taking them away. My parents, who had been so proud of their herds, watched their wealth wiped out in front of their eyes. Daraanle, my mom's favorite camel, turned thin and then died silently.

Droughts were a part of life for nomads in Bay region, but new forces in the world, from far beyond the land between the rivers, would make this drought different. That same year Somalia attacked Ethiopia in a war over control of the Ogaden territory, a part of Ethiopia that is populated mainly by ethnic Somalis. Somalia deployed troops to the border, and the tanks and military vehicles that left Mogadishu passed by my parents. My mom stood there, eyebrows raised, watching these strange moving things. My parents had never seen anything like tanks, they had never even thought about such a thing as a government or an army. They didn't know it, but under the dictator Mohammed Siad Barre, the founder of the Supreme Revolutionary Council, Somalia had amassed the largest army in Africa. Siad Barre was a general who had taken over the country in 1969, then cleverly used the Cold War to extract support from the Soviet Union. But none of this meant anything to desert nomads, who looked in the sky and prayed for rain.

The 1977 war, known as the Ogaden War, was the bloodiest ever between two African nations, with tens of thousands of casualties. The Somali army unleashed its heavy weaponry and Soviet-trained soldiers against the Ethiopians in a massive attack over the border. Somalia had Soviet T-35 and T-55 tanks against Ethiopia's older Italian tanks from World War II. In the beginning the Somalis advanced deep into Ethiopia, almost capturing the capital, Addis Ababa. But the Soviet Union also supported Ethiopia, which had a Marxist military regime, and tried to stop the war. When Siad Barre refused to back down, the Soviets abandoned Somalia and sided with Ethiopia, a much larger country. Then the war became global when China, Yemen, North Korea, Romania, and other nations got involved supporting either side. With the Soviet Union supplying the Ethiopian Air Force with advanced MiG-17 and MiG-21 jets and other weaponry, the Somali army was pushed out of the country and defeated in 1978. Siad Barre was furious; he expelled all Russians from Somalia. Wanting a buffer against a Soviet-backed Ethiopia, the Americans rushed into the vacuum and began to give military help to Somalia. If not for the American support, Siad Barre might have been driven out of power for his needless and costly war. Instead, he was able to build up his army again.

All these shifting alliances and power plays meant nothing to my parents. But the result—a small country with millions of guns and simmering resentment against Siad Barre for causing so much misery—would soon change their lives forever.

Meanwhile, the 1977 drought was the worst in Somali recorded history, wiping out lives and displacing tens of thousands of nomads. As the animals died, some nomads started moving. The nomads moved everywhere, mostly toward Kenya and Ethiopia. Some moved to the nearest cities with fishing and other opportunities. And so my parents decided to try for a better life in Mogadishu. After fifteen days of walking and begging rides, Nur Iftin and his wife, Madinah, set foot for the first time ever in a city with movie theaters, traffic lights, houses made of bricks, and citizens who spoke a nearly unintelligible dialect.

And statues! There was a bronze statue in the center of Mogadishu, high on a white stone column, of a colonial-era freedom fighter holding a rock. The statue was named Dhagaxtuur, which means "stone thrower," and it honored the rebels who fought the British with stones after World War II. My mom stood there waiting for the bronze man to throw that rock. Only a week later she realized it was not a real person. The green and red taxicabs that parked everywhere, the portraits of Siad Barre that hung on every street, caught them by surprise. They would later learn that you weren't supposed to say Siad Barre's name without adding the word *Jaalle* before it. *Jaalle* was a new word in the Somali language invented by Siad Barre, which roughly meant "führer" or "leader."

My dad's half brother Hassan, who already lived in Mogadishu, gave my parents a room in his house in the Waberi neighborhood. A mile from their house, to the east, was the Mogadishu airport and the beautiful green waters of the Indian Ocean surrounding it. But civilization sickened my mom. She missed the animals, her parents, the stories, the land, her freedom. She had not slept in weeks due to the sound of the airplanes taking off and landing. She kept looking up and wondering how on earth those things are made. Her first visit to the ocean made her remember stories from her parents, including one about something called a whale that can swallow a whole city. She worried about whales, and she wondered where the ocean ends. Using a toilet, going to a movie, and riding a bus were the strangest things to both my parents, probably the way so many things about America seem strange to me, like snow, cooking on a stove, or obeying traffic laws.

One thing that frustrated her more than anything else was buying milk and meat. In her nomad life these things were abundant; now she had to pay for them with money. Her first visit to the slaughterhouse brought her to tears. The meat dangled on hooks, flies landing on it constantly. Loud men with sharp knives yelled at everyone who stepped into the slaughterhouse, waving their knives in the air and promising the freshest meat. My mom was an expert on camel meat, and she could tell this meat was not fresh, but she didn't dare to question the scary butchers with their long knives and strange dialect.

During the drought many nomads moved to Mogadishu. The city people made fun of them. My mom remembers other women asking her to make sounds of animals. They were mocking her, but animals were her favorite subject so she was happy to make their sounds for the neighbors, especially the sound of her favorite goat, Eseey, which means "brown." The city women, who wore nicer clothes, did not want to be seen with Mom on the streets. To them she was a little embarrassing. They mocked her dialect, looking down at her whenever she said something in Maay. She was called *Reer Baadiye,* "the bush woman."

The neighbors said her house smelled like goat pee, from her clothes. To Mom the smell of goats and camels was like the perfume of her homeland, and it smelled like freedom. Also she had learned only a handful of verses from the Koran that her parents had taught her, just enough to pray five times a day. But the city women, who had studied at madrassas, knew the whole Koran. They played a sort of competitive religious game called *subac* where they would sit in a circle and recite the Koran like a round-robin. Each person would have to recite the verse that follows the last person's verse; to forget any verse would mean embarrassment. But none of those women could jump or run like my mom. They were too fat from all the city food, and they avoided sunshine so they would get lighter skin.

The women of Mogadishu were circumcised as children, but nomads don't practice female genital mutilation. So this was even more pressure on Mom. She was made to feel unclean by the neighbors. Eventually, she relented and bravely subjected herself to the cutting. Three neighbor women took her to the house of Hawa, a woman famous in Mogadishu for doing this. Of course there were no painkillers. Hawa usually circumcised little girls who didn't know what was coming and could be distracted for the cutting, like my brother with the airplane at his surprise circumcision. But of course my mom knew, like I did after seeing my brave brother. And so like me at my circumcision, Mom had to be held down as Hawa worked with that Topaz razor blade for some fifteen minutes while my mom screamed. Once Hawa declared that everything bad had been removed, the other women began ululating in joy. Hawa cleaned up with some warm water and sent Mom home. My dad, who knew of the procedure and approved, had to stay away from her for a few months.

It makes me so angry when I think about it. In my job as a medical interpreter in Maine, I often tell new Somali immigrants that they cannot mutilate their daughters in this country, which surprises them. This terrible custom is rooted in ignorance and will only change with education.

By now my dad had started making some money fishing, which eventually allowed him to rent a room with my mom and leave Hassan's house. Some of the men would go out in boats with big nets while my dad stayed on Uruba beach, waiting for them to return. When the fishermen came back with their nets full, Dad would carry the huge heavy fish, some as big as a person, on his shoulders. He would carry those fish a mile to the fish market at Geel-Laq beach. Some days he would make that trip dozens of times. After a whole day of that hard work he was supposed to get paid one Somali shilling, but he still didn't know much about money or coins and was often cheated.

At that time there were still Italians in Mogadishu. Before independence came in 1960, Somalia was two colonies: British Somaliland in the north and Italian Somaliland, including Mogadishu, in the south. So there was a long history of Europeans in Somalia, and in the 1970s and 1980s many still came to do business. They stayed in the big Uruba Hotel, today in ruins, where the women would sunbathe in bikinis. It was the first time Dad saw white people, and he couldn't believe they walked around almost naked. When he told my mom, she couldn't believe it either; she had to come and see for herself. Even then she didn't believe they were real people until she saw them actually breathing. Mom in her nomad life had heard stories about *gaalo,* the infidels. They are not Muslim, they are all white, and they are not clean. But she didn't know they had no clothes. She stayed away from the unclean white people she saw at the beach. She wondered, what are they doing here, and why don't they pray five times a day?

Everywhere in Mogadishu, my dad stood out in the crowd with his strong body and height. He had cut his long nomad hair short and shaved his nomad's beard, but he left his dark mustache and woolly sideburns. This look was very fashionable in Mogadishu in the early 1980s, especially if you also wore bell-bottoms. He would go out and strut around town. In that Uruba Hotel was a nightclub where dancers stripped and alcohol was served. There were more nightclubs than mosques in Mogadishu back then, all places where you could dance to funk music like on the American TV show *Soul Train* and drink at a seaside bar. Some Somali men and even some women (without a head scarf and wearing lots of jewelry) went to clubs to mingle with the Italian, British, and American businesspeople before the civil war. Eventually, my dad did go to the Uruba Club, though he never told my mom. He saw Somali women dancing with white men, which in a few years would become punishable by death. Today those clubs are rubble in the sand, a few broken pillars rising from the debris like the ruins of ancient Rome.

The fishing and dancing might have gone on for my dad until the wars came, but then one day he did something that changed his life. He jumped.

It was nothing to him, just jumping over a thorn fence, like he jumped in those games with my mom in the bush. But this jump was seen by a friend of his half brother Hassan who knew a lot about basketball. That game had become very popular all over Africa, and Somalia had leagues, amateur and professional, that competed against each other and other countries. Hassan's friend said that because my dad was so tall and could jump so high, he should try out for the national basketball team. But Hassan wanted his half brother to join the military, like himself. At that time under Siad Barre, Somalis were very patriotic; joining the army was considered a noble career. My dad had already gone through basic military training, which was mandatory for grown men in the city, and he was fine with being a soldier. Besides, he knew nothing about basketball, had never even held a ball. But Hassan's friend wouldn't give up. The Somali national team had been losing a lot of games, and they were recruiting new players. Having a winning team was another part of the patriotic spirit in the country.

So my dad tried out for basketball and was a natural. He towered over his teammates. He could jump higher and had strong hands from working with animals. His herding skills also made him very agile and gave him stamina. It didn't take long for him to get used to handling the ball. Soon he was nicknamed Nur Dhere, Tall Nur, and he was helping Somalia win games. Soon he stopped carrying fish and started making a lot more money playing basketball. The world changed swiftly for my parents. They learned how to identify and count shilling notes and coins and how to buy things like clothes, curtains, window shutters made of wood, a carpet over their dirt floor, a cupboard, and a shelf. Things only rich people had. My dad also learned to read and write Somali, which was unusual because nomad men and women were mostly illiterate.

By the time I was born, my parents had become the honored basketball family in the neighborhood. They were famous all over Mogadishu. Dad was traveling a lot outside the country, bringing medals home. He had a shortwave radio in the house and would listen to songs by famous Somali singers. My nomad parents had a lot of good things happening, but my mom missed everything in the nomad world. She thought that city life was hard and resented having to stay inside a house all day, cooking and cleaning, instead of herding her goats across the landscape, while Dad was out playing basketball. She was worried that her kids would grow up in Mogadishu not knowing anything about the life of nomads. The few women friends she made, like Maryan, had nothing in common with her. They all talked about popular Somali music and shows. Instead, she would entertain herself around the house by humming her favorite nomad songs.

Dad spent most of his time away from home, training with the basketball squad. Usually he returned on Thursday for two days (Friday being the holy day), still wearing his red Somali team shirt and bringing gifts of clothes and toys for us, sometimes jewelry for Mom.

Our neighbor Siciid visited often when Dad was at home.

They sat under the neem tree in the evening chewing qat leaves and talking late into the night. Mom was exiled to the house while the men talked, but from time to time she brought them tea. Siciid looked short and fat compared to Dad, a smile constantly fixed to his round face. Like Mom he told many stories and also jokes, and he provoked Dad into arguments, just for the fun of it. Siciid was a professional driver who earned his living delivering food and oil for the government. He came home after work smelling of fruit or oil or whatever he had been transporting that day.

Sometimes Dad took me to watch him train at the Horseed Stadium in downtown Mogadishu. Mom dressed me up with a nice clean vest and shorts. The court was behind a thick concrete wall; police with dogs patrolled around, fending off people who tried to sneak in to watch the players. Some of the fans would climb up a tall tree to get a view over the wall. They sat there for hours watching as my dad and his teammates, the best in Somalia, played basketball all afternoon. I had the honor to walk into the building with my dad holding my tiny hand in his big hairy one. People greeted him like a star and also gave me a gentle touch on the head. The police and soldiers saluted him like he was a general. Dad played for hours, and eventually I would fall asleep on the stairs, only waking on his shoulders as he carried me home.

The training ground was one kilometer from our house, and we walked home in the evening past the big KM4 traffic island, the Cinema Ecuatore, and shops and restaurants bursting with laughter, music, and discussion. People talked about concerts and plays at the theaters. The famous Waberi entertainment club presented great shows on Friday that would make people laugh a lot. There were famous comedians like Aw Kuku, Aw Kombe, and Aw Daango. Most would be killed or displaced soon, during the civil war.

In the old part of town, above the ruins of the medieval sultanates' castles, rose the white spires of the ancient Arba'a Rukun mosque and the Catholic cathedral, which had been built by the Italians. We could see the ocean beyond the Almara lighthouse, built of stone in the fifteenth century when Mogadishu was a major African port, and we felt the power of the sea breeze against our faces. "Mogadishu is a great city," I thought, "maybe the greatest in the world." The White Pearl of the Indian Ocean, they called it. I felt so lucky.

My earliest memories of Mogadishu always include my brother, Hassan. He was a hero to me, only one year older but always my protector from the other boys in the neighborhood who tried to bully me. Hassan was without fear and would fight with boys older than himself; sometimes he would fight with three at the same time, returning home with cuts to his body and dust on his clothes. On one occasion I was attacked by two boys who threw me to the ground, then punched and kicked me. I didn't tell my mom, but I did tell Hassan, who went after them and beat them. Even though I was smaller than Hassan, I ate more than he could, and I snatched food from his hands. Still he did not chase me. But we played fun games like hide-and-seek, *gariir* (a type of marbles game using rocks), and blindman's bluff.

Hassan went to the madrassa, where he learned the Koran with eighty other boys sitting on the sand in a shack. There was no paper; the students wrote on long wooden boards, using ink made from coal. They wrote a passage from the Koran in Arabic, memorized and repeated it, then washed off the ink and wrote the next passage. All day they did this. Mistakes were severely punished by the teacher, a scowling bearded man named Macalin Basbaas, roughly translated as "the teacher who uses hot pepper and scorpions to bite on wounds." Never was someone better named, though later we nicknamed him the Angel of Punishment. Hassan returned home bleeding from the beatings he got.

The madrassas were the only kind of school in Mogadishu, and there was nothing to learn there except the Koran. So my mom became my greatest teacher. She could cook, bake, and sing like any good Somali mom is supposed to, but what I loved most about her were the tales she told us about her nomadic youth. She would sit cross-legged under the neem tree with Hassan and me while our baby sister, Nima, perhaps a little more than a year old, slept with her thumb in her mouth. Mom would talk of her time as a herdswoman in the desert scrub, protecting the goats and the camels from lions and hyenas.

She told us about the day when a hyena suddenly appeared, growling and gnashing teeth. She chased it with her stick through the scrub before returning to the herd, knowing she should get the animals to the corral near her parents before darkness, when the hyenas would be at their most dangerous. But the pack had already scattered the herd. Without fear she chased them, for Somalis value their goats and camels as much as their own lives. A hyena leaped at her, pinning her to the ground, its sharp claws cutting into her neck. Luckily, her uncle arrived and started striking the hyena with a stick. Three days later, still in great pain, she was sent out again by her parents to mind the herd.

My head rested on her lap, looking up at the hyena scar on her neck. She still wore the necklace she had on when she met my dad—black beads made from hard, polished wenge wood, the sort worn by women in the bush but rarely seen in the city. I wondered how my quiet mom, who hid in the house when men visited, could chase hyenas.

The scariest story she told was about the night when a lion entered the hut where a relative was sleeping with his children.

This hut was made of discarded plastic and paper. A paper house is no match for a hungry lion, and that big cat dragged the man out into the bush screaming and crying while his children slept. Mom was one of the people who came out of the huts armed with spears, but when they reached him, he was almost dead. "There was a whistling sound coming from his neck where the teeth had sunk in," she said. I tried to imagine what it would be like to see dead people.

The story of the lion haunted me and gave me nightmares. I sometimes asked myself, "What if I was born a nomad?" Surely I would be killed by a lion. I hated death. I just wanted to live a good life like the one we had and hang on my dad's shoulders walking around town being cheered. Mom told us these stories not to scare us but to help us understand life in the bush, to appreciate it and remember the details. Her goal was to keep us from becoming city boys who know little about nomad life. She wanted us to not mock other nomads who came to the city but respect them and listen to their stories. We were also able to learn and speak the nomadic Rahanweyn dialect because Mom told all her stories in Maay. She trained us in the house and courtyard on how to fight, climb trees, and jump. Hassan and I could jump higher than most of the boys in the neighborhood.

One morning when I was around six, I woke up to see feathers covering the mat under the neem tree; a bird had been killed by someone's cat, Mom said, but all I could think of was a lion. "There are no lions in the city," she said, but I wasn't sure.

I asked Mom how the birds can be protected. "These birds are our guests," I said. "How come we can't save them?" She had no answer. After dark I went out to the tree and said to the birds, "I can't protect you from the lion tonight; may Allah be with you."

. . .

It was around that same time when Dad told our family that the basketball was finished and he would be staying at home now. I didn't know how basketball could be finished. There was always another game, on another day. Could there be no more days? Soon I began to notice people were tense and there were lots of changes in our routines. Siciid was now with us most of the time, returning to his own house only to sleep and spending long hours with Dad listening to the radio. His wife and children had left Mogadishu and gone to stay with relatives in the north of Somalia. Like Dad, he had stopped going to work.

Dad and Siciid talked about politics. Since the end of the bloody Ogaden War with Ethiopia in 1978, Somalia's economy was limping. Inflation was so high you needed baskets of paper money just to buy a kilo of Italian pasta (Mogadishans learned to love spaghetti from their colonizers), when you could even find it. People were angry at President Siad Barre, especially the people around Mogadishu who were mainly from the Hawiye clan. Siad Barre came from the rival Darod clan up north. There were five major clans in Somalia, but since independence the Hawiye and the Darod had nominated themselves as the only people who could be president or prime minister; members of other clans could only be members of the Parliament or the cabinet. Soon, instead of presidents and prime ministers, the Hawiye and the Darod would give us brutal warlords.

Before the Ogaden War, when he was still popular, Siad Barre managed to keep the Hawiye people under control, and he watched them carefully. One of their leaders, an army general named Mohamed Farrah Aidid, had been jailed for a time. Now he was free again and ready to fight his Darod rival, thanks to weapons and money he was getting from Ethiopia, which also hated Siad Barre because of the war. Aidid had whipped up the Hawiye of the rural areas, and that's where the fighting was going on, like a bunch of lions and hyenas in the bush. But how long could this fight stay out in the bush?

Of course I was too young to understand any of this, I didn't even understand that spaghetti came from a place called Italy or that no spaghetti would soon be the least of our problems. I just wanted to go to the snack bar. I begged Dad to take me, but for the first time ever I saw that his face was not happy. In his eyes I saw fear; I could feel it like the way I felt when boys in the neighborhood bullied me. This was a new thing to see in my dad, and while I understood it as part of something larger beginning, all I could think of was that everything I knew was ending.

He did not want to take me to the snack bar, he said.

2

The First Bullets

I wake up in Maine a grown man, but in my nightmares I am still a boy in Mogadishu after the basketball finished. What happened after the basketball is never in the past, it lives again every night in my sleep, and sometimes when I am awake.

Finally one day the fighters arrive, looting the shops and firing the first bullets of the bloody civil war. At night I hear bullets hitting the neem tree and the birds flying off in all directions. The next morning I wake up to see mattresses, beds, food, basketballs, and Dad's basketball trophies all packed outside. Dad is carrying the most important things in a gunnysack with one hand and a mattress in the other hand. Left behind are the *jiimbaar* and the wooden shelves that Mom uses to keep Dad's clothes clean and pressed. Sacks of flour, rice, and corn must be abandoned. Mom carries our clothes, our sister's formula, milk, and a few cooking utensils, plus Nima on her back, wrapped in a big scarf the African way. She is also pregnant with her fourth child. Hassan and I are trailing behind our parents on a dusty, scorching day with bullets and smoke all over the city.

After we walk just a few yards, I start crying to be carried.

Mom ignores me, reciting verses from the Koran, looking on both sides of the streets before we cross. I can hear gun and rocket fire in the distance; what I can see is looting and destruction. As we walk, I see huge padlocks on the gates of houses I know in the neighborhood; people have already fled. The locks mean they are hoping to return; maybe this will all blow over in a few weeks. Everywhere I see moms holding the hands of other kids my age, standing on the side of the road in shock. I hear screams and crying children. The small restaurant where I used to go with Dad, named for its owner, Hashi, is being looted. The food goes quickly; then two thin ragged men try to take the iron gate for their own house. Hashi belongs to the tribe of President Siad Barre, who has been ousted by these rebels, and Mom is worried about his whereabouts. There is a crowd gathered a short distance from the restaurant where a dead body is lying facedown—the first corpse I would see. It turned out to be Hashi's body. Rebels in civilian dress are laughing and throwing their arms in the air in triumph, smashing the windows of shops with their rifle butts before racing each other to collect the most valuable pickings. Most of them wear a *macawis,* which is worn mainly in the bush. That's how we know the rebels are not city people; they have come into town from the outlands and are probably seeing shops and restaurants for the first time, just as my parents had several years before.

When there is nothing left to loot from the shops, I see people being robbed at gunpoint. On every street, buildings are on fire. A rebel in a pickup truck is passing guns to a group of teenagers. One fires off his gun by accident, causing his comrades to scatter into porches and behind cars. They are spilling out of Toyota Land Cruisers with the roofs sawed off. The drivers honk and wave in victory as soldiers in the open cab shake their rifles in the air and dance. Some jump out and run after us, holding a gun in one hand while holding up their loose pants and *macawis.* Apparently, they have not yet looted belts. All of them are very black-skinned, much darker and thinner than the Mogadishans who have skin more the color of the supermodel Iman, also from Mogadishu. They call themselves nicknames based on their features, like gangsters I would see in Hollywood movies. Names I can hear are Daga Weyne (Long-Eared), Afdheere (Long Mouth), Ileey (One-Eyed), Gacmeey (One-Handed). The pro Siad Barre slogans on the streets are gone. Now the signs call him "Big Mouth" and "The Brutal One." The word *Jaalle* has been changed to *Faqash,* which means "Killer." The Hawiye militias are killing anyone who says *Jaalle.* You better say *Faqash.* Dad and Mom practice the new word and are ready to say it.

"They are giving guns out like sweets!" Dad says. "Who is in charge of these people?"

With the civil war spreading into the city, some people manage to escape by boats, airplanes, ships, and even cars crossing into neighboring countries. Most of these people who escape worked for the government. Some of my dad's own teammates got helped by their tribal affiliation to get to America, Canada, or the United Kingdom. No one has even contacted my dad. The country is divided by clans and tribes, and people help only people they are related to by those groups. My dad's Rahanweyn clan are the farmers and nomads who cannot help him escape. So my parents must use their nomad skills to try to save us. What nomads do is walk. We will walk to safety.

And so we embark on a walk that I will never forget. For years we called it the walk of death.

Seven miles of walking and we arrive at the house of our relative Mumin, who is a general in the Somali army. Mumin is my dad's cousin, he's the only man in our extended family to be in the army's highest ranks. He is educated, having studied at Lafoole University in Mogadishu before deciding to join the army. His house is behind a wall with a gate. Mumin appears at the gate not in his usual uniform but in a red T-shirt and black trousers, his hands nervously scratching at his mustache. The blue Somali flag is still flying over his house. "There's no one who can stop the fighting," he says. "No one is talking to anyone else, just fighting." He looks at the flag and shakes his head. He mentions that the government is still holding on to the airport, but President Siad Barre has already fled. The rebels seem unstoppable, and a general would be a certain target. "I must leave with my family because it's everyone for himself," he says. "I hope that you will be safe here." He wipes his fingers on my face and Hassan's, but our tears run harder.

"We'll be all right here," Dad tells Mumin. "We'll stay the night and move on in the morning."

So we are to sleep in the home of a general in the defeated army, while rebels shoot their way across the city looking for government officials to slaughter. It does not seem very safe. The rooms of the house are all packed with neighbors and Rahanweyn from all over the city, mostly women and children, so we must sleep outside. We lay our mattresses on the grass in the courtyard while Dad remains near the gate. I can hear the Rahanweyn dialect. People are scared; men like my dad are pacing back and forth thinking of what to do. He puts his hairy hands in his pockets searching for the last remnant of qat leaves to chew. My dad believes his thinking is better while he chews qat. No one is interested in him, no one is paying attention to the popular Nur Dhere, the handsome and famous basketball player. People are too worried for their lives.

It is an uncomfortable night of blasts and mosquito bites. The back side of Mumin's house borders on the largest Somali hospital, Madinah Hospital. Same name as Mom. That night the militias are busy looting the hospital, grabbing anything valuable to sell. We can hear the looting and shouting; they kick down doors and break glass, even tearing off the roof. We rise early to find bullet holes in the gate of Mumin's house, and we slip away quietly.

The road south runs along the sea. Out on the waves, white ships like whales move slowly in the distance. Later I find out these ships are evacuating government officials. On the land, cows, donkeys, stray dogs, and chickens move aimlessly through the crowds of people. A thin man is painting the letters *USC*—United Somali Congress, the main militia group of Aidid—in white on every wall. Someone else draws a rough face with a big mouth and labels it "Siad Barre."

Dad tells us to go back and stay at Mumin's and that he will go try to find Siciid, who maybe still has his truck and can take us to Baidoa, 150 miles from Mogadishu. So we go back to Mumin's house, again dodging bullets. While we were gone, the militias had come after emptying the hospital and looted everything in the house. Even the Somali flag is gone, lying in the dust in the street, torn through with bullet holes.

Three hours later, Siciid's black truck, stuffed with belongings, kids, and women, appears at the house—Dad sitting on the back side of the truck, the wind blowing his shirt, and so covered with dust I can hardly recognize his face.

We squeeze in, Mom crouching, holding Nima and me, Dad holding Hassan. We are off to Baidoa. Dad turns to Siciid and asks, "Do you have a couple leaves?" He's all out of qat. Siciid draws out a handful of leaves and hands them to Dad. He shovels them all in his mouth and chews like a goat as we drive on.

In about five hundred yards a group of rebels appears in front of us, ordering the truck to stop. One wavy-haired, thin, and dark man points his gun at Siciid. The gunman can barely talk with his mouth full of qat leaves as well. The cigarette in his hand is burning fast in the wind, the ashes flying into the eyes of Siciid. His accent is from Galgaduud region; he is talking fast and looking sideways with the gun on Siciid's head. Three others are pulling things out of the back. They take all the mattresses right away. My dad watches them take his basketball medals. My mom's eyes well with tears when they find her necklace of black wenge beads and other jewelry. The basketballs bounce down the road and end up as target practice for young rebels. Finally one of them picks out the red Somalia national basketball shirt and throws it down with the other possessions. My dad just sits there watching his career destroyed in front of his eyes.

"Who are you people? What is your clan?" asks a gunman.

"We are Rahanweyn," says Mom. Maybe they will let us go.

"Come out of the truck, all of you!"

Under her shawl Mom is concealing her bag, which contains money and almost everything else my family has left.

"What is under your garment?" he demands.

"Cosmetics," says Mom.

"Give it to me!" he yells, holding his gun to my head. Mostly I'm scared by how tight the gunman is holding me and how skinny his legs are. And because I'm just a little boy, what also scares me is seeing my mom cry. Never have I seen her cry so hard. He takes the money from her bag, throws it aside, and with a shake of his gun yells, "Be gone!" As a nomad girl, my mom heard stories of the end of the world. "This is what it looks like," she is thinking. The day the world ends, the sun rises west and sets east. Chaos starts, people kill each other, children get harassed. A scary creature appears. She is thinking the militia leader Aidid must be that creature. But she wonders why the sun is still headed the right way, toward the west.

. . .

With nothing left for anyone to steal, we leave Mogadishu on a thin belt of tarmac cutting through a landscape of red sand dotted with thornbushes. The road is crowded, and all of the traffic is in one direction: out of the city. Parked at the side of the road at intervals are more pickup trucks with teenagers dressed in tattered vests sitting in the beds. Many of them have thin cloth scarves wrapped around their heads. They are smoking cigarettes, some with their guns pointing toward the sky, others with them on their laps pointing at the vehicles passing by. Some are in groups celebrating, clapping, cheering, and singing songs. Some of the pickup trucks are already equipped with mounted machine guns on the beds. They are called "technicals" and would become very familiar to me. I watch one truck. The driver must be new behind the wheel because he pushes the gas too hard and everyone in the bed falls backward. They get up laughing, then shove and taunt each other like schoolboys. Sometimes I see them pointing their guns at each other and yelling in strange accents. It's like a game to them.

These are militias of the Hawiye clan loyal to Aidid. His forces are the ones looting the government buildings in the city and killing anyone they can find who is loyal to the government or a member of the Darod clan. They arrived at Mogadishu only a day earlier to participate in the uprising. My dad is famous in Mogadishu, and someone from the city who watched him playing basketball wouldn't deal with him like that. Siciid says he recognizes many of the rebels from his truck journeys around Somalia. They are the faces of nomads who used to lead camels, as my parents once did, but not from the peaceful Rahanweyn lands. These militias come from central Somalia, a place where nomads carry guns to guard their camels. Now they are driving technicals in Mogadishu.

"How did they get these trucks?" Mom whispers. "By selling milk from their goats?" I don't think she is being serious. As we continue, I see more vehicles being stopped by the militias. I see someone on the ground being kicked in the head; then I see a corpse. I start to see piles of corpses. One youth is showing another how to shoot a gun. The novice then turns to face a hostage and casually sprays him with bullets as if he were a signpost. Nearby I see a line of about twenty people standing, awaiting execution. I peep my head out of the truck to watch militiamen pushing more people to the line; then two skinny men shoot them all. Their terrible fate is our good luck: the rebels are too busy shooting the people they have pulled out of other cars to stop my family, and we move on. My mom is murmuring passages from the Koran.

Eventually, we are stopped at another checkpoint manned by about a hundred militiamen, where the air is thick with smoke from tires they are burning at the roadside. A gunman in the road fires across the truck; as Siciid lurches to a stop, they come from all directions, running toward us and climbing onto the back. Nima is crying, Hassan tries to hide behind the jerry can of water, I duck my head, avoiding the guns of rebels jumping into the back of the truck. They drag Dad and Siciid out of the truck and push them facedown in the sand. My dad's dark sunglasses are beside him; a rebel stoops and picks them up, blows the dust off the lenses, and puts them on his thin face. He shows his militia friends and smiles.

Dad looks toward us, widening his eyes and giving a small nod of his head to tell us to stay calm. The guy who took the sunglasses now sees my dad's watch and jerks it from his wrist. He runs toward another group of rebels, proudly holding up the glasses as they watch in boastful celebration. A woman who is not armed jumps into the driver's seat, where another lady and her kids are hiding. "You left a lady and kids here!" she shouts to the thugs; then she searches under the driver's seat of Siciid's truck but finds only a flashlight and a flare. Not satisfied, she turns to the mom of the kids and searches her roughly. She removes her scarf and puts her hand under her *guntiino,* but she can't find anything. "You just poor people," she says with a sour face and slips away from the truck, nothing to steal. She is a middle-aged lady, wearing a long, formal *dirac* dress with a military cap on her head—an odd combination, I am thinking. She disappears into the crowd of militiamen.

One of the younger fighters, who looks about sixteen, holds his gun to Siciid's head. "Let's kill them."

"No," says an older man. "Our fight is with the Darod clan."

The fighters turn their backs on us to argue our fate. Then they pull us up from the back of the truck and tell us to sit by the road. They grab Dad and Siciid and start to drag them away. Dad whispers, "Don't worry, I'll be fine." After twenty minutes under the hot sun, the militiamen tell us to go, but first they empty the truck of the rest of our few possessions.

Dad and Siciid appear from an alley and are kicked roughly toward the truck by rebels. They must have been beaten in the alley. Blood is trickling down Siciid's face, and Dad is also battered, but they manage to climb back into the truck, Siciid in the driver's seat, Dad in the back. "Are you aboard?" asks Siciid without looking behind.

"Yes, move on," says Dad.

Mom is sobbing. "Next time we won't make it! We will all die! I'm scared for the children, if we don't make it and they are still alive—they don't know anything. Where will they go? They'll die in the desert. Better to die in the city than on this road. Turn around!"

Siciid is unmoved. "The city is burning and there are more guns there than where we are going."

"We'll make it to Baidoa if Allah wills," says Dad, "so stay calm." Mom keeps reciting the Koran with a loud voice and keeps telling us that with her reciting we will be fine. She is wishing she had never lived in Mogadishu. *We should have stayed in the bush. Better to contend with the drought and the wild animals than this.* It is torture for her to watch my strong dad begging for his life in front of a guy half his size.

My dad is expecting death anytime. "I'm not afraid of dying," he tells himself, but he is worried for us and our mom. He too thinks this is the apocalypse.

Miles out of Mogadishu, there are no more roadblocks, just blowing sand, thornbushes, and lines of stones by the roadside. Later we turn off onto a dirt track and reach a bank of greenery—mango trees, banana palms, watermelon, and long grass—as the road reaches a river. A troop of blue monkeys descends from the trees onto the truck, looking for food; they are always stealing food from people. Their silver faces and blank orange eyes terrify me. Of course we have no food, and no one is interested in the monkeys except me. I look at their swollen cheeks and long fangs and realize I am more afraid of monkeys than guns. Every time the monkeys open their jaws wide, I picture myself getting swallowed. I clutch my mom's clothes tight, but my parents act like the monkeys are not even there.

We catch up with a family from our old neighborhood, a short lady with a round face and her three kids, all of them in tears. Dad peeps his head out of the truck; Siciid slows down and asks what happened. The lady says her husband has been taken at the checkpoint. He was a government soldier, and he was recognized by one of the militiamen. Dad and Siciid try to console her, but it only makes her cry more. She is sitting under a thick, tall acacia tree with storks on their nests on top, brushing her tears with her shawl. I am just watching the monkeys run around.

We reach the edge of the town of Afgooye, its small houses of whitewashed mud bricks with corrugated-iron roofs appearing from beyond the muddy Afgooye River. When my dad played basketball, he traveled this same road at least once every week. He and his teammates would stop by Afgooye to grab some fresh sweet papayas and mangoes. Crowds would build around my dad, curious about his basketball uniform, and he would wave. Today he is struggling to stand on his feet.

Siciid stops the truck along the roadside for us to relieve ourselves. My mom accompanies Hassan and me down near the river. As I pee, I keep looking around for monkeys that might snatch me from the ground and eat me. There is a woman celebrating the fall of the government, dressed in black and with her head covered; she chatters as we pee. The land all around is a farm. The trees are full of ripe mangoes and bananas. On the ground, fat round watermelons shine beneath a tangle of vines and leaves. The war has not yet engulfed Afgooye, but soon these abundant crops will be destroyed. The lady who is celebrating claims this is her land and says we may not eat her crops. I grab Mom, and as she looks down with her worn face, I touch my belly to show her I am hungry. She says she cannot do anything, but she fetches some water from the muddy river. It seems dirty to me, but I am thirsty, so I drink until my belly fills up.

The lady in black says government troops have regrouped in a town fifty miles away and are rumored to be heading toward Afgooye. She is anxiously awaiting USC militias before the government soldiers come. The atmosphere is tense.

The road continues along the side of the river. "Look at the crocodiles! Look, look!" Mom cries. Hassan and I have never seen crocs before.

One of them crawls back into the water, and to my surprise there is a man standing in the water close to it, his *macawis* tucked into his belt to keep it above the water. "What is he doing there?" I cry. "He'll be eaten!"

"They won't eat him. He is a *bahaar,*" says Mom, "someone who has a special friendship with them. He can ride on their backs if he wants, and they will visit his house by the river; sometimes they will stay at his house all night. But other people are not welcomed by the crocodiles; if anyone else comes close to them, they will be killed and eaten. If he stays among the crocodiles now, he'll be safe from the rebels." I wish we could stay with the crocodiles, but it is time to move on.

The dirt track joins the tarmac road again. The scorching sun cools slowly as it slips beneath the dusty horizon. It's not long before our truck reaches another checkpoint. Burning tires and boulders are in the road to stop the traffic. One of a group of soldiers wearing government military uniforms holds up his hand to stop the car. They still wear the badge of the government's Supreme Revolutionary Council, with President Siad Barre's image. They are not rebels! Dad jumps down confidently to meet them. War songs blast out of their cars, with lyrics encouraging the soldiers not to give up but to fight and recapture Mogadishu.

"We are displaced to Baidoa by the rebels," Dad says. The soldiers wave him back into the truck to continue the journey. On the way we see another truck carrying displaced people, stalled by the side of the road. The passengers wave and beg to board our truck, but Siciid moves on. He can't take the risk of bringing people who might be from rival tribes and cause trouble at roadblocks.

Another half an hour and we see a military vehicle blocking the road ahead—another checkpoint by soldiers loyal to President Siad Barre, with their flag still flying. They have tanks and heavy trucks with machine guns, also bazookas and ground-to-air missiles. Some shots ring out and we turn to see a group of half a dozen people fall to the ground, their bodies trembling as blood pours onto the sand. "These soldiers are the Marehan,"

Siciid murmurs to Mom. She knows what that means: The Marehan are the same tribe of the Darod clan as the president, but they are not regular army like the last soldiers we saw. They are the diehards loyal to their tribe, unlike many soldiers who burned their uniforms and disappeared into the bush when the rebels came. They don't care about the government, they are just seeking revenge against the tribes who kicked them out of the city. There are so many sides in this war, and I am too young to understand it.

Siciid turns the truck suddenly, but guns are now aimed at us from all directions. A bullet shatters the wing mirror close to me, almost deafening my left ear. Siciid stops the truck. Three soldiers run up; one strikes Siciid's head with the butt of his gun and drags him onto the ground. All three are hitting Siciid with their rifle butts. Mom pushes us down to keep us safe from the bullets. One man in a military shirt and hat but civilian trousers comes to the window where I am hiding. He looks down and with his dirty hands pulls my head to see me, but I hold hard. "Stupid child!" he says, then walks away.

Dad remains motionless, hidden behind the jerry can. A soldier looks at us. "Who are you?"

"We are a poor family," Mom pleads. "We are displaced to Baidoa by the fighting."

"Where is your husband?"

"I have no husband. He disappeared. They have killed many people, and the bodies of the innocents are all along the road." I look at the soldier's eyes and wonder why he wants to kill us. What did I do?

"Come down from the truck, woman, and bring your children down as well!"

"We will not! We have done nothing, we are just a woman and her children; why do you want to kill us?"

"Asalaamu aleikum!"—Peace be upon you!

It is my dad's voice. Dad decides to show himself, brave as always. "These are my kids and wife, I am taking them to the safety of the bush." But before he finishes what he wants to say, the butt of a gun smashes into his head. I watch in despair as the blood of my tall, strong, proud dad soaks into his shirt. Now he is on his knees in front of a tiny, dark militiaman.

Then a voice calls out from the group of fighters. "Nur Dhere!"—Tall Nur! A man runs over to Dad. In joy they shake hands and hug each other. My mom cannot hold back her tears.

"Ahmed, Ahmed!" Dad says. Ahmed is a traffic officer from Mogadishu and a friend of my dad's. He is as tall as Dad, with thick glasses and a large mustache. They start talking about their time during the peace together and remembering the games Ahmed attended, games that Dad won for the national team. Ahmed thanks Dad for a time when my dad gave him money. The soldiers, noticing this exchange, turn to the truck behind us. Siciid, still crumpled on the ground, utters prayers of thanks. The soldiers storm the next truck, and another one behind it. Ahmed and Dad are still talking. Ahmed asks Dad what he saw on the road and if the Hawiye militias are advancing south to Afgooye. For a moment we feel safe and unharmed, but we can hear the cries of the women being beaten in the next truck and imagine it happening to us.

Siciid joins Dad and Ahmed, who reaches into his pocket for a cigarette to share. They talk a few more minutes while Dad and Siciid take turns puffing on the smoke. Mom sits on the ground helping Nima pee. Behind us, soldiers are dragging people from the trucks and shooting them. Whenever the soldiers fire, I flinch and duck behind my mom. Ahmed keeps talking to my dad and Siciid while his fellow soldiers shoot and beat families in the trucks behind us. My poor mom watches with her hand on her head.

After a few minutes the cigarette is finished and we leave.

Mom's face is shining wet with tears of joy. "We've survived again!" she cries to Siciid when we speed off. "We have another day to live!" The road ahead is safer, and we are close to Baidoa. Ahmed had promised his soldiers would not attack Baidoa; he said they were going back to recapture Mogadishu and that the war would never reach Baidoa. My parents have smiles on their faces for the first time in days, but they should not have trusted Ahmed. Troops from his tribe would soon attack Baidoa and kill Rahanweyn people indiscriminately. Ahmed would carry a gun for another four years until being killed by Aidid's militias in a shoot-out in Mogadishu.

The only noises I can hear, apart from the humming of the truck's engine, are the braying of donkeys, the moos of cows, the bleats of goats, and the rhythmic sounds of the bells around the necks of camels returning from grazing. Our headlights reveal houses made of sticks and dung, between which there is just enough room for the truck to continue its journey. From inside a few of the houses I can see the dim light of kerosene lanterns. Dad is walking in front of the truck now, constantly stooping to move branches to the side of the track. Mom sniffs the dung and animal urine in the air and says, "I swear this is Baidoa." She starts humming songs for her animals, she's so excited to be home. She points out the termite mounds by the roadside. "When I was a little girl, we used to play on those," she says.

I hear a strange sound coming from close to the truck. *"Aeeyy! Aeeyy! Aeeyy!"* I am afraid, but Dad, Mom, and Siciid are not startled. I can't understand why my parents don't care about the sound until I realize it is being made by herdsmen leading their camels into a corral. An old man with a long stick appears behind the truck and walks slowly along the side. Soon

Dad catches up with him to talk about the camels. The old man pays no attention to our truck, he keeps saying *"Aeeyy!"* as he chats with Dad in the Maay dialect. He has a low fading voice; Dad knows the man has no idea about the fall of President Siad Barre and the invasion that is coming to Baidoa. Siciid does not know the Maay dialect, and he struggles to understand through their hand gestures.

We are so hungry. Thankfully, the man follows nomad custom by feeding us all with the fresh milk from his camel. Mom, Siciid, and Dad help with the milking. Mom puts a bowl on her knee as she stands on one leg. She uses both her hands to milk the camel, squeezing the camel's teats in her fingers. Dad gently strokes the camel's legs as Hassan and I watch the camel's face in wonder. We have never been so close to a camel. Its neck seems too large to be real, and it is chewing something, its fuzzy lips moving back and forth against crooked amber teeth. I think of the rebels with their brown teeth, chewing qat and biting on cigarettes, and I shiver.

The truck is almost out of gas, says Siciid, and there is no gas anywhere to buy, even if we had money. We lumber up to a fence built of thorns, and Siciid shuts off the truck. Dad gets out and knocks at the fence post repeatedly, but there is no reply. Finally he steps back, runs hard like he's making a layup shot, and jumps over the thorn fence.

"Who are you?" comes a deep voice from inside the wall in Maay.

"It is me, Nur," says Dad.

"Allah be praised! Where have you come from on this dark night?"

As the gate of thorns swings open, I am surprised to see that the voice belongs to a woman. It is Aseey, my dad's aunt. She is tall and strong, gap-toothed, and has protruding eyes. She is holding on to a big stick because she says the lion Fareey's pride is still active at night. She hugs us all in turn and pushes us down on a mat in the courtyard. Soon we are cross-legged and devouring white maize with beans. She says the Somali Patriotic Movement, a group of Darod tribesmen led by Omar Jess, a defector from the Siad Barre government, are on their way to attack Baidoa. They want possession of the fertile lands around the city and to occupy its strategic position in central Somalia. These militiamen were once loyal soldiers of the Somali government but have now formed their own faction. Most men are fleeing the city, because they are the main targets. Women fear rape. For the first time my parents understand that the conflict they thought existed only in Mogadishu is in fact everywhere. They don't know where to go from Baidoa.

Dad rises to his feet, looking at each of us in turn. He is smiling, but there is fear in his eyes. "If we wait until morning, all the roads out of Baidoa will be blocked and there will be no escape. Siciid and I must leave straightaway. Don't worry, we're all going to be okay." Dad is leaving to save us. He knows his presence with us could kill us all, because the militias are terminating men with their families all together. But they might spare kids with moms. The close calls we had on our trip from Mogadishu were enough to explain what would happen.

Dad and Siciid talk about what to do. Dad knows the bushlands well and Siciid knows the roads, a good combination. But they decide it is best to split up when they get out of town, making it harder to see them. They will walk into the bush, away from the gunfire. That is their only plan. Dad kisses each of us on the forehead, then leaves, pausing outside the gate to wave and force a smile. He returns in a second to grab a stick to fend off hyenas and lions, then walks out and down the road with Siciid, past the truck and its empty gas tank. I watch my tall dad disappear into the dark night.

3

Trail of Thorns

We are four now, with no dad. Five if you count the baby inside Mom. Just me, Hassan, Nima, and pregnant Mom. That night I hear gunfire. Aseey has gone away for half an hour and returns, saying she has seen bodies in the streets of Baidoa. We hear more gunshots, distant screams. Every shot worries us it might be Dad. Mom and Aseey are reading the Koran. The gunfire continues all night. I see red tracers across the sky. Bullets easily pierce the thorn fence around the house, one passing close enough that I can feel its warmth on my cheek. It is not safe to sleep in the cool of the open air, so we pile into the stuffy house, already crowded with other displaced people. Mom tells us we will leave in the morning by foot into the bush; I know from her stories that we could face wild animals, thirst, and hunger.

As the sun is rising, we creep through the thorn fence. I see the bodies of a man and a woman in an embrace of death. Just beyond them I see a woman on her back crying, blood coming from her stomach, stray dogs preparing to feast. Then shots thud against a wall beside us and we turn and flee back to the house. I am six years old and learning that nowhere in the world is safe.

For six hours we tremble inside the fence while listening

to the sounds of war. Finally a bazooka shell hits the fence in a fiery explosion. Aseey pushes Hassan and me behind a giant termite mound in the yard.

"Bring your men outside now or we will kill you!" says a dark, skinny man who stands outside the burning fence.

"There are no men here!" says Aseey, mimicking the gunman's Darod accent in the hope that buys a reprieve.

But gunmen force themselves inside through the remains of the fence, and they drag us roughly from behind the termite mound to our mom's side. I try not to move and I cry for the man to let my hand go, but he only pulls harder, then throws me violently onto the dusty ground and kicks me. It is a painful lesson not to argue with a gunman. When he orders me to stand up, I do so, silently. I can see that one of the men's hands is trembling on the trigger of his gun. They are scarred hands with small cuts, rough hands that tell of a different life in the country—the only tools that he possessed before a gun, the hands he used for pulling up thorn trees or digging graves. His fingernails curve inward and scare me. His Uzi, covered in dust, matches his dusty hands. The gun is pointed at my face. I stare into the dark hole where bullets come out.

A bright object drops into the sand. A bullet. I pick it up and hold it up to the gunman. It's the first bullet I have ever touched; it looks too small and shiny to cause all the bloodshed I have seen. "Uncle," I say, because in Africa children call adults auntie and uncle as a sign of respect. "Uncle, you dropped this."

At first he ignores me. "Uncle, Uncle, Uncle!" I plead. My Mogadishan dialect probably confuses him. Maybe the man thinks we are Darod.

He finally looks down and snatches the bullet. Maybe he's embarrassed that a small boy has found his bullet. Our eyes meet. His aren't the angry or threatening eyes that I expect; they are just tired and red. I can see the dust in his hair, the rough skin through several days of stubble, and I become aware of the powerful smell of sweat and dust from the man and his torn black shirt.

As I look up, I see his mouth open briefly revealing ugly brown qat stains on his teeth. He turns to his comrade. "Leave these women and children, we have to go."

We look at each other in silence for a few seconds before he leaves, still holding the bullet I gave him. Then he turns around and shouts, "You must leave as soon as possible because if I see you again I won't let you go! I will return at midnight, and if you're still here, I will kill you all!"

Twilight. Mom ties Nima to her back and grabs me and Hassan by the arms. Aseey paces around for a minute and decides to leave by herself. We say good-bye to her and head out into the darkening streets. Aseey herself would wander in the bush for a year, avoiding the gunfire and eating whatever she could find. When she finally returned to Baidoa, her house had been burned to the ground, so she left again, hiding in the bush until the Rahanweyn Resistance Army took back Baidoa a couple years later.

Mom leads with Nima on her shoulders, me and Hassan behind in bare feet—we never owned shoes even before the war—warily making our way past dogs chewing on dead bodies. We see more tracer bullets arcing through the night and flashes of light, and from time to time we hear the screams of women. Mom has known these narrow alleyways since her childhood, and she finds hiding places by the side of the huts whenever we see or hear any movement.

At the edge of the town we look back and see that much of Baidoa is burning. In front of us is the bush, that dangerous land of lions and hyenas. She points out places where she chased hyenas and herded goats in her childhood, but this time I am not ready to hear any stories; I am struggling to stay on my feet.

The bush at least gives us some concealment from gunmen. Instead, we must contend with the vultures and crows that are swarming everywhere, fighting with dogs over the flesh of dead human beings. As we move, the ugly scavenger birds follow us. Mom angrily shoos them away. We carry on in silence, even though the cuts from the thornbushes make us want to scream out in pain. Sometimes Mom stops briefly to pull us closer to her dress and shoo off more crows. Sometimes she stumbles in the dark over the undulations of the sand or a thornbush. The ride with Dad and Siciid in the truck now seems so much better. Mom is used to the bush, but we are not.

Overwhelmed by hunger, thirst, and fatigue, I am by now being pulled along by Mom. I have forgotten about Dad, my aching feet stumbling through the sands until finally I fall. Hassan sits down beside me. His lips are cracking. A film of dust coats his face. He no longer looks like my brave brother. Mom looks back and remarks that she can no longer see fires or hear bullets. "There may be predators and snakes here, but we are safe from the soldiers," she says. "We'll sleep under this acacia tree."

Mom tries to stay awake to guard us, but she is too desperately tired. Soon we are all asleep.

When the sun wakes Mom, she stands up quickly. "Look at all the footprints of animals, so many of them! We have slept near the den of the hyenas. I think they have gone to Baidoa to eat human flesh. Let's go before they return." Strange sounds fill the land, sounds I never heard in Mogadishu. I can't even tell if they are birds or animals, but Mom can tell. She even knows if the sound is a female or a male. She looks, smells, listens, and then knows which way to go. I am glad she knows so much about the bush and the animals.

We continue walking through the heat. I now have stomach pains and need to stop frequently. I scream all the time because my feet are bleeding, but Mom knows what to do. She makes us sit under a bush, Hassan and I squeezing close together for the little shade it throws. Mom goes off for a few minutes, then returns with some leaves in her hand. These are the *awrodhaye* plants, she says, good for wounds. We watch her chew the leaves, then put the paste on our foot wounds like an ointment. It feels so good. I always thought her nomad stories were like fairy tales; they seemed so far away from our city life in Mogadishu. But now we are living them, and I see how much my mom really knows about how to survive. And now, without Dad to lead us, I see how strong and brave she is. At that moment in the bush, as the *awrodhaye* leaves and my mom's spit soothe my cracked and bleeding feet, I vow that I will always survive like her.

Suddenly Mom stoops low, waving her hand in a downward motion to tell us to do the same. She used to do this when she spotted lions and hyenas, but today it is not an animal, it is a group of five militiamen dragging a short, middle-aged man along a track and yelling in Maay dialect. "They are Rahanweyn! Thank Allah!" Mom stands and walks toward them. "How are you?" she shouts in Maay.

All five of the Rahanweyn men look to be in their thirties, dressed in tattered shirts with missing buttons. Their eyebrows are obscured by layers of dirt. One is in trousers rolled up to his knees, revealing the dirt on his legs. They push their hostage against a rock and listen to Mom's account of our escape.

"There is no possibility that you can escape this way because you are heading toward their territory," one of the men says. "You will stand a better chance in Baidoa." Then he points his gun at the hostage, who begs for his life. "Forgive me!" are the prisoner's last words. The bullets throw the dust from his jacket against my nose and cheeks. These are the Rahanweyn Resistance Army militias, who will retake Baidoa later.

One of the men hands Mom a jug of water. Nima drinks first, then I, then Hassan, and finally Mom, who doesn't stop drinking until the jug is snatched from her. "Don't finish the water!" the man scolds her. They give Mom a few segments of mandarin orange but insist that she leave. So we set off again on foot, eating our fruit, knowing we cannot go back to Baidoa, and wondering if any place is safe.

By now my stomach pains have turned into diarrhea; Hassan isn't much better, so we need to stop a lot. Mom makes us chew the *awrodhaye;* it is bitter and sour but still comforting. One time as I'm stooping along the rough dirt path, a man approaches from the distance on a small wooden cart pulled by a donkey. When he reaches us, I can see that the cart is transporting the skin of a freshly killed camel, blood still dripping from it onto the path below.

"This is my last camel," says the old nomad. "I slaughtered it before it died."

The man is wearing a turban of faded red, and he has a little gray hair left. Mom asks him if he can give us a lift. He agrees. Mom thanks him and the four of us climb on the back of the cart and return to the outskirts of Baidoa, sitting on the bloody camel skin. We travel in silence, the only noise being the heavy breathing of the donkey struggling to lift the wheels through the sand. We keep moving through the thornbushes to bypass Baidoa; the donkey cart driver knows it is too dangerous to go into the city. Shots can still be heard, and along the path we can see bodies swelling and rotten. Two dogs are tearing at the stomach of a corpse, while two puppies play tug-of-war with a bloodstained sleeve.

Finally we reach the main road to Mogadishu, where we flag down a truck so crowded with people that it is standing room only in the back. The driver is a huge, strongly built man who agrees to let us on board, but he refuses a bleeding woman who begs him to take her to a hospital. "There is no hospital now," he says. "Who will be able to help someone who is bleeding to death?" The woman sits by the road, then lies down to die. "Today death is better than living," says the driver. "Let the dying die."

The truck is going to Mogadishu, from where we had fled only days before. What else can we do? We have no more strength to walk through the bush, and no food or water. But the road back to Mogadishu is not the same as two days earlier. Power has shifted into the hands of the USC militias, and the carnage is everywhere. The mango trees in Afgooye have all been destroyed. Even the crocodiles and monkeys are dead, rotting in the streets. Militias hide in the bushes, ambushing people and raping women.

Next to me on the truck is a woman carrying her dead child. She didn't want to abandon his corpse to be eaten by the dogs. Hundreds of flies are landing on the dead boy's face, then lighting on my own filthy face and eyes. We are riding in a banana truck, and the smell of bananas mingles with the stench coming from all the people in the open bed where we are standing. Everyone is trying to find a banana to scavenge, but there are none left. The luckiest ones find a few banana peels and eat those. Mom finds none for us. She doesn't bother to complain that she is pregnant; no one can help anyone else.

The road is blocked with boulders and burning cars, and the driver threads the truck through the debris. At one point he stops to move some corpses blocking the way, dragging them off the road into the scrub. The stiff ones he just kicks to make them roll like a barrel.

"My son!" cries a woman, leaping from the truck and falling face-first to the ground. A body on the road is her son. Blood is coming from her mouth as she pleads with the driver to carry her son's corpse for burial. The driver refuses, saying there is no room for corpses. He gets back in the truck and starts to drive away, leaving the bleeding woman hugging her dead son by the side of the road.

"Mommy! Come with us please!" She has other children, still alive, on the truck, which is pulling away. "Mommy!"

The truck stops and reverses slowly. The woman gives her dead son one last hug, then returns to the truck and sits in silent grief for the rest of the journey. We pass by many more corpses on the road. Mom looks closely at all of them, looking for Dad or Siciid.

We drive on for more than 120 miles. My stomach throbs. I am barely conscious, aware of the flies, the heat, and the pain and of Mom's trembling hand holding on to my own. I am aware of the checkpoint that the truck is approaching and of the gunshots that hit the vehicle, but by now I am prepared to accept any outcome, even death.

Then I am aware of the driver on the ground, pleading that he is of the Darod clan like them and is taking sick people to Mogadishu. He is offering the gunmen money. I am aware of harsh, merciless faces looking at him, aware of the dirt and smell of their faces but not seeing any shape to them. You can't know what clan or tribe someone belongs to just by looking at them. You can tell only by their speech, so people learn how to fake accents. Maybe the driver is pretending to be Darod, I don't know. But my mom could fake any accent, she is prepared for anything.

I realize that the vehicle is moving again and that it has turned off the road to follow rough tracks where there would be, we hoped, no more checkpoints or militias. But then, less than twelve miles from Mogadishu, a bullet shatters the side window and explodes in the driver's head. The truck veers wildly off the road, then shudders into a ditch and finally stops at an angle. Everyone panics and stumbles out of the truck, people pushing and shoving. A woman throws me off the truck and I land on the ground. Mom struggles to keep us together, holding Nima tight. I take one last look at the truck and the driver who moments earlier was kicking bodies off the road, now himself dead. Mom knows we too might die any minute, from a random gunshot, and she is thinking our dad is dead by now, but she says she will die herself before she leaves our bodies to rot on the road. The rebels who shot the driver are running toward the truck. Mom takes our hands, me and Hassan, Nima on her back, and we walk again into the blazing bush. We are four, going on five, and we cast our feet and our fate forward into the breeze that rises from the sea, toward the White Pearl of the Indian Ocean. With our brave mom by our side, we will live or die in Mogadishu.

4

City of Women and Children

Mogadishu had become a city of women and children, a city of graves. The streets were littered with bullet casings and unexploded bombs. Exhausted militiamen roamed the empty neighborhoods, roofs and doors gone, carrying the goods they looted going from house to house, leaving nothing behind. The great capital city of the nation had become the valley of death. It was hard for my mom to see the ruin of this city where she had arrived a few years earlier to find a better life. We stood there—Hassan, me, my pregnant mom with Nima on her back, and no dad, all of us dazed. We could not believe what guns could do to a whole city. And the smell. Blood has a smell, metallic and musty like the smell of coins in a dirty pocket, and you can smell it when it covers the streets and turns rusty in the dust. That and the rank odor of smoldering buildings. The smell of death.

With my brother and me trailing behind Mom, we passed the bombed-out Cinema Ecuatore, the ruins of restaurants and clubs. There were no more signs touting the shows of local comedians. There was nothing to laugh about. We finally got to our house. It was a ruin. Rockets had pierced jagged holes in all sides of our rooms. Gone was the furniture my parents had proudly bought with Dad's basketball earnings. Gone were the wooden window shutters, or any windows you might shut. Gone were the shelves. Rebel soldiers had been using what was left of the rooms as an outhouse, there were stinking piles of shit swarming with flies everywhere. The neem tree was still standing, covered in dust. Underneath it was the shattered frame of the *jiimbaar* bed on which I had been born, littered with birds' nests and branches.

Hassan and I were so glad to be home we did not care about the mess. But Mom said no. "We cannot stay here," she said. She knew whoever was using our house as a toilet would kill us when they came back. A gunman in the distance was already signaling us to move on, his weapon pointed at us. I could see his mouth open; I could not hear what he was saying, but his gestures were enough to convince us he was about to shoot. Mom told us to keep walking. Hassan and I lingered, but after a few minutes we finally walked on.

Mom kept noticing landmarks that had disappeared. "Look!" she said. "Ahmed Gurey is gone!" Ahmed Gurey was a sixteenth-century imam and general, a national hero. His bronze equestrian statue, brandishing a sword in the middle of the KM4 circle was gone, probably melted down for the metal. Mom, the nomad girl who once thought statues were real people, now shook her head in disbelief that a statue could disappear.

Our walk was interrupted by a gun battle as two groups of rebels in pickup trucks met suddenly in the road. We ducked behind the chassis of a burned truck. After five minutes the gunfire stopped, and we came out to find bodies on the ground. One of the men wasn't dead but badly injured, bleeding and crying for help. A truck with gunmen sitting in the bed drove by fast and finished him off with a hail of bullets. Dust blew off the ground where the bullets ricocheted. Mom could tell by their speech that these opposing gunmen were all from the same tribe. The entire skirmish, the blood and the agonizing death, was probably caused by someone refusing to share a cigarette. We fled.

Our bare feet were bleeding from running on the rough ground in the baking sun. In our search for a place to stay that night, all we could see were people ducking from gunfire as they crossed the streets. Sometimes we would catch up with another confused family, a mom and kids like us, never any men, and together we would sit on the side of the road. It felt so good to sit after a long walk. Hassan removed tiny stones from my feet as I lay on my back. The *awrodhaye* plants that Mom used to treat my wounds don't grow in the city, so we had to bear the pain. My sister, Nima, was lucky to be on Mom's back mostly.

Many Somalis made it to North America and Europe, where they found a better life and watched the carnage in Somalia from afar. One of them was a boy my age named Barkhad Abdi, who escaped with his family to Yemen and then to Minneapolis. He went to college in Minnesota, then was working in a cell phone store in a mall when he auditioned for a part as a Somali pirate in the film *Captain Phillips* starring Tom Hanks. Now he is a famous actor and lives in Hollywood. He had very good luck.

And then there were people like us, mostly women and children, returning to Mogadishu because we had no other place to go. We were trapped.

Soon it was dark. With no electricity the city became pitch-black. Gunshots rang from all corners and dogs fought over dead bodies. Mom was still trying to find us a place to spend the night. She had one place in mind: under the KM4 bridge, a place where a road tunneled under the main artery. It was a few miles' walk, but when we got there, Mom was right: it seemed quieter in the dark tunnel. We heard only the distant gunshots and the soft wind of the night. Mom spread her scarf on the dusty road. We were all so tired. Hassan and I rested our heads on the scarf; Mom cuddled Nima. The waves of the ocean, the cool breeze, and the chirping crickets sent me into a deep sleep.

But that tunnel turned out to be not so quiet. Our sleep was interrupted by dogs that growled as they scavenged. Finally, at dawn, when there was a little light over the horizon, I opened my eyes to see Mom and Hassan standing in the tunnel crying, *"Lailaha ilallah!"* There is no god but Allah. They were standing on top of a graveyard. We had not noticed at night, but now we saw the place we had slept was where bodies had been hastily buried by people on the run. The bodies were fresh, not yet rotting, still in clothes that could be seen just under the thin layer of dirt covering them. One woman's body was half exposed. Dogs tugged at her feet. There was flesh everywhere. It looked like roadkill on U.S. highways. We fled again, retching from the scene.

For weeks we slept on the streets with the dead. Mom would sing the lullaby "Huwaaya Huwaa" in her weak voice, but with our empty bellies the song was not sending us to sleep. With a few hours of napping we continued every morning, only to expect to join the dead. We got used to the corpses, but we could not get used to our painfully empty stomachs. After days of no food or water, I would try to piss and couldn't, only blood came out. We ate whatever we could chew—unripe neem tree fruit that tasted like bitter olives, lizards we could catch. Nothing was too disgusting, even dead skin we peeled off our feet. We were sick with dysentery and dehydration, and we were not alone. As many people were dying from disease as from bullets. Mom tried to comfort us, telling us stories of her nomad life as we rested on her scarf at different places every night, but I could not pay attention to her stories. When Nima cried for milk, Mom tried to breast-feed her, but no milk came out. Our little sister was shrinking from malnourishment.

Meanwhile, Mom's belly was growing big with her baby. Her lips were cracked dry. The bugs sucked blood from her skin, and she scratched every second. The old wounds from her fights with hyenas opened up and began to seep blood from her neck, hands, and legs. The baby would come soon. Bad timing—our newest sibling was on the way to hell on earth. No one expected this baby to make it. Mom was scared for the labor.

Khadija Ahmed was the only neighbor we could recognize still remaining in the city. Her family was brave and decided not to leave Mogadishu, but her husband had been killed in their house just a few days earlier; the family was in mourning when we arrived. We met Khadija as she was clearing some rubble on the street. Mom and Khadija hugged, surprised to see each other alive. Khadija had three living kids, a boy named Abdikadir, who was almost my age, and two older daughters, Fatuma and Fardowsa. Another son, Kaafi, about a year older than my brother, Hassan, had been killed by a sniper on the street. Fatuma and Fardowsa, both in their teens, helped their mom fetch water and clean the house.

Khadija decided to take us in. She had given us some water and porridge, but none of us could swallow the food, we were too dehydrated. My soul wanted the food but my body could not. It was a big relief to finally be able to sleep in a room, even if the roof was pierced with bullet holes. The walls were made of cardboard, but at least the dry dust off the streets was no longer hitting our faces and we were not sleeping on graves. Every night before we went to bed, we sat quietly in a circle under the dark sky of Mogadishu with the stars blinking. Sometimes they would disappear in the bright flare of the tracer bullets and bombs, only to blink on again when the light of the gunfire dimmed. Fatuma, the elder daughter of Khadija, helped us forget the pain with her riddles. Some were religious, about the Prophet Muhammad or his wives. Others were problems of logic.

"A man wishes to cross a river with a goat, a bundle of hay, and a leopard," she said. "There is one small boat that can fit only one thing at a time. If he carries the hay first, the leopard will eat the goat; if he carries the leopard first, then the goat will eat the hay. If he carries the goat first, he will have the same problem on the other side when he brings either the leopard or the hay. How does he do it?"

I thought about that riddle for what seemed like hours, gazing up at the stars. Somalis believe each star represents a person who died. I looked at the brightest star and imagined my dad winking at me from heaven.

"He takes the goat first!" said Fatuma, snapping me back into the circle. "Then he goes back and gets the leopard."

"But the leopard will eat the goat on the other side!" said Hassan.

"Ah, no," said Fatuma, "because now he brings the goat *back with him*! He leaves the goat on the first side and takes the hay, then goes back and gets the goat."

"No!" said her sister, Fardowsa.

"Yes!" said Fatuma, very seriously. "It's true."

When the militias of the Hawiye clan entered Mogadishu and deposed President Siad Barre, they were united in that cause. But in late 1991, once Siad Barre had been defeated and the government destroyed, the Hawiye splintered into two tribes, the Abgaal and the Habargidir, and they began fighting each other for control of the city. This was the second phase of the civil war, known as the Four-Month War. This fight would turn out to be even worse, because by now there were so many weapons in Mogadishu. It would end in the total destruction of the city, and it began just as we arrived at Khadija's house.

Mom and Khadija were out every day clearing bodies from the streets, trying to bury them properly. This was for both respect and sanitation. Hassan and I slowly recovered from our dehydration and were able to eat a little porridge. I became good friends with Abdikadir. We played war games, making AK-47 rifles out of tree branches and shooting at each other. We could make very realistic gun sounds with our mouths, because we were hearing real guns every day. We cut the top off a three-liter jerry can and made it into a model of a "technical" weapon truck, using flip-flop soles for tires. We set it on fire, pretending it was hit by a rocket. We cheered. In this way we coped with our deep and constant fear and insecurity. Together with Hassan and Khadija's girls we also played hide-and-seek in the empty houses surrounding us, jumping from window to window, hiding behind debris. Whenever a house was blasted, we would run to it and hope to find new hiding spots.

But the porridge soon ran out, and we had to scavenge in the streets for any food. We became so weak that we spoke in whispers, unable to vocalize. I looked at Hassan and realized his eyes were sinking into his head, his skeleton was clearly visible. Every evening, Mom and Khadija would return with so much worry on their faces. By now the militias were fighting into every corner of the city, trying to take control block by block. They had rocket-propelled grenade launchers and automatic machine guns that almost deafened us. The war sometimes got so close to our house that we could hear fighters cheering and sometimes wailing when they were hit, the bullets zipping past our room. Abdikadir and I looked through the bullet holes in our walls, watching the action.

Sometimes the war moved into other quarters of the city, giving us a moment to peek our heads out and see what the streets looked like. We slowly stepped outside, peering in wonder through the smoke and dust. All we could smell was gunpowder and blood. Our only toys were the bullet casings that littered the street. We learned how to count using those shells, and we learned which guns had fired them. "This is AK-47; this is *Dabajeex*," which is the Somali name for the Russian PK machine gun. We could name every bullet and weapon. We even made up our own nicknames for weapons, calling unexploded hand grenades *anuni* (durian) because they looked like that spiky fruit. These *anuni* would often explode, killing or maiming people. Today on the streets of Mogadishu you can see many people with limbs missing from *anuni* explosions.

The war continued, leveling what remained of the crumbled city. Soon came a new misery: Mogadishu and all of Somalia faced their first drought since the one in 1977 that forced my parents out of the nomad life and into the city. The 1992 drought was even worse. All my grandparents survived the drought of 1977 but could not survive this one. Only later did we learn that they died, all four of them, after all their remaining animals were wiped out and they could not find water or food. Their wealth, their bravery, and their pride were gone. The Iftin family that once boasted of hundreds of animals had vanished from the earth as if in an apocalypse. No one ever found my grandparents' graveyards. They died like they were born, in unknown places. Everything in between was herding animals.

Khadija called us orphans because we had no dad. Now we had another orphan in our family. My new baby sister was born during the Four-Month War. Khadija helped Mom deliver in the middle of the night using a flashlight, while Hassan and I waited outside the room, curious. Amazingly, the baby came out breathing and healthy. Unlike when I was born, Mom did not have people visit, or bring herbs, food, and clothes. There was no rest for forty days. The day after Sadia was born, Mom was forced to go out and find food for us.

She was getting weaker. I could see that our mom had swollen feet, her skin was darker than ever, and she was no longer the beautiful nomad girl whom my dad had fallen for. Hunger, sleepless nights with the baby, and constant worry had beaten her down. Madinah Ibrahim Moalim, brave daughter of her brave parents, was giving up the fight. She could no longer care for us.

At least Hassan and I had friends. Nima was all by herself. Girls in Somalia don't usually play outside with other girls. They stay in with their moms learning how to cook so they can be married when they become teenagers. Now, with my mom so weak and no food to cook anyway, Nima would sit outside by herself in a daze, eating sand to fill her empty stomach. My brother and I, now eight and seven, knew that if our family was to have water and food, we would need to get it ourselves. Our mom had kept us alive this far; now we needed to keep our sisters and her alive. This was not anything we discussed or planned. When your belly aches from hunger and your lips crack from thirst, there is nothing to say. You just do what you need to for survival. And so we put aside our games of hide-and-seek and our bullet-casing toys and got to work.

The only place to get water in our quarter of Mogadishu was the well pump at Madinah Hospital, three miles distant along a road lined with sniper posts. This was the same hospital next to Mumin's house where we had spent the night when the civil war broke out. Now it was a ruin, the roof gone and the main operating room being used as a militia meeting hall.

Much of the grounds had become a graveyard like everywhere else in Mogadishu, though at least here the dead were buried properly. This was where Hassan and I had to walk with our twenty-liter jerry can. When we arrived, the line for the water tap was hours long, in the glaring sun. The rebels that controlled Madinah were themselves former hospital workers from the Hawiye tribe, and they were not as bad as the street militias. They minded their own business while we filled up our cans. We would put the can in the line and then try to sit in the shade of a tree or building, keeping a close eye on that can or someone would cut ahead of us. It felt so good when our turn came and we finally had freshwater. The can weighed forty-four pounds full, but it was round, so we could roll it home, especially since the road that way was downhill. But there were snipers sitting in the windows of the old Ministry of Planning, shooting at people for practice. They did not distinguish between kids, women, and old people. Hassan and I kicked and rolled that jerry can and ran along the edge of the ministry wall, crouching to avoid being seen by the snipers. The bullets that hit the wall above our heads sent dust into our ears. As we moved out of range of the snipers, Hassan would stop and search me for bullet wounds, then I would do the same to him. Even when we were that young, we knew that sometimes you don't feel a bullet until you see the blood.

One day our mom had the idea that we should fetch water at night, when the snipers were unable to see us and there would be no line at the pump. The gates of Madinah Hospital were closed, no one was allowed to enter after dark, but Hassan and I found a spot around the back of the hospital where a rocket had destroyed part of the wall. Through that hole we were able to creep in quietly with our jerry can. The hospital militiamen who tolerated water gathering in the daytime would likely not be so kind to children sneaking in at night. Being careful not to speak, we filled up the can while hoping the sound of the crickets covered the squeak of the pump handle. We could not roll the full jerry can on the hospital grounds, it was too noisy, so Hassan and I lifted it a few feet at a time, resting our arms in between, until we reached the hole in the wall. On the road home we could hear the snipers cursing in the windows of the ministry; they could hear the can rolling down the road, but they could not spot us.

One morning we woke to the usual sound of gunfire but also to the voice of a man in the house. He wasn't yelling like a fighter. Who was this male visitor in the city of women and children? We rose and saw to our dismay that it was Macalin Basbaas, the neighborhood Koranic scholar. The Angel of Punishment was back from the bush and ready to reopen his madrassa. Our mom and Khadija kept asking him, how did he survive? His answer was simple: *"Alhamdulilah!"* Praise be to Allah!

He was wearing a long white clerical *kanzu,* and he carried a bundle of hard sticks in his hands—the switches he used on his students, which he apparently never traveled without. Mom and Khadija were nodding at his words. They talked a lot about the war, though for a few minutes they argued about the day of the week. (No one knew for sure.) Then he led us all in a long prayer. I remember the words: "May Allah save the children to grow to be religious leaders for this country." Then we raised our right hands up and said, "Amen!" With that prayer, Hassan and I as well as Khadija's kids had been signed up for the madrassa. War or no war, learning the Koran must go on. Even the gunmen who tormented us had studied at madrassas and could recite the holy words. Lessons would start immediately, and we left with Macalin Basbaas for his mud-walled school.

There were only ten students including us at the school, all of us sitting on the dirt with our wooden writing boards on our laps. From that day on, Hassan and I as well as Khadija's kids bore, besides war, thirst, and hunger, the daily beating of Macalin Basbaas and his hard sticks. Any mistake in our lessons, which consisted entirely of memorizing the Koran in Arabic, rather than our native tongue, was an excuse for a beating. Each day I memorized several verses of the Koran by heart. The first few chapters are short, and they are mostly verses I had learned at home from Mom. But each day that passed they grew longer and harder to memorize, and the flogging doubled each time we made a mistake. I felt I needed magic to carry them all in my head.

The Angel of Punishment sent us home every evening bleeding from our wounds. Hassan was not big enough to carry me as I got weaker and weaker from the daily beatings, but he would at least hold me up as I sat during lessons. The teacher's cruelty was not unusual or personal; all madrassas relied on corporal punishment. In fact, parents expected it as part of a rigorous education. When we got home, sometimes I could not open my mouth to describe my pain, but all Mom could see was that her sons were learning all 114 chapters of the Koran. We had missed so much school because of the war, and now was our chance to catch up on memorizing God's holy word, to learn discipline and mental strength. She did not care about the beating, she cared about the three verses of the Koran I had memorized for the day. I was angry and felt betrayed, but the madrassa was the only type of education available to us, and children who excelled at the Koran could someday become clerics, a position of high status in Somalia. In that culture, in those terrible times, this was her way of looking out for us. Anyway the wounds from the beatings would heal, and if they didn't, better to die memorizing the Koran than from a sniper's bullet. Because on days when there was no madrassa—praise be to Allah!—we still had to kick that can of water past the snipers.

In early 1992 the Four-Month War ended in a stalemate. Exhausted militiamen, still holding guns, sat in the beds of their technicals, chewing qat, on every corner of the city. Most of these rebels were loyal to Mohamed Farrah Aidid, who was much respected by the majority of his tribe on the south side of Mogadishu, where I lived. Aidid's rebel organization, the USC, controlled twelve of the sixteen districts of Mogadishu. The rest, mainly in the north of the city, were controlled by the warlord Ali Mahdi. Between Mahdi's forces and Aidid's forces, "green lines" were established that divided the city. Meanwhile, Aidid moved deep into inland Somalia with his soldiers, grabbing land and killing anyone armed who was not on his side. One of the places Aidid seized was Baidoa. When Aidid and his militias entered the town, they met the dying and starving faces of the Rahanweyn; the drought had hit hard in this area. Aidid's militias remained in town for the next two years until the locals armed themselves and pushed back against them.

The famine drove many from Baidoa and other areas into Mogadishu. They arrived by foot, thousands every day. The streets were filled with women and children begging and dying, very thin and ill. Many headed straight to Madinah Hospital for water. The queues at the single pump got longer and longer, hundreds of people.

Meanwhile, the stalemate did not mean the fighting stopped, it just became sporadic and unpredictable. Usually the opposing sides would send up their rockets and shells at night, exploding in neighborhoods as we cowered in our beds, hoping we would not be among the unlucky ones who got hit. By day the rebels who had been shelling us all night hung around our streets, laughing and chewing qat.

I could recognize some of the faces among the newly returned, people I had known in the city before the war. I saw the same kids who used to bully me, jealous that my simple Rahanweyn dad was a basketball star; now they were back with their uncles in the militias. Now they bullied all of us. Hassan, who once put them in their place, now had to stand there and take it as they punched him in the face. If we fought them, we would surely be killed by their uncles. So we were bullied every single day. This was the new order of Mogadishu. Families harassed other families. Guns ruled the city. Even kids carried around pistols and shot people. Hassan and I were more scared of teenagers than of older militiamen. There were no laws, no rules, justice did not exist. Somalia had become a failed state.

Our Rahanweyn clan had always been stigmatized by the more powerful Hawiye, but now in the lawless city we were threatened every day. Clan became the only thing people talked about. Hassan and I learned to speak only in the Mogadishu accent, to disguise what tribe we belonged to. When someone asked us for our tribe, we even lied and said we were Hawiye. Our mom and Aseey had used the same tactic to save our lives during the flight from Mogadishu. So we were learning from them how to survive. But they were nomads from the bush. Hassan and I were born in Mogadishu, and we felt like guests in our own city. People who had never set foot in Mogadishu before the war were ruling the streets.

When we weren't carrying water or attending the madrassa, Hassan and I roamed the streets in search of food for our family. Everyone in Mogadishu said the same thing: "Eat anything that does not eat you." The struggle was to survive another scorching day, and every day the chances were slim. It felt like all the curses of the universe had descended upon us. First war, then natural disaster, then disease. There were no working hospitals, no clinics or drugs to treat malaria, typhoid, dysentery, and cholera. All became things you just had to live with, or die from. Mogadishu had become a city of walking skeletons, not unlike pictures of Holocaust survivors in World War II. Somalis called it *Caga Bararki,* "the time of swollen feet." Everybody's feet had blown up like balloons due to severe malnourishment and fluid retention. It became hard to walk, but we had to walk to get water. So our mom used cactus thorns to pierce and drain our feet.

In this way Hassan, Nima, and I were able to stand on our feet and also run, but our newborn sister, Sadia, was not even able to sit up. She was so tiny and thin, just skin stretched over bones, and struggling to breathe. Hassan and I watched every day as Mom let Sadia suckle on her breasts that could not even produce a drop of milk. We watched as Mom lifted up Sadia's tiny body, trying to make her comfortable. We watched as she bathed Sadia with warm water, putting drops in her mouth. Nothing helped. Khadija was often in the room with Mom, discussing what they could do to save the baby. Finally there was only prayer. Mom had tears in her eyes as she whispered into Sadia's face, "Please, Malakul Maut, Angel of Death, take Sadia with you. There is nothing more I can do."

Many times Sadia went quiet and we thought she was gone, but then she came back breathing again. Finally, one Friday morning, Malakul Maut visited our house and decided to take Sadia. When Sadia started rolling her eyes, Hassan and I avoided watching and started digging the grave for her in the front yard of Khadija's house.

Makeshift mass graves had popped up everywhere in Mogadishu. To earn money, men would dig graves seven feet deep, then guard the hole with shovels and wait for people to come with their dead charging a few coins to accept the bodies. Hassan and I watched as the men with spades and the families of corpses argued over the price of burial. The men were saying they buried the bodies properly, it was hard work, and they wanted money in return. Hassan and I discussed how we would handle this if our mom died. Definitely we would not have money to pay the men for a proper burial. We knew we would only be able to cover her with a little sand, like everyone else with no money did, leaving her body exposed to the dogs.

So we tried to dig as deep as two little boys could for baby Sadia. We had to be careful because Khadija had other bodies including her own son buried in the same spot. Right away our shovel hit the foot of a dead person; we kept moving around until we found a small space unoccupied to bury Sadia.

By the time the grave was ready, Sadia was dead. I looked at my baby sister and kissed her on the forehead. We wrapped her in a small white scarf and laid her in her tiny grave before sunset, when the dogs would start roaming the streets. Mom cried tears of sadness but also tears of joy because she knew Malakul Maut had carried Sadia's soul up to heaven, and in Islam a child's death means protection for the mom from hell. Then we poured sand all over her until we could no longer see her. No one came for condolences. Hassan and I shared the death of our sister with friends and people in the neighborhood, but no one expressed sorrow or even cared. Death was everywhere; it was not a big deal. It was nothing to talk about. After a few prayers we got on with our own survival. In a few days Sadia's grave disappeared into the dust; she did not have a grave marker, just sand.

Lucky for our sister she had left the cruel world of guns and bloodshed. She was now in heaven eating sweet ripe fruit and floating on a river of milk and honey guarded by the angels. The rest of us trudged on with our daily struggles. Every morning we got up and made sure everyone was still breathing and alive. Mom prayed and read the Koran for another day of survival.

The stories Mom told us about heaven, life after death, and the privilege of being a Muslim child encouraged us to not fear the end. Mom talked about the rivers of milk and honey, the beautiful endless good life in heaven. No wars, no bullying. It made us feel guilty for living in the hell on earth, like we had done something bad to deserve it. Another thing our mom told us that made us strong and kept us going: "Allah is watching us." She said all our struggles and difficult days were tests from Allah, and the strongest and most faithful would be rewarded in heaven. So every morning Mom reminded us to pray to Allah, and Hassan and I spent five minutes praying.

It turned out that unlike the citizens of Mogadishu religion was surviving the war very well. With all the people returning from the bush, small mosques were popping up on every corner. The madrassas were now packed with students. Macalin Basbaas stood in his school, under a thick roof of sticks, and supervised our daily Arabic reading of the Koran. On school days Hassan and I walked down to the madrassa with a container of black ink, our adrenaline pumping as we got near the entrance. Macalin Basbaas was always torturing a student for minor mistakes. If you were one minute late for school, you would get twenty minutes of beating. If you had not memorized the lesson of the day, you could be hung by your wrists for hours.

The morning after Sadia died, Hassan and I thought we would be forgiven for being a little late, but Macalin Basbaas did not care. That day he beat us so bad that I thought of quitting the madrassa, but I knew it could never happen, because Mom would disown me and anyway Macalin Basbaas would come down the street and find me and drag me back to school, with another beating for sure. There was no escape. In Somalia, madrassa teachers are second in rank after dads. What they say cannot be rejected even by the parents. Still, even the Angel of Punishment allowed students to leave early and find water and food for their families. The end of the class in the afternoon was always a happy moment for us, but the next morning the beatings would resume.

5

Arabic to English

By late 1992 some rain had finally come to Somalia, and people were selling food on the street—small piles of tomatoes, bundles of sugarcane, ears of corn—which they had brought in from the countryside. We desperately needed coins to buy some of this food, so Hassan and I hatched a plan to make some money. We tried hawking on the streets, selling anything we could find. First we collected firewood from near the airport, where the drought had killed so many trees, leaving piles of dead sticks. We collected them and ran after people, begging them to buy our firewood. But no one would buy. People had so little money and could collect firewood themselves. So we came up with a different plan: selling water. At this point we had two twenty-liter jerry cans, so Hassan and I would split up. He would get water for families in the city too afraid to risk their lives crossing by the snipers and willing to pay a few shillings for the chore. With the second can, I would get water for our family. Hassan learned he could move faster, and earn more money, by carrying his water can on his back, lashing it around his forehead with a scarf. But eventually this caused him so much back and shoulder pain that he screamed in agony every night. We needed another plan.

The militiamen were all addicted to qat, which they chewed constantly and which energized them to fight. The qat came into Mogadishu by boat and by land, a lot of it from Kenya. I remembered my dad chewing qat before the government collapsed; he was always happy when he was chewing. That's when he took me to restaurants and bought me things. I knew some of the militiamen might also be in a happy mood while chewing, so Hassan and I would sneak behind them and pick up the leaves they dropped, which we could then resell. We joined a group of other kids who roamed the streets day and night collecting loose qat leaves that militiamen would drop or that had been left behind at the stands where women hawked their bundles of leaves.

Eventually, we grew bolder. When the fresh qat entered the city escorted by trucks full of militiamen, we ran after the trucks, jumping on and stealing leaves from the rebels while they were not watching. Many times the butt of a gun would hit me and send me tumbling off the moving truck empty-handed. But other times I ended up with some fresh leaves that I could sell on the streets. Many times my stash was later taken at gunpoint or with a knife on my neck. But sometimes I was lucky to get some cash.

Of course there was no government to print currency, so before long the paper shilling notes still in circulation had become torn and tattered. When the rebels did give us money for loose qat, they always paid with the filthiest, shredded five-hundred-shilling bills they had—basically money they felt was useless. The market ladies selling food would not accept these bills, so Hassan and I devised a plan. We learned from our mom, wise woman of plants, about a plant called the apple of Sodom whose leaves and twigs contained a milky sap like glue. We collected these leaves and squeezed out enough sap to carefully glue the shredded bills together. Then we waited to do our shopping until dusk, when it would be harder for the ladies to see the money. This usually worked.

It felt like bringing a medal home as we walked into the house with maize, milk, and fruits for our family. Mom cooked the maize, put it in a bowl, and added milk. Hassan, Nima, and I sat in a circle surrounding the bowl. Mom would not eat until we were full. She always ate just the little bit that stuck to the bottom of the pot, scraping every last bit of it out.

Nima had sunk further into what seemed like insanity. She mostly spent her days outside the house, digging ditches in the sand with her hands, as if she wanted to make her own grave and get in it. Sometimes she sat right on top of Sadia's grave with her cheek on the sand, like she was communicating with our dead sister. When Hassan and I arrived home, Nima would run and hug us. In the conservative Somali culture, girls never associate with men, even their own brothers, but Hassan and I refused to accept that and always allowed our sister around us when we were home. She was not going to the madrassa, but Hassan and I taught her the basics of the Koran by reading to her in Arabic, and she picked up some verses, even though she had almost no energy left.

With so much of the city destroyed, people moved into houses they found in the neighborhoods whose owners had either died or never returned. Old buildings of universities, schools, and hospitals became makeshift refugee camps. But some people also returned to their former houses, including a woman named Falis who would change my life.

Falis was a tall, dark woman in her twenties. Like many sophisticated Mogadishu women, she wore makeup—including eyeliner and a bright yellow foundation made from ground turmeric. In peacetime she had been fat, which in Somalia is a sign of beauty. Many men chased her. But during the war she came back skinny, and she was worried that her beauty was gone. She had been lucky that her house survived the war, in part thanks to having relatives in the militias who guarded it while she was gone. Before the war Falis had a good job as the ticket seller at the Cinema Ecuatore; she remembered seeing my dad on weekends, hanging out with his friends in those peaceful days. When she came back to Mogadishu, she was able to get a television, some videocassettes, and a VCR, which she had set up in a shack attached to her house. With a gasoline generator and fuel she had somehow secured from the militia forces, she started a makeshift cinema and dance parlor, hoping to charge a few coins for admission. At first she wouldn't let us kids wander in, but we could hear the sounds outside her door while she was testing the equipment. One of the tapes she played over and over was the Michael Jackson music video "Thriller," and I would dance with other boys to the beat from her courtyard. I loved that song so much.

One day when I was out there dancing, Falis came out to hang posters of Rambo, the Terminator, and Chuck Norris, which she had saved from the Cinema Ecuatore. I stared at the men in the posters—big strong Americans, flexing huge muscles, not like the skinny people in Mogadishu. I didn't understand what an actor was or that the men called Rambo, the Terminator, and Commando might have other names in real life. I just went and looked at those posters every day, imagining what those strong people must be like. Sometimes rebels would come up to the posters and spit on them, like they were picking a fight with the men in the posters. But whoever these men were, I knew it would be a fight the rebels could never win. The weapons the movie people carried were much bigger and shinier than anything the militias had in Mogadishu.

Falis needed help getting that shack cleaned up and ready

for people to watch the movies. Because I was outside the shack all the time, looking at the posters or dancing, she asked if I would help. For the first time I was allowed inside. The shack had a dirt floor and was filthy. I got to work, climbing up into narrow corners and pulling off spiderwebs, dusting off the TV screen, cleaning the cassettes, fetching water, and arranging where people would sit. Finally the space was ready. I was so excited that I was going to see the people on those posters in a movie!

The first movie Hassan and I saw was *Commando,* starring Arnold Schwarzenegger. I sat with my jaw practically on the dirt floor, my eyes popping out. The audience cheered, laughed, and applauded whenever an action scene happened. Of course none of us knew any English, we couldn't understand anything they were saying, so whenever there was a bit of conversation in the movie, we shouted at Commando to stop talking and shoot to kill. Everyone hated the talk; they wanted shootings and killings and bloodshed, just like real life in Mogadishu but better. People would wander out of the shack during the talk and come running back when they heard the gunfire. Others stayed but just talked to each other during the dialogue until the action started.

I stayed. I never talked to Hassan or anyone during the dialogue. I loved the action best, but I also had a burning desire to know what they were saying. So I sat there, glued to the screen. I watched the actors intensely as they talked, trying to read their lips. I picked up words and phrases that were repeated often, most of them related to guns and death. I learned to recognize words like "shoot" and "kill." I realized I had some ability to hear the words easily and remember them.

Hassan and I went back to watch movies whenever we weren't at the madrassa or fetching food and water. Falis let us watch in return for sweeping the dirt floor. We saw *Rambo,* and

The Terminator, and *The Delta Force.* All action movies. I got to know the scenes by heart, exactly what would happen and what Commando or the Terminator or Rambo would say. I met new friends in the movie shack, Mohammed, Bashi, and Bocow. At the end of the day, when Falis said she was closing, we would walk home and quiz each other on the movie, reminding each other of scenes, talking about what we liked. We would act out scenes, throwing rocks, jumping over debris, and pretending to speak English. I read Arnold's lips and moved my mouth the way he did. I drove my mom crazy saying "I'll be back!" over and over again. I didn't even know what it meant, but I knew it sounded cool.

For the first time in years, since going with my dad to the basketball games, I felt truly happy. I had no more strong dad to look up to, but now I had these big strong action heroes giving me so much excitement. I wanted Commando to come to Mogadishu and kill all the militias in the city.

Hassan and I still had to feed our family. How could we go to the movies and make money at the same time? We hit on the idea of selling popcorn and peanuts in the video shack. We didn't even know Americans buy popcorn when they go to movies; this was just an idea we had. We borrowed ten kilos of raw peanuts in the shell from a market lady, who agreed to the loan when we told her our plan and promised we could pay her back more than she could make selling them raw. We got some corn kernels the same way. Hassan and I shelled the peanuts and roasted them over a fire at home. We popped the corn in a kettle of our mom's. Then we carried our basket of peanuts and popcorn, still warm, to the video shack and sold it all. Even Falis bought some. We were able to pay back the market women, buy food for our family, and watch a movie.

The movie shack became a second home to me, and Falis became like family. I even started calling her aunt. Hassan and

I started skipping the madrassa to go to the movies and sell peanuts and popcorn. We lied to our mom, telling her in the morning we were going to school, because she would never agree to let us do that. She thought movies were evil and not a place for good Muslims. But we weren't alone. Many students were skipping the madrassa to watch the movies. One day Macalin Basbaas showed up at the video shack and found five of us watching *Commando* when we should have been in school. He dragged us out and marched us back to the madrassa in a rage. "Allah will send you to hell for going to the movie!" he screamed. "You will be punished in hell! Allah hates you!"

The punishment on earth was beating, and hanging by the wrists for a day. The Angel of Punishment stripped off my clothes, tied me to a pole, and beat me for a whole day until my body was covered in blood. I can't say what was more painful, the beating or my arms being pulled from their sockets as I hung. All I could think of was the torture scene in *Rambo: First Blood Part II,* when Sylvester Stallone is captured. I tried to be strong like Rambo, but it was hard in real life, and I screamed for help. Macalin Basbaas's hard sticks on my skin seemed even worse than bullets.

After that I had to stop going to movies for a while. Instead, my friends and I formed a gang called Weero. *Weero* is the Somali word for "war," and our gang played war games with slings and rocks. We attacked another group of neighborhood boys who had formed their own gang. Unlike hide-and-seek, this war play was dangerous; you could lose eyes or break bones. Also if you hurt a kid in the same tribe as Aidid, you could be shot and killed. I was always careful to know my opponents in these games.

The best place to play war games was inside the Horseed Stadium, because it had a smooth concrete floor and bleachers. The rockets and guns had not done much damage to that thick concrete. The best thing in there was the echo that came from the concrete, so when we released the sling, the snap of the ropes was amplified like a gunshot. This had been the home of the Somali national basketball team, the same place where my dad trained and played, carrying me proudly on his shoulders every weekend. Now everything was destroyed and looted, including the Somali flags that had waved inside and outside. On the walls that still stood were painted guns of all kinds. Some families from the countryside had settled in parts of the stadium, they had set up tents. When we played in there, they always tried to chase us out of what they decided was now their home.

Soon enough I was going back to the movies; no beating by Macalin Basbaas could keep me away. In those movies I learned about a world beyond Somalia and Islam. I had never seen a map of the world. I didn't know the difference between Europe and America. I had no knowledge of geography or history, only what Macalin Basbaas had taught us in Arabic about Islam, Saudi Arabia, and Egypt. But in the movies I saw so many brave soldiers and beautiful women. There were no ruins, the streets were clean and nice; the wars were always fought somewhere else. No one chewed qat and spit or dug graves in their yard. There was lots of food. I thought, "Whoever these people are, they are great!" I prayed to Allah that I could meet some of these strange foreigners. Maybe it was wrong to pray for infidels, but it worked.

By December 1992, the world could no longer sit back and watch the starvation in Somalia. Humanitarian aid had been coming in for months, but the warlords grabbed all the food and medicine for themselves and gave none to the people. The situation got worse until finally the United Nations decided to take action. Led by the United States, twenty-eight countries organized a military task force called Operation Restore Hope. The goal was to supervise the distribution of food and supplies.

In Somalia we call Americans *Mareekans*. When I heard these *Mareekans* were coming to Mogadishu, I asked my mom who they were. I didn't know the people in the action movies were *Mareekans*. "They are huge, strong white people," she said. "They eat pork, drink wine, and have dogs in their houses."

This sounded like the people I had seen in the movies. Whoever they were, the militiamen looked worried about their arrival. Many rebels started burying their guns; some fled Mogadishu. There was confusion and tension everywhere. I couldn't wait to see *Mareekans* land in Mogadishu! Hopefully, they would look like actors in the movies and would spray bullets all over the militias.

And so at midnight on December 9, the thunderous roar of Cobra helicopters and AC-130 gunships filled the air. From the ocean came the buzz of hovercrafts, unloading tanks and marines onto the beach. Our house was close to the airport and the sea, so all these sounds woke me up right away. Through the bullet holes in our roof I could see the gleaming lights of the planes, accompanied by the roar of tanks along the roads. My mom, Hassan, and Khadija were all up, even Nima.

I was eager to see the troops and the helicopters in the morning. At dawn Hassan and I, holding hands, walked down to the airport past streets that used to have sniper nests. There were lots of Somalis in the street, all of them headed the same way, toward the airport. As we got closer, the sounds of the Cobra attack helicopters became deafening. We joined a group of other excited Somalis, some standing on the walls, others on top of roofs, watching as big Chinook heavy-lift copters took off and landed. We could see warships in the distance on the blue ocean; everywhere around the airport, marines in camouflage were taking positions and setting up gun posts.

Someone said the *Mareekans* had rounded up the rebels who were controlling the airport and seaport. The crowd got bigger and bigger; we shouted, laughed, and cheered in excitement. Security perimeters had already been set up, blocking entrances to the airport. The *Mareekan* flag was waving, stars and stripes. That's when it hit me: *I had seen that flag in movies!* These *Mareekans* were the movie people, and this was a real movie happening in front of us!

Commando must be here, I thought. This is it. This is the moment I had been waiting for, to meet Commando and watch him blow away all the militias! Helicopters dropped a shower of leaflets with photos and information about the troops. I picked up several of them. "United Nations forces are here to assist in the international relief effort for the Somali people," it said in Somali. "We are prepared to use force to protect the relief operation and our soldiers. We will not allow interference with food distribution or with our activities. We are here to help you." Because not so many Somalis could read, the leaflets also showed an illustration like a comic book of a U.S. soldier shaking hands with a Somali man under a palm tree as a helicopter flew past. I couldn't wait to shake hands with Commando.

Everything was moving so quickly—the tanks, the soldiers, the planes. We jostled for positions to watch the movie that was happening in front of us. Except there was no gunfire. I kept waiting for the battle to start; I wanted the Chinooks and Cobras to blast away at the rebels. But everything was peaceful. Then I remembered it's always like this in the movies. First you see all the heavy machines and helicopters gearing up for action, then the battle comes later. I wanted to see the militias face these troops, but the rebels I had known since we returned to Mogadishu were now walking around unarmed, acting like regular people. They didn't dare to face Commando.

I watched all day as the marines took positions, more and more of them coming. Two men in uniform waved to let us cross the airport runway up to the sand dunes, so we could watch as the hovercrafts brought more and more marines from the sea. Humvees and tanks roamed noisily but never fired a shot. I was getting impatient for the battle to start. We watched as the troops pulled out their stuck Humvees from the sand dunes. Hassan and I grew bolder and edged close to the troops. I stood there with my mouth open, watching them drink from a water bottle and smile at us. I made a sign asking for water, and the white guy in uniform went into the Humvee and handed me a plastic bottle. Then we made eating signs with our hands to our mouths, and they handed us tasty marmalade, bread, and butter. The Commando look-alikes even spoke to us in Somali, but all they could say was *"Somali siko!"* Somali, move back!

One of the marines threw a chocolate candy to me. I grabbed it and swallowed the whole thing. When I got home and told Mom, she gave me a hard slap.

"You must not eat pork!" she said.

I told her I didn't think it was pork, it was sweet, but she didn't believe me. How would she know what pork tastes like?

Night came again, and Mogadishu was noisier than I had ever heard it. But for the first time in two years, there was no sound of explosions and gunfire. We were surprised how the marines lit up the airport. Lights came from everywhere, helicopters, tents, cars. It looked like daytime in the middle of the night. We were not allowed to get too close to the airport at night—*"Somali siko!"* the marines yelled over and over. But for the first time my friends, my brother, and I could go out on the dusty streets after dark and play games, laugh, and talk. We counted the helicopters as they flew over, and the big gunships that circled over the city. Falis's movie theater could now stay open at night, but we did not go. For the first time in years, outside was even more exciting than the movies.

One morning my brother and I woke to see sand-colored Humvees parked in the streets of our neighborhood. The troops were going from house to house searching for weapons. There were marines on every corner with their guns pointed down, standing tall. They looked so fit and clean in their uniforms, which had no holes or missing buttons. They were not chewing qat or spitting. They were not arguing with each other. I stood there trying to imagine the America that these people came from; that place must be gorgeous. Then a beautiful, tall lady marine exited a house near us and walked our way. She had a huge smile on her face, but Hassan and I ran back to the house and stayed close to our mom and Khadija. We weren't sure what was happening, and we did not want our mom to be hurt. The lady came in and used sign language to communicate that she wanted to search the house for weapons. Every step she took I was following her, my mom struggling to pull me away. Her straight brown hair reminded me of white women in the movies. Before she left, she smiled, said something, and came to me, stretching out her hand. I shook my head no and backed off shyly. I wanted to touch her, but I was too scared to get into trouble with my mom and Somali culture. Normally we don't shake hands with women, specially a non-Muslim. The soldier wasn't angry, and she handed me some chocolate bars. My mom grabbed them away, thinking it was pork, but we convinced her it was candy. Even she ate some.

As the marines drove off, I ran after the Humvees begging for more. One marine took off his mirrored sunglasses, and I saw he had blue eyes! He was like an alien. Next thing we knew, sweets were raining down from the Humvees. Other kids and I fought over them, and then chased the Humvees some more. Finally one stopped and I quickly climbed up, trying to reach a marine's sunglasses. I was curious and wanted to see if he also had blue eyes. He was as big as Commando. He pointed his M16 rifle up and away from me, then stretched out his arms and lowered me back to the road. I shouted, "Rambo! Commando!" hoping he would respond. He laughed and waved and said, *"Somali siko!"*

Lots of food was now coming into the port under troop escort, and distribution centers opened in Mogadishu. Hassan and I went to one of the food kitchens in the old ministry building—the place we had crawled past every night and day to avoid snipers while bringing water. Now the snipers were gone and the gates were open, hundreds of people queuing for food. Hassan and I waited in line every day, holding bowls in our hands to get nutritional porridge for our family. Streets closed by the Four-Month War reopened; the green line was eliminated. Convoys carrying food and escorted by U.S. troops roared down the streets, some of them headed off to Baidoa. With all that food and no warlords, people started flooding back into Mogadishu. The city of women and children now had men. One of them was our dad.

He went first to our old house, inhabited only by the flies that feasted on the shit of the militiamen. He wandered the streets confused, checking in the distribution centers, searching for anyone he knew. He looked at every family sleeping on the streets, hoping to see us and wondering if we were still alive. In the city where he once was a basketball star, no one recognized Tall Nur; people ignored him. The celebrity athlete was now homeless, hungry, and sick like everyone else.

He walked down to the Mogadishu beach to see if the fishing business was back, but he was chased away by new faces who claimed they were the only people fishing now. All the other faces he saw on the streets looked either scared, angry, or hungry. His feet were burning. He put on some discarded flip-flops he found along the road—two different sizes, but he didn't care, anything to shield his feet from the burning ground. Dad was almost ready to collapse when he ran into Khadija's daughter Fatuma. She led him to our house, where Mom and Nima were taking their midday nap next to each other with bellies full of porridge.

When my mom saw her husband walk in after three years, she thought she was seeing a ghost. This man in front of her looked sort of like Nur Iftin, but different. He was so thin and dark, his eyes sunk deep in his head. The skin was peeling off his hands. He had rashes, cuts, and bruises all over his body, which was caked in rusty blood. His hair had grown long and was matted with dust and mud. His shirt was torn everywhere.

Hassan and I were at the madrassa memorizing our lesson for the day when Fatuma came and told us. Macalin Basbaas, and the other kids who had believed Hassan and I were orphans like most of them watched us sprint out of the school.

We had forgotten his face during the past three years of the civil war, and like our mom we felt we were reuniting with a ghost. I still remember the smell that was coming from Dad. It was definitely the smell of death, the rusty smell of blood and dust. Hassan and I sat at his side. Our mom went out to fill a bucket with warm water for him to take a shower, but he was too weak, so she bathed him herself. Every time Mom touched his skin with the water, he screamed in pain. His long, muscly legs looked like sticks. Mom fed him with porridge that Hassan and I brought from the distribution center. Hassan cut his hair and trimmed his long beard. I washed his clothes, all he had was a *macawis* and the torn shirt. Mom put a straw mat in the corner of the house. He covered himself with a piece of cloth and slept deeply, waking only to pray five times a day. Hassan and I went out to bring more water and food home. Even though many men were returning to Mogadishu, when it came to getting work done, it was still a city of women and children. The men were still too weak to help.

After a few days, when Dad felt able to stand and speak, Hassan and I walked him to a local clinic run by the United Nations inside the airport. It was only a fifteen-minute walk, but Dad had to stop and rest every minute. An Asian man gave him shots, penicillin tablets, and vitamins. Back home, Dad finally told us all that had happened during his treacherous journey deep in the bush. After he left us in Baidoa, he walked for days into the bush, land he once crossed as a nomad with his camels. He saw the places where he dated our mom and the land where the lion Fareey used to roam. Dad told us he actually prayed to the lions to protect him from the militias, but for months he did not see one lion. He came across dead hyenas and other animals. It seemed like the lions and other predators had fled the severe drought.

Dad was far from the gunfire, but he did encounter other people. He met a group of Rahanweyn men sitting under an acacia tree. They had killed a gazelle and were sharing the meat over a fire. After discovering they all spoke the Maay dialect, they shared their meat with him. They were nomads who had never seen the city, so my dad's stories of his basketball games, the clubs, and the beach were all like fairy tales to them. They stayed together for months, constantly moving and hunting, sharing the meat according to nomad tradition. At times they hummed, sang, and danced, and at night they slept with only one man awake to guard their camp. Like my dad they had all lost contact with their families, but they did their best to enjoy the few months they spent together as nomads again.

One day they heard gunshots and had to scatter and run for their lives again. Dad eventually caught up with one of the men. They walked for days and nights, unsure where they were going. At times they came across corpses of women and children with bullet wounds. Dad thought for sure that we were dead by now. Even if we had escaped the militias, the harsh environment would surely kill us. As he told us the story, his eyes had tears, but he was not actually crying; it was some sort of allergy. Water ran down his eyes for months

The night the U.S. Marines landed in Mogadishu, Dad was looking up at the stars, still hiding in the bush, not knowing what was happening in the city. A few months later he was able to return to Baidoa after he heard that Australian and American troops were there, providing food and nutrition. He was queuing for food in Baidoa and kept asking people about us. But no one answered him. You don't ask about people in Baidoa; you pray they have reached heaven, because they are probably dead.

He stayed in Baidoa after reuniting with a friend there. His friend had a bullet injury on his knee, and with no treatment the wound had gotten worse and infected. The man could no longer walk. Dad cut some traditional herbs to treat it and brought him food from the distribution centers. On other days, Dad walked into the bush around Baidoa, trying to see if he could find us out there. He stumbled upon dead kids and women, some of them too difficult to recognize. He had to roll over the bodies to see if their faces were ours. Some bodies were only parts, so he couldn't be sure if they were us. Finally he gave up and assumed we were dead. But after hearing that lots of people had returned from Baidoa to Mogadishu, he decided to go back to the city and look for us there.

After Dad told his story, we told him ours. He was not surprised that our mom had done everything to make sure we survived. He was sitting with his back against the tree trunk, but he leaned forward and looked at Hassan and me, telling us how proud we made him for the way we had helped our mom and sisters.

It would take a long time for his health to return. Sometimes he talked to Mom about life in the good times before the wars—their life in the bush and in Mogadishu. Sometimes he paced back and forth in the house reading the Koran. He was not sure what to do in a city where his beloved Horseed basketball stadium was now being used for war games by children and a camp for displaced families. It was Hassan and I who had taken the full responsibility of feeding our family every day, including our dad, the once-famous national athlete.

The year had changed to 1993, my ninth year of life. The U.S. troops and the star-spangled banner were now accompanied by blue UN helmets and flags of countries from all over Asia, Africa, and Europe. Many nonmilitary people also came to the city to help. We would see them jogging, and swimming in the green waters off the beach. One woman, some kind of aid worker, jogged every morning near our house. She was white, had long hair, and smiled and remembered my name. I made sure to get up every morning and say hi to her when she passed. I watched her listening to music on her headphones and stretching. Sometimes she would sit and play games with me, my brother, and Nima. She always brought us snacks like peanuts, candies, and cookies, and she also brought painkillers, antibiotics, and other medicine. She explained what they were for and how to take them. I think I fell in love with this woman;

it wasn't romantic, but I just wanted to stay close to her. If I knew her name today, maybe I could find her in America, but I called her only what we called all non-Muslims, *gaalo,* or "infidel." One day she came to the madrassa, just to visit and say hi. Macalin Basbaas refused to shake her hand. Then one day we stopped seeing her. Soon we realized no one was jogging anymore.

The warlords were getting restless; they wanted the city back. Aidid had a radio station and was telling Somalis on the air that they should fight the "occupation" of Mogadishu. On June 5, UN forces went to the radio station to seize weapons. Aidid thought they were trying to shut down the broadcasts, and he ambushed the troops, killing twenty-four Pakistani soldiers. That's when things got bad. On July 12 the Americans sent Cobras over a house in Mogadishu where they thought Aidid was hiding and blasted it into rubble. He wasn't there, but dozens of other people were killed. Aidid claimed the Americans had killed women and children, and he started to whip up Somalis against the infidel "invaders." The Americans said only Aidid's soldiers had been in the house, but the seed of resentment against the foreigners had been sown. Aidid wasted no time, planting roadside bombs in August that killed four American soldiers and wounded seven others. The Battle of Mogadishu had begun.

I had been waiting so long for this moment! I wanted to see the American troops in action and how they fight. Hassan and I were so excited for war we ran toward whatever corner of the city where we heard explosions or gunshots. Soon Cobras and Black Hawks were swooping down everywhere, hovering over buildings where militiamen were hiding. I looked up and cheered whenever the helicopters shot at a building; to me it seemed like the greatest movie. I stood on the streets and watched militiamen yell at each other, jumping from house to house and hiding in narrow alleys. We watched them take positions as helicopters hovered over them.

I thought the airplanes and helicopters would scare the militias away, but instead the huge, strong American men of the movies were being chased by Somali rebels on the streets. It was not what I expected. Soon everything had changed. We were no longer welcome near the marines; there were no more candies or cookies. For the first time the marines were aiming their guns at Somalis and pushing them around, even us kids. They looked nervous.

It is hard to explain why so many Mogadishans turned against the marines and cheered the militias. The rebels had been killing us for four years, stealing our food, and shitting in our houses. The Americans had been so kind. For sure it was partly the U.S. attack on the house that killed so many civilians. And at this point we were so familiar with death and destruction that this new battle seemed like a basketball game or a soccer match; it wasn't even real life. People filled the streets, rooting for their home team. I too fell in with the crowd. I yelled out to the militias to let them know which side the helicopter was coming from. I threw rocks at helicopters. I ran with the crowd, repeating their cheers: "Up with Aidid! Down with America!"

The battle continued for weeks. The foreign troops slowly withdrew to the airport. Militias loyal to Aidid ruled the ground, but the foreign troops ruled the skies with their helicopters. At night it was hard for the Somali militias to see, but the helicopters with their infrared lasers were able to fire at their targets. Every night from our house I watched militiamen changing positions, shooting at helicopters. For a few minutes it would be dead quiet, then the helicopter would swoop down again and fire back. I believed my mom's prayers saved us from the helicopter cannons, but now I think it was the pilots' precision.

On Sunday, October 3, Aidid's forces shot down two Black Hawk helicopters with Russian rocket-propelled grenades. I heard the booming explosions and columns of smoke rising about a mile from our house. Naturally, I ran as fast as I could to watch this new action unfold. Everything was so dusty I could not see much or get very close. A crowd was dragging the bodies of dead Americans, and people said others were still alive, trapped. The rescue operation lasted until the next day. Sixteen Americans died and more than three hundred Somalis. A few days later I was playing hide-and-seek in the remains of one of the Black Hawks.

Five months later the Americans left Mogadishu. It was March 1994, my tenth year. The skinny rebels with their ugly brown teeth had beaten back the movie-star marines. The Americans and the UN troops left so fast they didn't even take their stuff. They left behind malfunctioning helicopters and vehicles, boots and uniforms. I joined a crowd that went to the same spot where the *Mareekans* had first invited us to watch them land on the beach in hovercrafts. This time we were looting the stuff they left behind, even the boxes of medicines, tablets, discarded syringes. We stuck the syringes into our hands for fun. We ate the tablets. Was it looting if they just left it?

The same militias whom we had cheered against the foreigners would soon turn on us again—stealing our food and shooting at us for sport. I felt shame that I had cheered against the Americans, the people who came to help us from the country of my dreams. But I now realize that I was lost—a nine-year-old boy caught between the teachings of Macalin Basbaas, my mom and her view on infidels, the American troops and their kindness and food, my love for my brave dad and the glorious Somali basketball team, and the American movies I loved.

I stood on the beach, picking through the discarded camouflage uniforms with the American names sewn above the pockets. I held them up, hoping one would fit my skinny little body. My friends Mohammed, Bashi, and Bocow laughed. I looked at them and scowled.

"I'm not Somali," I said. "I am *Mareekan.* I was left behind by the marines. And they will come for me soon."

6

The One They Call American

The city of women and children had become a city of refugees. The streets swarmed with former herders and farmers, most of them Maay-speaking Rahanweyn from Bay, Bakool, and Lower Shabelle regions, the places my parents came from. They had come to Mogadishu for the food brought by the UN forces and to seek work like fishing, or porterage at Bakara market, or digging people's latrines. When the Western troops left, the ancestral lands of these new arrivals had been overrun by the warlords and they could not go home. Now they were stuck in Mogadishu, a city run by tribal militias who hated them.

The Hawiye of Mogadishu did not know much about the refugees and assumed they were mostly criminals. Some of the very poorest Rahanweyn were in a subclan known as the Eelaay. They wore amulets around their necks and arms and often lived by begging instead of herding animals. Because of these Eelaay people, the Hawiye assumed that all Rahanweyn were beggars—similar to the way many Europeans think of all Romany people as shiftless "Gypsies." To many Mogadishans they were all disgusting.

My mom often went out and met the Rahanweyn refugees on the streets. She helped them find spots to build makeshift camps. The first place she could think of was out past the airport. The road from the airport to Lower Shabelle region was empty and treeless, with harsh sunshine and dust blowing from the sea breeze continuously. No one would bother the poor refugees there, she figured. Within one day, they set up over a hundred makeshift tents of sticks and plastic bags, but the next day the militias came and destroyed it all. Some of the refugees spent the day sitting on the open ground, one side facing the Indian Ocean and the other the endless sand dunes.

Their despair was like my dad's. He had no plans, and he never left Khadija's compound. Her family could give us only one room, and Hassan, Mom, Nima, and I crammed into it. There was no space for Dad, he had to spend the night outside exposed to mosquitoes. So we took shifts: he slept during the day in our room when we all went out; by night he sat outside in the courtyard, swatting mosquitoes and praying. Gone forever was the strong man who jumped over fences, chased lions, and scored hoops. Whenever he stood, he leaned on a stick, his tall body bent in half. I helped him get to the bathroom, take a shower, and dress. The brave dad who carried us on his shoulders, in his basketball jersey, needed help with everything. Hassan and I sometimes jumped through the window to sneak out and escape the work. I would go to the movies, and Hassan would disappear with his friends. We would be out all day and come back with so much to do for Dad. We had to wash his clothes, trim his hair, and walk him around the house.

My dad could not understand why all this had happened to him and his family. When he had money and played for the national team, he had always given to charity, given money to the poor, helped everyone. Why did he deserve this misery? Had his prayers not worked? Had he given less than he was supposed to? He did not know why Allah put him in this misery. But his faith was stronger than ever, he prayed five times during the day, he even prayed extra hours. He could not go to the mosque, but he had a prayer mat in the house. The prayers kept him alive, but he had so much guilt. "I used to go to movies, went to clubs, and traveled abroad," he told me once. "God might be angry with all that sin." He believed those sinful things could explain why he suffered and lost his wealth. And it was a message to me not to go to movies.

One night while Dad was in the courtyard kneeling near the fire, uttering prayers, a loud knock came at our tin gate.

"Who are you?" said an angry voice from outside.

"Why don't we know who you are?" yelled another voice. "Open the door or we will kill you!"

Dad got up and knocked at the door to Khadija's house, trying to wake her up. She was Hawiye like the men at the gate and could maybe calm them. But the militiamen were impatient and kicked down the gate. Khadija got up quickly and managed to get herself between the militiamen and Dad. By now we were all awake. I was standing there watching as the men pointed a gun at my dad's face while Khadija tried to stay in between, putting herself directly in the line of the barrel. With our Mogadishan accents, Hassan and I stood close to the militiamen and kept yelling, "He is our dad, please leave him!"

The militiamen seemed very angry. Before they came to our house, we heard gunshots in the neighborhood; they had shot and killed a Rahanweyn man, a beggar who was sleeping on the streets because he did not have a place to stay. They asked Dad what his clan was.

"I am Rahanweyn."

But Khadija told them we were Mogadishans first. "These kids were born here. They don't know about clan," she said. Luckily, they walked away, but the harassment of the Rahanweyn continued and grew worse. All of this was nerve-racking for my dad. Already weak and confined to the house, now he was worried that if he ever did get up the strength to walk around, he would be attacked by Hawiye gangs. So he retreated further into his small world and his bored mind.

Part of the problem was that Rahanweyn were not allowed to carry guns and so were defenseless. In almost every Hawiye house in the city there were guns, even houses where no militiamen lived. When Siad Barre's government fell, the citizens stormed into the government arms stockpile. There were more guns in the city than people. There was more ammunition than food. It became a thing to own a gun to save your life. Most people slept with a loaded AK-47 sitting next to them.

Khadija brought home two guns, an AK-47 and a SAR-80 assault rifle given to her by a relative who had plenty of guns and wanted to get rid of some. Khadija, her son Abdikadir, and her daughters, Fatuma and Fardowsa, all took turns shooting at a bucketful of sand set up at the corner of the house. Abdikadir and I carried the AK-47 outside, walking around to show it off.

Some of the Rahanweyn beggars would come to Khadija's house early in the morning around five to beg for a cup of tea. Mom was usually up at this time making tea for my dad, and when the beggars came and spoke in their Maay dialect, she would respond in Maay, *"See hayteng?"* How are you? *"Hadhawaw fadheew."* Come in, have a seat.

Mom and the beggars would get into deep conversations as they sipped their hot tea in the house. Khadija did not understand Maay, so it was easy for Mom and the beggars to talk about how bad life had turned under the Hawiye militias. They talked about life in the Bay and Bakool villages, the animals, the nomad life. Many of these beggars in Mogadishu had been some of the wealthiest people in their villages; they owned hundreds of camels, cows, and goats—assets they thought would never disappear. But like my parents they had not even a chicken today, nor a place to live. They bragged about their past life. They talked about fighting hyenas, lions, and cheetahs. They were warriors who fought with knives, spears, and bows. They had no idea why God had abandoned them and left them begging on the streets.

Their conversation would come to an end as they remembered that they had to be on the road again to find food for their children, who were sleeping on the streets. But every morning they came by to chat with Mom. Usually Dad was asleep, but he sometimes woke up to join the conversation.

Then one day none of the beggars showed up. Mom went out to see what had happened. Down the street, around a corner, her beggar friends had all been killed by a sniper; the killer piled their bodies on top of one another and was yelling, "They were burglars, I shot them!" For sure they were not burglars. Mom returned home and prayed for them to enter heaven.

Most Rahanweyn men returned to the harsh life in their villages, which the militias also controlled. The women remained behind and did all the dirty jobs; they dug out latrines and removed shit, carrying bucketfuls of shit on their shoulders and dumping it in the sea. They begged or hawked on the streets. I heard later that only one out of four of their kids survived to adulthood. But they showed strength and perseverance.

Hassan and I could identify with these beggars because we would have been like them had we not been born in Mogadishu and received the goodwill of our neighbor Khadija. Still, no one else we knew let beggars into their houses, and Hassan and I were a little embarrassed by it. By now we had started to distance ourselves from our parents. We had no stories of our own to tell about the villages, or the nomad life. All we knew was Mogadishu. We had a Mogadishu accent, the neighborhood was our home, and all our friends were Mogadishan. We had become so unlike our mom but especially different from our dad, who could not blend in at all. He pined for his village, and Mom hoped for the same. They waited for two things: the rains to return and the Aidid militias to withdraw from Baidoa so they could go home. Hassan and I were home in Mogadishu, and we hoped we would not move to a village in the bush.

Every day I walked out to the airport, hoping to see the American marines coming back to rescue me. But all I saw were the tread marks of their big tanks in the hot, soft tarmac of the runway. Discarded U.S. military boots were still scattered across the sand dunes, drying in the fierce sun of Mogadishu. The airport had been closed since the troops pulled out, and quickly the militias turned the terminals into a butchering place for people they did not like—dragging their victims inside and shooting or hacking them to death. Their jeeps, mounted with automatic machine guns, parked in the middle of the runway as the militiamen wandered aimlessly around the airport, not sure what to do. There was no commander they listened to, no schedules to follow. Their days were always the same: wake up every morning, get qat, sit, and chew. We gathered around them every afternoon when the sun cooled down a bit and they were too busy chewing their drug to mind us. They usually had plenty of qat that could fill their cheeks the whole day, but the next day they would have to ride fifty kilometers out of the city, to a makeshift airport where the qat flew in from Kenya and Ethiopia, to escort the shipments into Mogadishu. Their technicals, loaded with leaves, barreled into Mogadishu with engines screaming, like teenage drag racers trying to impress each other. This juvenile display of power reminded us every day that these were the rabble that had kicked American marines out of the city. They were so unorganized they never figured out how to use the main airport, because Aidid and Mahdi, the rival clan leaders, couldn't agree on how to run it.

Other than sheikhs, the only role models for young men in Mogadishu were these rebel soldiers with their guns, their cheeks full of qat, and their endless bickering and cursing. I didn't chew qat, but I cursed every day at my friends for fun, and they cursed back. Our fiercest obscenities were related to pigs and dogs, two animals much hated in Mogadishu. "Son of a dog!" "Son of a pig!" "Your dad is a dog and you are a dog!" Everyone would get very angry when associated with these dirty, satanic animals that cannot be touched. When I saw Americans kissing dogs in movies, I'd make a face like sucking on a lemon. "How do they trust the dog?" I asked myself. "What if the dog bites them?"

One day Dad called us out to the courtyard. "I'm going to take a walk around to see if my brother Hassan is still in his house," he said. Dad had not left the house since the Americans and United Nations left. So this was a big step, but one filled with danger. In Mogadishu under the warlords it was very dangerous to knock on people's doors, especially for a Rahanweyn. None of us had been to our uncle's house since we returned to Mogadishu, we didn't know who was living there

But Dad found the courage to walk to the house. Leaning on his stick, in his worn-out clothes, his hair a mess from our homemade haircut, he looked like one of the Rahanweyn beggars. People avoided him on the street. Unfazed, he shook his head and took small steps toward the KM4 circle. He stopped briefly every few steps to catch his breath and then kept moving, looking around. Everything had changed, no more clubs and restaurants, no cheering fans slapping his back.

Uncle Hassan's house was there, still standing, with some

damage to the roof and walls. The back side of the house was gone. The green tin door that my dad remembered was not there; instead, a gate of thorn branches covered the entrance. He stood there hesitating, deciding whether to move the thorn gate and go inside; many houses had been looted and taken over by militiamen and their families. Who lived here now? Dad stood there waiting for any movement, or someone to come out. It was very quiet inside. He didn't hear a single noise except the flapping of the tin roof, which had come loose from the rafters.

After a long wait he heard some noise inside, the sounds of kitchen cleanup and distant chatter. He didn't know if it was Uncle Hassan's family. He came closer to the gate and looked through it, but he could see nothing in the courtyard.

"Salaam aleikum!" he finally said. No answer.

"Is Hassan here?" he yelled.

Then Uncle Hassan's daughters came out to see who was asking for their dad. They did not recognize my dad.

"No," they responded as they looked at him, studying him.

But Dad recognized them and cried out their names. "Salada! Anab! How are you? It's me, Nur!"

At that point Dhuha, Hassan's wife, came out and joined the girls. They all welcomed Dad inside. Everyone cried; they hugged.

They told Dad how Hassan had been killed by a bullet, or two, or three, or six in his head. No one knew how many bullets, but someone knew he was shot in Beledweyn town. Dad had no more tears to cry. His own parents had starved to death or were eaten by animals, who knows? His other siblings had gone missing and were presumed dead. Dad reminded the grieving family that his brother Hassan was by now in heaven and that we will all die and go where the dead are.

"We are happy you are here for us," said Dhuha. In Somali

culture a man must take charge when tragedy strikes a sibling's family. Ideally, he is supposed to marry the wife of his deceased brother, a union of mercy called *dumaal.*

But Dad was in no position to be the man of their family; he couldn't even be the man of his own family. Even if it were possible for my dad to care for Hassan's family, he was in too much danger as a Rahanweyn man. With the wars still happening, and men being killed daily, our dad might be next. He reminded Dhuha about this, saying he did not want to cause more grief to her family.

Dhuha said she understood, then invited us to come and stay in the two-room mud house that had been built on Uncle Hassan's property. This was a relief to us, because now Hassan and I would have our own room. Dad, Mom, and Nima would stay in the other room. Nima had turned seven, but she looked somehow both younger and older—small and frail from years of malnutrition, and already missing some of her permanent teeth. And she was still struggling to speak well.

Now we woke up every morning alongside family members, and Dad had stories to tell every day, which made him feel better. He and Dhuha would sit and talk while Mom and Dhuha's kids were busy doing the chores. (Dhuha was older than my mom and also had two grown daughters, so she was excused from housework.) Sometimes we shared sweet tea with cloves, cinnamon, and camel milk. Only one full kettle was made at a time; everything was measured, from tea to water. We were told we could shower only once a week with a three-liter jerry can, and we were given just five minutes each to use the bathroom. The most difficult rule was that everyone had to be at home no later than seven in the evening. Mogadishu was completely lawless, and crime in the city was high at night; even people without guns were using knives to slit throats, and there were burglars who jumped into houses. Dhuha asked our dad to be the guard at night. It was one way he could still be the man of the family.

Our new room was so much better than Khadija's tin-and-cardboard shack. The mud walls at Dhuha's absorbed the heat during the day and released a bit of cool air at night. The room for Hassan and me had only one straw mat, no furniture, no beds. But it had a wood-framed window, and we could sneak out through that window and come back in without anyone noticing us. We had to be so quiet because the wall between our room and our parents' room had cracks and holes from bullets and rockets, and we could be heard when we came in or when we talked. Always when we lay on our mat talking, Mom would yell at us to go to sleep.

It was pitch-black in our room at night, we had no electricity or lantern and could not see each other, but we could see the glittering stars through the small window. As we both lay on the mat on the dirt floor, Hassan talked about Kenya, Yemen, Europe, and America. "Arnold Schwarzenegger and Sylvester Stallone visit Kenya on their vacations," he said. Which definitely is not true but gained my attention.

"Nairobi is like New York," he said. "They have highways, nightlife, clubs, music, movie theaters. And a lot of white people." Many years later I would see New York and realize how different it is from Nairobi, but at the time I imagined either city was no closer than the stars we saw through the holes in our roof.

"I want to leave Somalia," said Hassan.

We were talking at night while lying on our mat, as usual.

"You are dreaming," I said. To me leaving Somalia seemed impossible. First, I could not imagine going anywhere while Hassan was still around. How could I leave without him?

Besides, at that point I was not unhappy with my life. Life in Somalia was harsh, but it was all I knew. You wake up in the morning with no plans and no future. Every day is the same. They come and go; months come and go. No New Year's celebrations, no holidays, no birthday parties. Even the Eid was nothing to look forward to in war-torn Mogadishu. The Eid is the biggest Muslim celebration, after the last day of Ramadan, like Christmas in the West. In good times, kids get to dress in brand-new clothes and buy toys and sweets. But since 1991 the Eid in Somalia was just like every other day. No clothes, no toys, no sweets. All we had was our mom telling us stories about the fun Eid holidays we had before the war.

While many people like my brother dreamed of moving abroad, I found peace sitting at Falis's video shack watching movies. The things I saw in the movies seemed unreachable, but at least I could learn the language they spoke. I had been paying close attention to what the American actors were saying. Nobody else cared. The only Western language people in Mogadishu knew was Italian, and not much of that. Falis and everyone else at the movie shack wished the movies could be in Italian, or maybe Arabic. English might as well have been Chinese. But I wanted to understand it. I would walk up to Falis as she was busy collecting money and ask, "Falis, please could you turn up the volume today?"

She would look at me and laugh. "Why would you want to hear that crap? You don't even understand a word."

But I did. I sat very close to the speaker. I had been making progress on picking up words. Sometimes even when the dialogue was in English the movie had English subtitles, which made it easier to learn how to write the words. I also learned about the culture. The movies often showed kids' rooms decorated with posters of rock and movie stars, which inspired me to decorate my own room. I collected old, worn-out posters I had found in the ruins of the Cinema Ecuatore and other buildings—posters of Michael Jackson, Madonna, Sylvester Stallone, Arnold Schwarzenegger, Bruce Willis. Falis gave me some posters that she was going to throw out because they were torn. I would glue them together using the sap from the apple of Sodom plant, and then we used that sap to glue the posters onto the clay walls of our room. Using a piece of charcoal from the madrassa, I wrote on the walls the English words I had learned from movies, plus movie titles, names of stars I liked, and some daily phrases I taught myself, most of them swear words. I liked it when actors in the movies swore.

Fuck you.

Bullshit.

Get the fuck out of here.

Motherfuckers my name is Abdi American, I am a powerful man. Be careful.

Rambo, Terminator.

I'll be back.

I also wrote a notice on our wooden door: "Stop. No coming." I meant for people not to come into our room, but of course no one would ever be able to read that. When Mom saw the walls tattooed in English, she gasped. Then she saw the poster of Madonna in a bikini hanging next to where I slept. This was the last straw. She slapped me hard on my face and yelled, "*Lailaha ilallah!* There is no god but Allah! Nur, come see what they did! I will kill these two boys!"

In Islam it is sacrilegious to have any pictures of the human form, much less Madonna in a bikini. To my parents, we were inviting the devil into their home and pissing off the angels that stick with us until death. Raqib and Atid are the two angels that sit on our shoulders, invisibly writing down all of our actions, thoughts, and feelings every single day. On the day of judgment we will be confronted with all the actions the angels have put down, and Raqib and Atid will be present in front of God as witnesses.

Mom ran from the room, yelling it was a sin hole and if she stayed a moment longer she too would be damned by Allah. She talked to our dad in the other room, then they both came back in. Dad was furious.

"I never expected this!" he said, pointing at the poster of Madonna. "What is this? Is this why we sent you to the madrassa? Are you out of your mind?" They both kept yelling at us for being evil and littering our home with infidels. Finally Mom tore off all the posters and erased all the words as best she could. When she told Macalin Basbaas, we were whipped. Even after all that, Mom was angry because you could still see the words we had written because the charcoal was hard to erase completely. So I was forced to scrub the walls with water and get rid of the notice on the door. From this time on, whenever something bad happened, I was blamed for bringing evil to the house. One time a stray bullet hit the roof; my fault. Another time Nima was coughing and wheezing and I was blamed for it. The things that I wrote and the posters just became a huge problem for me in our house.

Even while I was scrubbing English off my bedroom walls, I was writing new words on the walls of abandoned houses where no one could scold me. I especially liked the walls at Horseed Stadium because they were smooth concrete—perfect for charcoal. The letters came out in dark black. I wrote, "I am not lost," which I learned from the movie *Die Hard.* Then I painted the American flag, a huge one, on the wall with the stars and stripes. Boys looked at the words and wondered what it meant, so I translated for them. The next day I went back and saw that they had erased it all by smacking it with their sandals, which made the charcoal dust fly off. I was so mad I wrote "shit" and "fuck you" on the wall. They asked me what it meant. I didn't know, only that in movies it's what people say when they are angry.

No one gave me credit for all the words I taught myself, not even my parents. Learning Arabic or reading the Koran was the only thing they wanted me to do. But I had my brother at my back, himself inspired by movies. We found joy in talking about movies, English, actors, singers. We practiced English more than we practiced Arabic. We didn't have enough vocabulary to say much, our grammar was not perfect, but we got better. We collected English words from old worn-out magazines that had probably ended up on Mogadishu streets after libraries and schools were looted in 1991. My parents used these magazines to start cooking fires, or as napkins, but I used them as textbooks, underlining phrases and words I thought were good. I noticed they used many prepositions such as "over," "down," and "up," and we were confused about when to use them. So Hassan and I practiced, building our own sentences. "*Down* here, *over* your head, get *over* to Mom." She came to check our room every day to see if we had smuggled in posters again. In the madrassa I was frisked every morning. It was embarrassing; no other student was inspected. Macalin Basbaas always said that the devil dwelled in me, but I didn't care.

Every night after Dad listened to the BBC Somali service, Hassan and I would tune in to the six o'clock English-learning program by the Voice of America called *New Dynamic English.* The show featured two characters, Max and Kathy, who talked about American culture, U.S. cities, and how to speak American English. The shortwave broadcast had a lot of static, and the lessons were hard to understand sometimes, but we listened carefully anyway. When Mom or Dad found out, they would snatch the radio from us and tell us, "Go say the evening prayers. Go to the mosque."

We went to the movies instead. Hassan and I held hands

walking in the dark to the movies and back. We would get home after nine; by then our dad was the only person awake, reciting his regular prayers, or sitting in a corner of the house in the dark with his head leaning against his hand, looking up in despair and boredom. Mom and Nima were deep asleep after a long day of washing dishes and clothes, cooking, and cleaning. We would tiptoe into our room from the window and quietly spread our sleeping mat. Other times Dad would be with Dhuha's family in their own house in the front of the courtyard, and then Hassan and I could come through the latched wooden door, which we learned how to open by reaching through the cracks and pulling the latch.

Friday was the weekend in Somalia, the only day off from the madrassa. In the morning heat of the city my madrassa mates and I gathered under the shade of neem trees. Often we played *mancala*, a type of sowing game using stones and small holes in the dirt, played in the West as a board game. We had to stop the game at noon, when the mosques of Mogadishu all rang the call for the important Friday prayers, called *Qudbah*. Before going into the mosque, Hassan and I had to clean our arms, legs, head, and ears. Huge crowds of mosque goers filled up the streets, except the militiamen, who sat in the beds of their technicals ignoring the call to prayer. The rest of us had to sit through an hour-long lecture by the imam before we stood up for the prayers. In the lecture, the imam talked about how sinful it was to watch movies, how non-Muslim nations were planning to eliminate Islam by trying to spread their languages including English, their culture through movies and songs, and soccer. Hundreds of men in the mosque all nodded, my brother and I as well.

Macalin Basbaas was always seated in the front row very close to the imam, an exalted position. He never missed one Friday. He even arrived five hours ahead of time. One day he took the microphone and mentioned many names of his students who go to movies, and he asked for the hundreds of men to pray so that the sinful students would return to the Islamic culture and stop watching movies. My name, of course, was among the ones mentioned. When the prayer ended and men started pouring out of the mosque, an imam took the mic and asked for those whose names had been mentioned to stay behind. I did, along with two other friends and several other students I didn't know from other neighborhoods. It was three o'clock in the afternoon, a time when the heat of the day radiates through the walls of the mosque and turns it into an oven. We sat on the floor, sinful sweating boys. Six men, short and thin, their beards almost touching their chests and with fierce eyes, surrounded us and started their harangue.

"It is the devil, the devil is taking advantage of your weakness!" one yelled, so loudly that his spit was almost landing on my face. "You are all weak! That's what the devil likes! Now you are serving the devil against Allah! You go to movies, the devils smile and Allah frowns. You need to quit now! Start coming to the mosque for the five daily prayers. We will also provide lectures on how to defeat the devil. Come to the mosque!" His eyes were like they had caught on fire, he threw up his hands as if he were talking to the devil himself. He was so threatening we couldn't say no. We all agreed. But the next day I never showed up. Outside the mosque, the imams had no power. Not yet.

Anyway, I was more afraid of my mom and Macalin Basbaas than of the imams at the mosque, but I kept going to the movies. We also played with our dangerous slings, shooting at birds, cats, dogs, anything that was not human. And we played soccer. We could not afford a real soccer ball, so we made our own from old clothes, rubbish, and shredded plastic, all tied together to look like a ball. Our goalposts were made of sticks. We had no cleats of course; we played barefoot, tackling each other and scoring wild goals to the cheers of our teammates and the boos of our opponents. There were many places in Mogadishu where we could play soccer, but we had to hide from our parents and madrassa teachers, so we played near the beach by the airport, away from their sight, and away from the militias. When Mom asked where I was, I always told her I was at the mosque reading the Koran. I made sure to clean the dust off my feet but leave a spot of dirt on my forehead, which indicated I had been bowing and praying. She looked at my forehead, sighed, and smiled.

Nights were always good for several reasons. Macalin Basbaas never came out of his house at night, and the wandering sheikhs stayed in the mosque. It was a good time for my English practice at the movies. Liberated for a few hours from the Islamic surveillance, I sat on the dirt in front of the TV screen, savoring the freedom. My friends would come find me, now appreciating my basic English skills. They sat close to me because it was my job to tell them what the actors were saying. My translating got pretty accurate; people knew this because events in the movie happened the way I predicted, based on the dialogue. "They are planning to kidnap the little girl!" I would shout. And the girl gets kidnapped. My friends would applaud, not because the kidnapping happened, but because I said so. I became known at the movie shack as the translator. Little did I know that someday I would be working as a paid interpreter in Maine.

Outside the movie shack, life went on at the madrassa. Children graduate as soon as they have memorized the entire Koran because that is the only point of instruction, so I was motivated to study hard. We had to completely memorize over six thousand verses, and we had to know which verse is next to which without looking at the book. I was surprised to find myself able to memorize easily, just like I was memorizing English, and do the recitation with Macalin Basbaas. My parents were so proud of this, and they waited eagerly for the day I finished madrassa, because they had plans for me. They wanted me to follow in the footsteps of Macalin Basbaas and all the other fashionable long-beards in the city who carried Korans, not guns, and gathered around mosques every day. In a city where people die every day from guns and diseases, I would be prepared for it by being sinless. This meant no movies, no women in bikinis, nothing but the glorious Koran.

But I had other plans. Falis had started letting me into the movies free of charge—without having to sweep the floor—because I could attract a crowd who were enthusiastic to hear my translations. They encouraged me to learn more and listen. It was fun to have a crowd all leaning their heads toward me when I shouted out in Somali what the actors were saying. Unlike at the mosque or the madrassa, in the video shack we could talk, shout, play, or even just move around. But as soon as the movie ended, we ran home because we had to be up at six in the morning to go to madrassa, and first we had to memorize the lesson for the next day, which of course we had not done while watching the movie.

Learning English and American culture started as something for fun, an escape from the miseries of our life. But soon it became more than entertainment. I was discovering the world beyond Somalia and learning that I could make my own decisions about my life. I discovered that the American accent is not like the British, and I could tell the difference from the way Americans talked in movies and the British announcers spoke on BBC Radio. I learned from movies that no one is above the law, not even leaders. That people are held responsible for their actions. In movies the police would chase thugs and arrest them, something that never happened in Somalia. I learned the freedom of women doing things men can do. In some movies I could see kids going to school in buses the color of Falis's turmeric makeup; I wanted to go to a real school in a turmeric bus and learn things besides the Koran. I learned that not all Americans are white, there are black people there who stand shoulder to shoulder with the whites. In Somalia there was no black and white, only black. We don't even look like the Arabs who many Somalis claim to be. There were no laws, and even if there were, the militias would have been above them. I realized we had fallen behind the rest of the world, but I had no idea when Somalia would catch up to the way life was in the movies.

When I asked my parents why Somalia was behind and in a total mess, they always replied that it was Allah's will. He put us in this mess, he is the only one who can get us out of this. How can you argue with that? But somewhere in my head I told myself, "Allah is not responsible for this mess, why would he do that?" Somali militias were the ones who bombed our house, killed my uncle, and shot at us while we went to fetch water. It was not Allah.

The learning continued for me. I learned that all white people are not the same, they don't speak the same language, they don't use the same money, they don't live in one country, they don't even have the same religion. Some even don't eat pork.

"Mom, there are some white people who don't eat pork," I said one day.

"Shut up!" she said.

"And, Mom, America is not next to Somalia."

"I said shut up!"

One night as we lay on our backs on a mat looking up at the stars, I told Mom, "The moving stars are not lucky stars; some of them are satellites."

"What is a *satellite*?" she asked.

"They are moving machines or ships crossing the skies."

"You are being misinformed, Abdi, shut up!"

"Mom, there are nine planets among the stars too."

"The Koran tells us there are seven," she said. "Shut up and don't try to say anything about that." I went quiet and kept listening to Mom's stories of how the blinking stars are our ancestors trying to communicate. But this time I did not believe her.

Today I communicate with my mom on a cell phone connected to a satellite. I wire her money every month thanks to other technology. Hopefully, she does not look at the stars the same way now.

I don't blame my parents; they had been trying to make me be a good man, even though being good can take many forms. Whenever I started arguing with my mom about things like satellites, she blamed the movies. "Those evil movies that you go to are making you very stupid!" she would say. "You have let the devil take over you!" She was especially mad that the movies were distracting me from becoming her dream son, a sheikh.

Even though my mom despised my movie habit, I earned a new privilege: because I was near graduating from the madrassa, I was now allowed to bring my friends to our house. In my room we talked endlessly about stories in the movies. They listened as I spoke English and tried to teach them. "*How are you, how are you doing, how is it going . . .* these are all the same," I told them. "They all mean the same." Mom occasionally walked in and angrily told us to talk about the Koran or go to the mosque. We would leave, walk in the direction of the mosque until out of sight, and then do something else.

Sometimes we went to the Sufi mosque, where they didn't even care if we spoke English. The Sufis were not so strict; they just minded to their chants and ceremonies without telling people what to do. Macalin Basbaas never went to that mosque, he cursed the Sufis as evil, but Hassan and I liked to sneak in and listen to the chanting. It was so peaceful and mysterious. I fell in love with those gentle people. Later the radical Islamists destroyed their tombs and erased their culture from most of southern Somalia.

By 1996, the video shack was no longer the only entertainment in Mogadishu. The warlords still fought and shot their guns constantly, but some culture and normal life were returning to Mogadishu. One big change was public transportation. Some men who returned to the city had converted Toyota pickup trucks into buses by putting seats in the back, charging a few coins for rides. These buses, called *xaajiyo khamsiin,* meant we could explore parts of the city beyond our neighborhood. The drivers risked their lives every single day, negotiating through roadblocks manned by dangerous militias. Some went as far as the border of Kenya.

At first my favorite place was the grounds of the former presidential palace, which was now a playground for kids. I walked from the palace to the Parliament building, which had become a camp for displaced people because there was no Parliament, then on to the beautiful Catholic cathedral. The bishop of Mogadishu, an Italian, had been killed by militias while he was saying Mass in 1989; the church itself was later destroyed by Islamic radicals in 2008. But in the 1990s you could still go in and walk around, listening to the echo of your footsteps in the great hall.

Outside the cathedral was the famous Via Roma, named because it had many fine buildings with arches and terraces and tall shady trees. On one side, in front of the skeleton of the former central bank of Somalia, tall coconut palms swayed in the breeze from the Indian Ocean. I walked up the road toward the beach, past convenience stories that had opened in renovated buildings. Owners were standing at the doors calling out to passersby. On the walls they had painted pictures of popular snacks like *bur* (sweet doughnut holes), *bajiyas* (savory doughnuts made from crushed and skinned black-eyed peas with onion, garlic, and tomatoes), and especially samosas, the fried meat-filled pastries that al-Shabaab would later ban because the triangular shape was considered Christian, I guess like the Holy Trinity.

I loved to go to a candy store on Via Roma called Xalwo Shakata. One day, after stuffing my face with sweets, I heard strange music blasting out of the entrance of the building next door. A small wooden sign, written in chalk, read, "Al-Faghi Studio and Stereo." On the wall were photos of Michael Jackson and Stevie Wonder, and someone had written their names in Anglicized Somali: "Maaykal Jaksan," "Stiif Wandhar." The wooden door shook with some kind of loud music; a crowd of people were practicing wild dance moves in front of the building. Some people walking by covered their ears with their hands. The music was not Motown or soul, which I had heard before in movies and on tapes. I just stood there in awe. I tried to go inside, but the DJ wouldn't let me; I guess it wasn't for kids. But I could hear the music outside and twist my body like other people on the sidewalk. A crowd had built up, everyone dancing and laughing, and someone told me the music was American and called hip-hop and rap, and also some music from Jamaica called reggae.

This was the beginning of my new life. Al-Faghi became my favorite place to go every day, practicing how to dance with the crowd on the sidewalk. When I got home, I practiced by myself. Tupac Shakur and Bob Marley became my favorite artists after Michael Jackson. I decided if I was going to talk like an American, I should also dance like one.

I got myself a cheap boom box and some tapes. Soon I

felt ready to show my dance skills in my neighborhood. Mom would find me on the streets dancing with the boom box and scowl. "Stupid boy!" she said. I had to sneak the boom box into our room through the window and hide it by digging the dirt and burying it under the mat so that when Mom came in she would not see it.

The hip-hop culture was spreading fast into Mogadishu. All the young people who weren't trying to become sheikhs started wearing hip-hop fashion that we saw on television and posters. The people who ran Al-Faghi were young men who had just returned from Yemen and came with some cash to establish a music store. Similarly, the Bakara market was booming with small clothing businesses. The clothes were brought in from Kenya, Yemen, and Ethiopia, worn and old but not torn. For just a few shillings I was able to buy a black baseball cap that said "Titanic" and baggy denim jeans. I found a few plastic bracelets to wear on my hands and a bandanna for a do-rag head scarf. With my cap twisted sideways and my pants sagging below my waist, I practiced walking with a ghetto swagger; my friends Bashi and Bocow did the same thing, and we called ourselves a posse. This was all good timing, because I was starting to get interested in girls, and by now in Mogadishu girls were falling only for boys who could dance and who dressed in jeans.

The new hip-hop culture disgusted the Somali elders, who started calling us *saqajaan*—idiots—but we weren't trying to impress them. My dance skills and ability to speak English made me popular with all the young people in the neighborhood. Soon people were coming to my house asking my mom, "Is Abdi American here?" She was so mad when she learned I was the one they call American. To her American meant Christian. She would definitely want me to be called Abdi Saudi Arabian. My friends Bocow, Bashi, and Mohammed now regretted not paying as much attention when we all sat at the shack watching movies. They were still just regular Somalis on the street, while I was becoming the neighborhood star.

Around this time Hassan and I started to drift apart. For one thing he couldn't play soccer: when he was very small, he had been bitten on the foot by a poisonous snake, which my dad then killed. The snake bit off some of his toes, and the venom caused a bad swelling and infection. From that day he always walked with a slight limp. Nor did he go to movies as much as I did. But he had his own friends, Mohamed, Daud, and Hussein, and they got interested in raising pigeons.

Hassan had caught a male and a female pigeon and pulled out enough of their feathers so they could not fly. They laid eggs and had chicks and also brought other pigeons home. Soon we had hundreds of pigeons in the house to take care of. Hassan and his friends would race them—carrying them away from the house, letting them go, and seeing which would fly home first. Our male pigeon Gariirka was always so fast and clever and surprised everyone, winning over and over again.

Hassan should have been ahead of me at the madrassa, but he lost interest in memorizing verses. Finally the pressure became too much for him; he defied our parents and Macalin Basbaas and dropped out of school a little before graduating. When a student drops out, his parents disown him. My mom told Hassan not to come back to the house again. Just like that, my brother was living on the streets.

7

Buufis

One late April morning in the year 2000, I woke with a smiling face and walked to the madrassa at six. There I wrote down the last lesson on my board—the end of Surat al-Bacarah, the final Koranic chapter. I was so excited! This meant I could graduate from school and go anywhere in the city, dance, and watch movies, without worrying about Macalin Basbaas and his beatings. I had memorized all 114 chapters of the Koran—fluently reading 6,266 verses in perfect Arabic. The day I came home from my last lesson, Mom had a huge smile on her face. As a gift she had bought me a white *kanzu,* the robe worn by sheikhs, and a *tisbih,* the necklace of Islamic prayer beads. I never put them on.

A few days later we gathered for a brief party at the madrassa, ten of us who graduated that day, looking forward to a world without the Angel of Punishment. Macalin Basbaas made a very long speech, still holding his bunch of sticks tied together in his hands, ready to administer some last-minute pain.

"This is the moment that your parents have been waiting for," he said. "Not as much as we have," I thought.

"This is the beginning of your future. You all need to go out and spread the word." That meant Macalin Basbaas wanted us to open madrassas of our own or be at the mosque permanently every day. And for some graduates, this was a dream. They dreamed of going to Saudi Arabia or Egypt to pursue Islamic studies. But I had other dreams on my mind. "If those who want to be sheikhs can dream of a foreign country for Islamic studies, why can't I dream of America?" I wondered. "If they have been inspired by speeches from the sheikh, why can't I be inspired by the English words in the movies?"

Macalin Basbaas droned on, but my mind was somewhere else. By early afternoon all of us graduates were running all over the streets, our joy multiplied by a thunderous sky ready to deliver much-needed rain. I felt very accomplished; I had survived seven years of beatings from Macalin Basbaas. Was it possible to learn the Koran without beatings? I felt certain I would not have succeeded without the threat of those sticks. But when I saw and felt the scars across my body, I realized I could never beat children like that. I could never be a madrassa teacher.

To celebrate graduation, we went to Falis's video shack with no worries about waking up at six the next morning or reciting the lesson for the day. The movie was a new one for us, called *Coming to America,* starring Eddie Murphy as an African prince who goes to America to find a bride. I translated as usual.

Little did I know, while I was at the movie celebrating graduation, my mom had been chatting with Dhuha and some other women in the neighborhood. As usual Dhuha bragged about her three sons, who were older and had become sheikhs. They dressed in robes, went to the mosque all day, and read the Koran. Other women talked about their sons opening new madrassas and teaching the Koran to a new generation of Mogadishans.

I got home in the evening to see Mom and Dhuha sitting happily. A glass of camel milk with two cubes of ice melting in it was on the short leather stool next to Mom. Dad had slaughtered a chicken, he was pulling the feathers out. It was a graduation gift for me. I sat down, happily drinking my milk, hungering for chicken meat. They never told me how they got that chicken. Mom was massaging my head as she continued the conversation with Dhuha. I went into my room and saw a fresh cloth spread on my mat, a gift from Dhuha. Then Mom walked into my room with Dhuha.

"Abdi," she said, "tomorrow you need to go back to the madrassa and start as the assistant to Macalin Basbaas."

I felt like someone had fired a gun at me.

"We arranged it all with Macalin Basbaas," she continued. "He will be waiting for you tomorrow."

"But I need a break from the madrassa!" I protested.

"A break?" she yelled. "You don't need a break at all; you need to go to Macalin Basbaas tomorrow! You are not a student anymore but you can have your own madrassa someday, and to do that, you need to stick with him. He will show you the way to be a sheikh."

"Mom, I don't want to stick with Macalin Basbaas!" I stormed out of the house.

Mom kept pressuring me to go back to the madrassa and practice more, to be sure I wouldn't forget what I had learned. She also insisted that I go to the mosque regularly. I withheld my anger, but the final straw came a few weeks after my graduation, when the Tabliiq knocked on our door.

The Tabliiq are proselytizers in the Muslim world—pious Sunni men who come to houses dressed in long robes and turbans. They knock on any door where young men live, asking the young men to travel with them around the city and encouraging them to go to the mosque daily. When they came to our house to take me, I refused to go. To my mom I was now a lost cause. Gone forever was her dream of my being a respected sheikh with a shaved head who hates music and reads the Koran all day. My parents kicked me out of the house. I was fourteen years old, and I went looking for my brother.

By day Hassan hung around Zobe Square, which was crowded with elders and militiamen who gathered to talk about politics and clan rivalries. They cursed at each other and then cursed America and Israel for the invasion of Palestine. Hassan idled around nervously, always looking over his shoulder for militia recruiters. He was fifteen and so tall for his age. Now that he was old enough to carry a gun and chew qat, his choices grew even narrower.

And now I was out on the streets with him, dodging the militias and ducking when we heard gunfire. We traveled all over the city but knew to avoid certain high-crime areas. The northern Madinah district, where the hospital was located, had been taken over by a crime gang called Ciyaal Faacali. These young men had emerged from the ashes of the civil war, with no police or laws to stop them. They not only robbed people but also committed brutalities not seen in the southern parts of the city. They would hold up their hand and tell a person to pick one of five fingers. Whichever one you picked, they would name something you had to do, like drink mud or swallow a battery or even a bullet.

To avoid the street gangs, people were crowding into the safer southern part of town, where we lived, which became dense with people and stores. Two movie theaters opened, the Cinema Mogadishu and Cinema Ducale. Stereo stores popped up in other neighborhoods, selling cassette tapes and sound systems and even making recordings. My friends and I went to one of these stores to record our own rap songs on a tape. We rapped in a mix of Somali and English, describing a girl with hair like an ostrich and a walk like a camel. We sang English chorus lines like “She’s the best!” “Come to me, babe!” “Dance with me, babe!” I felt like I was part of this new musical revolution and that we were creating something amazing.

My parents were still mad at me, so I never went home. I

slept on the streets at night, covering my head with the shirt I was wearing. By dawn the early-morning prayers broadcast from speakers on the minarets woke me up. My friends Bocow and Bashi had also been evicted from their houses, and they stayed with me on the streets.

Even though many people had returned to Mogadishu, there were still empty houses, most of them crawling with giant bugs, littered with trash and shit, and stiflingly hot at night. We hung around in those houses sometimes to eat and talk, but it was much better to sleep outside in the fresh air. I would sneak around to the back of our house when I was hungry, peeking through the holes to make sure Macalin Basbaas wasn't there. Sometimes I heard his voice and I made a run for it. When Mom was taking a nap and Dad was listening to the BBC Somali service, I would quietly jump in the window. I looked around for food, sometimes there was maize left over. I scooped the gruel into my pockets and jumped back outside, out to the street, to share with my friends in the empty houses. They did the same for me, sneaking into their houses to steal food. We walked to the beach to wash our clothes in the ocean.

I had not asked to be thrown out of my house, but now I was happy to pursue my own dreams, to live my own life without fetching water and food for my family, without Macalin Basbaas. I still prayed, and I respected the Muslim teachings about charity and justice. I consider myself a good Muslim to this day. But I had seen from the movies what was out in the world, and I wasn't going to live in a mosque.

Starting in 1998, Somalia had some good rainy seasons that soaked Mogadishu. I remember my mom saying it rained because the warlord Aidid had been killed just a year before, during a shoot-out among his own clan. With the rain new life would quickly emerge. There were butterflies and dragonflies floating around everywhere; small lizards came out to feed on the new insects. The rain also brought back the flowers and their sweet fragrance, scents I have not found anywhere else in the world since.

But the rains also came with mosquitoes that carried malaria. It was getting hard for me to sleep outside, with the sound of mosquitoes in my ears followed by their painful bites. I decided to come back home. My mom saw the scratches on my body, the bites, sores, and bruises all over my face and hands. My brother, Hassan, also came home briefly, devoured by the insects and looking sick with malaria. Sleeping in our old room, with the rain hitting the roof, felt like floating on a ferryboat. Hassan and I stood in our courtyard during downpours, filling any container we could find, even cups and bowls, to collect drinking water. When the rain stopped, we had to scoop the water out of the rooms of the house; it was everywhere because the roof had so many bullet holes.

Everyone seemed to be forgetting about the war. Nomads like my mom were happy because to them rain was a sign of prosperity. She started humming the nomad songs for her goats and called out to her flock, even though they were gone forever. She ran around in the rain, laughing. I couldn't remember the last time I had seen my mom happy like that. Mom would sit with me sometimes to see if I had changed my mind about going back to the madrassa, but whenever she mentioned that school, I would get mad.

With no more Koran lessons, I could spend even more time learning English. I recorded the sound from the movies on a cassette player, then replayed it constantly, listening to the words. I practiced English freely on the streets, talking either to myself or to my brother or to my friends. I told people that in America you feel free, you can be a singer or an actor, anything you want. I still joked with my friends that the marines left me behind, and they laughed at me. But they stopped laughing when I started teaching English to a group of boys and girls in the neighborhood.

I put together the lessons myself, trying to think of easy ways the children could learn. Lesson number one was introductions:

BOY: Peace be upon you.
GIRL: Peace be upon you too.
BOY: How are you today?
GIRL: Fine, and you?
BOY: I am fine. Thank you.

Lesson number two, second day:

BOY: Where were you born?
GIRL: I was born in Waberi. And you?
BOY: I was born in Wadajir. When were you born?
GIRL: I was born in 1989. And you?
BOY: I was born in 1988.

I must have been fifteen when I started teaching English, for the few coins my students could afford. It was something many people thought I could not do, but the three students I had on the first day soon turned into ten. The lessons were repeated every week until each student memorized the passages—just like I had learned the Koran. So my madrassa training had not gone to waste. Unlike Macalin Basbaas I did not beat my students; in fact I encouraged them to have fun. I would ask two students to stand up and face each other and practice the lesson by having a conversation. During the lessons I would wear my blue jeans, my new long T-shirt, and sneakers. As I taught class, I would swagger and move around like a rapper. The students seemed to think I was so cool, this Somali guy who speaks English and dances like Snoop Dogg. I thought I was pretty cool too.

By the turn of the new century Mogadishu was divided into two economic classes: those who had relatives abroad, and those who didn't. Our family was in the second group. The lucky others crowded every day into Xawaaladda Barakaat, the money-wiring office in Bakara market. A man with a long beard sat behind a closed door and spoke to people through a glass window, flanked by three men armed with AK-47s. The man asked for their names and the name of the sender. Then he asked where the money was coming from, always faraway places Hassan and I dreamed of seeing called Minnesota, Seattle, London, Toronto.

Somalis who had made it to those places were lucky to escape the country. Eventually, they had been resettled in North America and Europe from refugee camps in Kenya and Yemen. They found jobs in the West cleaning hotels, stacking shelves at Walmart, and driving taxicabs. And they proudly sent hundreds of dollars back to their relatives in Mogadishu. We all knew they must be getting so rich. The civil war was now going on for ten years, and with no government or treasury the Somali shilling had become a worthless currency. The U.S. dollar was now the money of Somalia, and it was flooding in through those wire transfers called *hawala.* People left that window with fifty dollars, a hundred dollars, two hundred, three hundred.

I had no one in America, not even a distant relative. I felt it was unfair for me not to be able to collect dollars, while people who did not even respect America or speak English could go there and get American dollars. Here I was, Abdi American, and I had never seen a dollar in my life except in the movies. I wanted to see one in real life, but as people left the window, they clutched their dollars tightly and walked fast to their houses. I could never see them.

Next to the remittance window was a telephone center where people called family members in North America or Europe. "Thank you. I received the money. God bless you!" people said. I wanted to hear the voices of the people on the other side in case you could hear Americans talking in the background, chattering in English. Maybe I could hear Arnold Schwarzenegger! Mostly I wanted to talk in English to someone who lived in America. I sat there daydreaming, imagining what I would say: "Hi! How is New York? I love America. I want to come!"

People who got money from America and Europe ate freshly cooked beans, rice, meat, and eggs. At our house we were struggling just to get corn. Our mom went out every day to work, walking miles into Bakara market to get a porter job for people who bought sacks of rice with dollars received from abroad. Mom would put the whole sack on her back, trudging miles to the rich person's house. With the cash she made, she would buy food for us.

Dad had gained back much of his strength, but his mind was always somewhere else. He managed to wake us up at five o'clock every morning to perform the dawn prayers with him and then read the Koran. But one morning in September 2000, Dad didn't call us. When we finally got up, he was gone. Mom said he had left in the night, to Bakara market to catch a bus to Baidoa. He told Mom it had rained a lot in Baidoa and he hoped to start farming there. Also, he heard on the BBC that after Aidid's death his militias had withdrawn from the city; the Rahanweyn had learned how to carry guns and had retaken

Baidoa. Mom was praying for his safe passage, her forehead on the floor, as Nima made tea.

I think my dad left mainly because he was lost and bored in Mogadishu. There was no work for him, he felt useless. And he had given up on me and Hassan becoming sheikhs. Maybe he could be something in Baidoa. His departure was not the same as when he walked into the bush that night in Baidoa almost ten years before. Back then we were all so scared to lose him; we didn't know how we would survive the war. Now things were different; Hassan and I were the men of the house. He left without saying good-bye, probably because he was humiliated.

In truth I was a bit excited that he was gone—first because I hoped he would do better in Baidoa, but also because I would get a break from his harsh scolding about my new lifestyle and from praying with him and always bathing him and trimming his hair. It was like another freedom to me. Strangely, my own dad had become something else to me. None of my friends in Mogadishu even had dads, they lost theirs in the wars. Mine was alive, and I knew I should be grateful for that. Instead, I was grateful for more freedom.

Mom hummed her nomad songs and prayed for Dad as she scraped the maize from the pot. She had not protested his departure, in fact she encouraged him to leave. It would be less stress for her; she would not worry about him getting shot in Mogadishu. "When your dad settles in Baidoa, we will all move there and start herding animals," she said with a smile. I walked outside and thought to myself, "She is crazy." I wasn't sure we would ever see Tall Nur again.

Meanwhile, I hated growing older—not because I was afraid of getting old, but because each year added to my potential to end up in trouble. I had watched boys turn into feared militia fighters when they became teenagers, killing people and chewing qat. Once you enter that life, there is no going back.

The choices were so narrow. You could become a sheikh and call the mosque your home, or you could carry a gun. To me, either was going down a dark path to a world I did not want to live in. My mom did her best. She woke up early every morning and forced me to get up and pray. My prayers took two minutes; hers lasted two hours. Even though she could not read the Koran, she prayed in Somali. On and on. She prayed for our family, for food on our table, for farms and livestock in Baidoa. None were answered. "Allah has plans for us," she always said. Meanwhile, Hassan was making his own plans.

My brother had returned to the streets after his malaria bout, and he had been hanging out more often at Zobe Square with the men. I would walk down Zobe Street and see him and his friend Hussein sitting against a wall, hiding from the baking sun. I would sit next to them and talk about life.

"I want to leave Somalia," Hassan told me one day.

"You have been saying that for years," I said. "You are still dreaming."

"Now it's for real," he said. "Now I will do it. I have the *buufis.*"

Buufis. That was a word meaning "temptation to leave," and it was being used by young Somalis who had seen all the money coming in from abroad and wanted to get their own life away from Mogadishu. Hassan was still dreaming, but his dream was growing bigger.

"Where would you go?" I asked.

"I don't know. Maybe Kenya, Djibouti. But I want to leave Somalia." Young men his age were leaving for Yemen, Kenya, Dubai, Saudi Arabia. These places were by now dealing with so many Somali refugees that it had become a crisis, and they were putting people in refugee camps. Hassan told me that if he left Somalia, he would earn money and send us some, fifty or a hundred dollars a month; that would help our family stay together. These things Hassan told me sounded good, but I did not want him to leave us; we would miss him, but also we would be worried for him, because in Mogadishu there was no communication system. If he left, how would we ever find out about him?

Nearby, a crowd of elderly men were engaged in the regular *fadhi kudirir* debate, a Somali custom where men (never women) gather over tea and talk about clans, politics, animals, and other important topics. They were talking about how great the refugee camps were in Kenya and Yemen. They said the camps were a gateway to America. Some of them had sons and daughters who had made it to the United States, Europe, or Canada. One bragged that his son was a taxi driver in Seattle, sending hundreds of dollars back home, then another described how his own son worked as a truck driver in Minnesota and was paid thousands of dollars every day. Many were sure they would soon be going to America through something called family sponsorship. But first you had to go through the refugee camps.

"Everyone who is sending money from America had been through those camps," said Hassan. "Once in the camps it is easy to go to America. It only takes something like three months, and while you wait you get food from the United Nations. It's heaven!"

But without money for transport, Hassan was stuck in Mogadishu. He looked out over the Indian Ocean and asked Allah for wings to fly across it to America. I told him that beyond the blue waters of the Indian Ocean was heaven, that's where the dead end up. The ocean divided the dead and the living. He laughed at me. "No, Abdi," he said. "There is life beyond the ocean."

I told Hassan how much I missed him at the house, how our family had survived through the wars and the famine, and how we now barely saw each other during the day. How we were all taking separate ways, including our dad. Hassan didn't say much, but I could tell he was also sad.

One morning I went to see him at the wall. Hassan was listening to the elders engage in a heated debate about the new American war in Afghanistan. The men had been cursing the United States and praising Osama bin Laden. They were organizing protests against the war, and against America. "This is a war between Muslims and non-Muslims," said an elder, throwing one hand in the air as if he wanted to go fight the war himself while holding a cup of tea in his other hand. The crowd nodded and all said, "Yes!"

I placed one hand on Hassan's shoulder. "Come home, brother," I said.

He did not protest. We walked home together. When I reached out for his hand, he held mine tightly.

Back home, Hassan didn't say much, but I could tell he was thinking of a better way we could all live. "There is life outside Somalia," he finally said. "We can do something. People who are sending dollars from abroad are just like us. They left Somalia and now they have jobs."

Mom looked at him and said, "I wish you were abroad."

"Mom, I will leave," he said. "I need your blessings. We are now grown up, Abdi and me. We can either carry guns and kill people or leave and send money back to our mom and sister."

He was right. If I was not enjoying movies and soccer and dancing at weddings, I would be as bored as Hassan and also recruited by the militias. It was then I realized how wrong my parents and Macalin Basbaas had been in trying to stop me from going to movies, learning English, or dancing. I knew that movies and music had saved my life.

Hassan asked for Mom's prayers. I remember her looking him in the eyes and saying, "I would like to see you leave. May Allah be with you."

That's all Hassan needed, Mom's prayers. That, and money to get a ride to the border. So we started selling the pigeons. I sat on the side of the street with a boxful of birds, selling them for a few cents each. After two weeks almost all of our pigeons were sold. We got a total of ten dollars for the birds and two dollars for some wooden scooters that we had built with our hands.

At dawn on a Sunday morning in September 2004, Hassan walked out the door with twelve dollars and a plastic bag containing a blanket to sleep on.

"Be strong," said Mom. "You will make it."

I walked with him and his friend Hussein to Bakara market, to see him off. Again Hassan and I held hands the same way we had done as children when we walked up the hill to Madinah Hospital, dodging sniper bullets and rolling jerry cans of water back down. This day we held tighter; I felt like I did not want to let go of my brother, but I knew I could not let him stay. He felt the same way. I saw tears in his eyes for the first time in years. Hassan had been strong enough to sleep on the streets of Mogadishu, go a whole day without eating, but it was hard for him to imagine living far away from Mom, Nima, and me. He would not be flying home at night like the pigeons. He was on his way out from our family, maybe forever, and we all knew it.

We walked deep inside the dusty market. Then, through the shouting of the hawkers, we heard our mom's voice coming from behind.

"Hassan! Wait!"

She could not stay home; she decided to come say good-bye to her son.

When Hassan saw Mom, tears soaked his face. I watched as my brave mom and brave brother hugged and cried.

"Do you want to change your mind?" she said.

For a minute I thought Hassan would decide to stay, but finally he released Mom and said, "Let's keep walking."

Soon we spotted the car that would take Hassan to the border of Kenya. It was a green Mercedes, parked in a narrow alley, but it was hard to tell it apart from the surrounding market stalls: its roof was piled with hay, bags of corn, and luggage all tied together. The front passenger seat was loaded with baskets of fruits. A live goat was bleating under the hatchback, its legs tied together. The driver's door was missing and the hood was gone; it seemed like a car in a Hollywood movie crash scene. I couldn't believe it would actually move, much less travel hundreds of miles on potholed roads. So there was a gamble: it was the cheapest ride Hassan could find, but if it broke down in the bush, there would be no refund, and he would probably die of thirst in the desert.

Two women in the rear seat looked angrily at Hassan. "We don't want him in here, put him in the back!" one of them yelled at the driver, who was standing at a nearby stall, eating bread and drinking tea. He was missing one arm, probably from a gunshot, and he barely had any teeth in his mouth. He lit a cigarette using his one hand and laughed through his qat-stained tongue and cracked lips. He did not care who sat where as long as he got his money.

The driver opened the hatchback and indicated that Hassan should climb in with the goat. The two women in the backseat smiled. They would not have to share their space with a man, which was sinful. So Hassan squeezed into the hatchback and curled up with the goat. There was goat shit everywhere. And of course this car had no air-conditioning, so it would be an oven under that hatchback window across the bush. But Hassan didn't care. He was finally escaping Somalia, the place he called "a roofless prison," under the airless hatchback window of a ruined Mercedes-Benz, with a goat.

When the market lady who ran the tea stand started bothering the driver to pay his bill, as well as his breakfast bill for the last three days, he stubbed out his cigarette and said, "Let's go." But the engine of the car would not start, the battery was completely dead. It took five guys pushing to kick the motor into life, spewing a cloud of black exhaust. The breakfast lady ran alongside the car demanding money from the driver, who argued with her. "Next time!" he shouted.

I hugged Mom as we watched the car trundle through the crowd of porters and shoppers, past the pyramids of tomatoes and peppers, the driver honking nonstop. The car turned from the market alley in to the busy main road. Under the hatchback, Hassan stretched his hand out from behind the goat to high-five us. Then my brother disappeared.

8

Wedding Vows

A burning-hot day in March 2004, me and my friends Bocow and Bashi high up in the branches of a neem tree. We were looking out across the city for smoke. Where there was smoke, there was food, and we were so hungry. Then we saw it, a big fire, lots of people. Probably an arranged wedding. We climbed down, grabbed our boom box, and crashed that party. Time for some food and dancing!

With more money and more men in the city, weddings were happening almost every week in Mogadishu. For less than three hundred dollars you could put up a nice wedding, providing lots of cow meat, camel milk, fruits, and dance music. Except for very strict Muslims (who had not yet taken over the city), a wedding without dancing is considered incomplete for Somalis—like eating maize without camel milk. But most of the traditional Somali musicians had been killed or had fled during the fighting, so there was no live music; you had to use a boom box, preferably with fresh batteries so you could play it really loud. There was nothing on the radio, only cassette tapes, and people with a lot of cassette tapes were in demand for weddings, especially if they also knew how to dance and could get the party going.

By this time I had my boom box and some tapes, and everywhere I went I was twisting my body, gliding and moonwalking to the music. About once a week I would get hailed on the street to perform at a wedding. People yelled my new name, Abdi American, at every corner of my neighborhood when I passed. I would show up with my group of dancers and play music for the crowd.

One day I received a request to dance at a big wedding in the neighborhood. The groom was living in the United States. He called the girl's family and told them that he would sponsor her to come to the United States after the wedding. The family was so excited that they put together an amazing wedding—five cows, two sacks of rice. There was a space for me and my two friends Bocow and Bashi to dance on the floor that evening. I was relieved it took place at night because by then the madrassa would be closed and Macalin Basbaas would be back in his house. I walked in with my boom box, two tapes in my hand. As the music started and my friends and I began dancing, some people walked out of the room disgusted by our sinful moves, but others were cheering and clapping. The bride was sitting in a corner; she had a smile on her face. She definitely liked the music and dancing, but I'm sure she was mostly happy to be moving with her new husband to Minnesota. "She is lucky," I thought.

After that wedding the bride's dad gave me a few American dollars, the first I had ever held in my hand. It was enough to buy maize and camel milk for our family. Not everyone could pay me to dance, and usually I did it for free. Most important, I got a reputation. Girls would come to my house, walking past Mom and Dhuha into my room just to chat and flirt with me. When I was out, Mom told me girls she didn't even know were coming to our house asking for me. One girl left a message in Arabic at our door, written in charcoal on a wooden board. It said "I love you." And wherever I went to dance, girls came, watched, and clapped. When I walked on the streets, girls shouted, "Abdi American!" I just waved and moved on.

Of course the girls always looked their best at weddings, wearing traditional Somali printed *diracs* but also modern Western garments of different colors. They braided their hair, painted henna tattoos on their hands, put on makeup and perfume, and showed off bracelets and other jewelry. Most of them were shy and had never danced at all, much less with men, which their parents would usually forbid. They would mostly just sit and watch us dance, ululating and applauding.

One afternoon we walked into a wedding celebration, dressed in our usual California street gang attire of head wraps, plastic bracelets, baggy jeans, and hats. I set up my boom box and played my latest tape, brand new to Mogadishu: "In da Club" by 50 Cent. The ululations and shouts from the women were so loud, they loved this new song. Then a beautiful young woman stepped onto the dance floor. She had a big smile, and her dark brown braided hair flowed down her neck from under her head scarf. She was wearing an orange *dirac* in a *maqbal* pattern of brilliant flowers. The dress fit perfectly around every curve of her body. She coyly swayed her body sideways, covering her face with her colorfully painted hands. This girl obviously did not know how to dance, but I thought she was so brave to be the first to try. Some of the wedding guests cheered her, but others booed. Another girl in the crowd yelled, "Stupid girl, sit down!"

I moved closer to encourage her. The music was loud. She leaned in to my ear to say something.

"I can't dance," she said.

"I can teach you," I said. "What's your name?"

"Faisa."

Of course I could not touch Faisa's body, because people were watching. This was Somalia, not the movies I had seen where men and women dance while holding tight. But I could smell her perfume from where she stood. I can still smell that perfume. Then the girl who had been scolding her jumped onto the dance floor, grabbed Faisa by the hand, and dragged her outside the building, yelling at her. "I will tell Dad, I will tell Dad!" she screamed.

So there was a good sister and a bad sister. Their dad was Sheikh Omar, an important cleric in the Waberi neighborhood. You could see him everywhere, he wore a long beard dyed bright orange with henna. He led the five daily prayers at the mosque, and also the important Friday prayers. Sheikh Omar was also a judge mediating divorce, marriage, and child support cases according to the Koran, which he knew not just in Arabic but also in Somali. He had ten children from four different wives. Faisa's half brothers ran mosques and madrassas; another brother lived in the United States and sent money to the family. Sheikh Omar also coordinated the annual hajj pilgrimage to Mecca. Fortunately, he was too busy to pay much attention to his daughters, which is how Faisa and her sister were able to dress up and go to weddings where dance music was played. But listening was one thing. Dancing was another.

I watched the door for a while. When Faisa never came back, I went out to look for her. I found her sitting by herself, fanning her face against the late afternoon heat.

"Asalaamu aleikum," I greeted her. Peace be upon you.

"Wa'aleikum salaam," she replied. And unto you, peace.

She stood up, smiled, and said she was happy to see me. Sweat was running down my head to my back, partly from dancing but also because I was so nervous. She told me she had to go home before sunset, and it was already five o'clock.

"I want to see you again," I said.

"Okay," she said, offering to meet up the next day and adding that she hoped I could teach her to dance.

"Could you come to Aargada Arch tomorrow at four o'clock?" I asked.

I knew I would not be able to teach her to dance, because we had no private place to hang out. She would never come to our house, because her dad would never allow it, and Omar would certainly not invite me to their house. And in Mogadishu, even what happens inside is not private, everything can be heard behind tin or mud walls. A boy and a girl cannot date; only marriage is allowed. So what Faisa and I wanted to do was strange. Still we could try.

The next day at four o'clock I was standing under the Aargada Arch in my new denim jeans, a new T-shirt with an American flag, and a new taper-fade haircut inspired by the U.S. Marines in Mogadishu back in 1993. The arch, at the KM4 circle, was built by the Italians during their colonial occupation of Somalia. Surrounding the circle were once landmarks such as the Cinema Ecuatore, the former embassy of Egypt, and the Naasa Hablood hotel. Now most had been destroyed, but the arch remained. Faisa appeared walking down Maka al-Mukarama Street with a smile, looking happy to see me.

We walked together enjoying a cool breeze from the sea. Of course we could not hold hands, we just walked side by side. I could not take her to a tea shop or a restaurant; all I could do was take her to Hamarweyne for a walk through the old part of Mogadishu, down the streets with coconut trees on each side and the Indian Ocean beyond. I talked to her about my dad's basketball games, how life had been good for us before the war.

She talked about how they survived during the mass displacement in 1991 by fleeing to Jigjiga in Ethiopia, then returning six years later. Now she was curious about the music of 50 Cent I had played at the wedding. "How did they create such a sweet thing?" she asked. "Where do those people live?"

I told her they live in America, the same place as my nickname. She started calling me Abdi American. We talked about how she could join my dance club, but our conversation was cut short when Faisa realized it was five thirty and again she had to be home before sunset.

Our next meeting was the day before Ramadan. She had prepared *bajiyas* and samosas specially for me. We walked again down the street, me taking bites of the *bajiya* as Faisa talked about her family. Faisa did not eat anything while we were walking; Somali girls are too shy to eat on the streets. Her story was interrupted by a group of hungry street kids who had followed the smell of the fresh snacks and begged for some. I gave everything to them.

Faisa looked me in the eyes and said, "You are so generous."

I told her that the kids reminded me of my childhood, when hunger was an enemy that can make you eat anything. There was no way I could not give it to them.

We talked about fun things we could try to do together. There were not many options. Men could go to restaurants or sit in tea shops. Faisa could not do any of that, but we decided to walk on Uruba beach. Hundreds of young men came to that beach to swim every day, but there were never girls there. Unlike the restaurants it was not strictly forbidden for women to go to the beach; mostly they stayed away because it could be dangerous for a woman around all those rough boys.

I felt I had to take Faisa to the beach. In movies I had seen a place called Venice Beach in Los Angeles, where people in love could walk and swim and have fun. Mogadishu was no Los

Angeles, and we did not enjoy the carefree life of those actors, but this war had gone on for thirteen years, and I was sick of it. I wanted life. I already danced on the streets and spoke English; why not go to the beach with my girl? I knew the dangers that could come from bringing a girl in a crowd of boys who had been raised in the war and thought assaulting girls was fun. So I organized my posse of friends as bodyguards. They followed us with machetes, rocks, and sticks. In this way I found myself in heaven, walking down the beach, shirtless, side by side with Faisa. It didn't take long for crowds to build and stare at us.

Faisa trusted in me and stayed very close to my side as she waded into the ocean in her clothes. Every time I saw guys moving close to her in the water, I jumped up and used my best Mogadishu gangster dialect to shout, "Stay away, motherfucker!" I had perfected a good Mogadishu accent, so everyone thought I was from the Hawiye tribe and probably had militia connections. It was Faisa's first time in the ocean, and whenever the waves rolled in toward us, she would race back to the shore in terror, like it was something alive chasing her. But her shock turned to excitement. Going to the beach would become our favorite thing to do. I would write her name on my arm with a piece of charcoal, like a tattoo. She wrote my name on her arm too, but she always made sure the ocean had erased it before she went home.

Faisa was not a movie buff like myself, but sometimes during the day (never after dark) she came to the movies with me anyway, sitting close as I translated. Sometimes I think she was bored. Girls like different movies from guys, I was learning.

Many times Faisa was not allowed to go out of her house, especially when her dad was around. I tried to go see her, but it was impossible; he would sit near the door and watch who came in and out. Sometimes I worked up the courage to sneak around the side of their house and come to the window of

Faisa's room. She would stand there whispering to me to leave, it was too dangerous for her if anyone found out she was talking to me from the window. I insisted I wanted to talk to her, that I missed her presence.

One day her sister learned that I was stalking Faisa at her window. When she told her dad about this, all hell broke loose. Sheikh Omar marched over to our house and found my mom.

"Your son is *faasiq*!" he told her. That means a dissolute person who commits sins. "He will end up in hell!"

He went on to tell her he did not like the way I dressed, the way I talked, and the dancing. To him, everything about my life was just an evil act.

"Where is this bastard boy's dad?"

Mom felt embarrassed that she had no husband in her house.

"If you can't stop this boy from stalking our girl, we will take measures against him!" Then he stormed out.

When I came home that evening, Mom was waiting for me at the door. She hit me with a broom, then her sandals. She was so angry that she started pinching and biting me. "Stay away from Faisa!" she said. "Her dad came here threatening me!"

Soon my relationship with Faisa was known on every corner in the neighborhood. I found myself in the same situation as Leonardo DiCaprio in *Titanic.* I did not know where this would end, but I knew I would have to fight for Faisa. She had been under surveillance from her family, so we could not meet. Weeks passed and there was no sight of her until one day she was allowed outside when her parents traveled to visit family. She was at the market buying bananas and tomatoes when I ran into her.

"I miss you so much," she said.

"I miss you too."

Against all odds we agreed to meet at Aargada Arch again,

before her parents returned to town. She told her sisters she was going to do shopping. This time she did not bring any snacks. She told me she had twenty minutes to chat and then she would have to go back. But she had an idea. Her parents were on their way back to Mogadishu in two days, and she had been told by her sisters to go gather fruits in Afgooye, where I had seen the scary blue monkeys as a boy fleeing the war. They needed to welcome their parents back with fresh food. So we agreed to meet in Afgooye.

I took a bus by myself. It was the first time I had been down that road since our flight to Baidoa a few days after the war erupted in 1991, and it brought back terrible memories. This time the road was much different. There were about sixty roadblocks where militias robbed travelers, including bus drivers and their passengers, but it was not as crazy as the last time. By now the rebels were experts on how to use guns and shoot people, so they didn't need to practice randomly on innocent travelers.

But I didn't care; all I could think about was Faisa. I had seen enough movies; I knew what I would do when we met.

I would kiss her for the first time.

Of course it would not be like a Hollywood kiss, long and with hugging. That would scandalize her. Faisa did not believe in kissing on the lips, because she had never seen people do that. I told her people in the movies do it. "Stop, Abdi American, those are not Muslims," she would say.

I was standing under an acacia tree close to the river when Faisa got off her bus. When she saw me, her eyes widened with her smile, and I saw she was wearing eyeliner. We greeted and walked along the riverbank. Blue monkeys chattered in the trees above us.

"Faisa, I want to kiss you," I said. My heart was beating so fast as I waited for an answer. She coyly giggled, covered her smile with her hand, then shyly turned and walked toward the river. I knew that meant okay, so I took her hand, but she resisted.

I was walking behind her, begging, "Just one time," when suddenly she turned and came running toward me, stumbling on her feet and throwing herself in my arms. I was sure she had changed her mind, but actually she had just seen a crocodile in the river.

"I thought the croc was coming for me!" she said, pulling away when she realized there was no danger.

I guess not all the monkeys and crocs had been killed in the early days of the civil war, so this was a new generation of war wildlife. We kept walking, me shooing away the monkeys and throwing rocks at the crocs as she collected papayas, mangoes, and bananas hanging from the trees. The fruit trees along the river were like "pick your own" at an American farm stand. You gathered fruits in a basket, then paid when you left. It was a beautiful spot; it felt like a peaceful world with no civil war. Best of all, it was a private place, out of sight of people, especially her family. The only sounds we heard were the splashes of the crocs and the squealing of the monkeys jumping from tree to tree. A perfect day for a kiss. Faisa was standing there, still protesting, but I felt she was showing enough shyness to suggest it was okay. I came close and gave her a quick peck on the cheek. Her skin was soft and she smelled like heaven.

Kissing Faisa on the cheek that day was a moment in my life that I will never forget. First kiss, first time. I know she liked it, but she told me I would have to wait for the next kiss until the day of our marriage.

"When will that be?" I asked.

"I don't know," she said. "Only Allah knows."

Maybe only Allah knew, but I had a pretty good sense that marrying Faisa would be a challenge. Her dad might get over his hatred of me if I came up with enough of a dowry, but the bigger problem was that we were not even from the same tribe. It was not impossible for a Hawiye girl to marry a Rahanweyn boy, but it would have been very hard. In fact it would be a long time before I saw Faisa again.

Someone returned from Kenya who had seen Hassan in the refugee camps in Wajeer, which our dad's sister Amina had also reached. This person carried a letter to me from Hassan. It was handwritten in English:

> Abdi it is Hassan I am doing well. I am in Wajeer Kenya. Our car broke down somewhere near the border with Kenya and I had to walk three days to get to the border. I met lions and hyenas on the streets, scary and remembered Mom's stories. Anyway, everything is good with me. I am trying to get to Nairobi. The refugee camp here in Wajeer is very hard, really tough like Somalia people are dying from hunger. I heard Nairobi is a good place that I can work at least. Abdi there is something called Hotmail. You can create an account on the internet, create one and lets talk there and my hotmail address is hansiftin@hotmail.com. Say hi to Mom and Nima.

Back at home, life was so different with both Hassan and Dad gone. When I came home at night after watching a movie, the house was dead quiet because Nima and Mom usually went to bed around seven. When Hassan was home, he stayed up and we chatted in English. Now I was in our room all by myself, lonely and bored. Nima was now fourteen and had been practicing her regular daily chores starting from dawn, from making tea to washing clothes. She did not have friends like me; her only companion was Mom. Nima was tall like all the children of our tall parents, and like every other girl in the city she had been putting on eyeliner, coloring her nails, and putting henna tattoos on her hands. After Hassan left, Nima and I grew closer; we entertained each other at home playing *gariir* and hopscotch.

One afternoon some strange guests came to visit. They were five men all dressed in long white robes, their beards reaching their Adam's apples. They were spotlessly clean except for the fresh dust on their foreheads, which signified they had been to the noon prayer at the nearest mosque. At first I thought maybe they were Tabliiq, coming back to enlist me to preach the word of Allah, and I prepared to run. But when they arrived, Mom ran back into her room, put on her hijab, and came out smiling. She offered the five of them to sit on the mat.

"Nima, prepare the tea for our guests," she said.

"Okay, Mommy."

I was dressed to go out and see what movie was on at the shack, but the men invited me to sit next to them. "I heard you graduated from madrassa," one said. His name was Omar, and he was short and maybe about thirty years old. "Congratulations!" he said. "It is one big leap. We are proud of you. What are you doing now?"

"Nothing," I said. *Definitely nothing these guys would want to know about.*

He pointed to my hair and told me I should trim it down, I looked like an infidel. And my jeans and tank top were not proper dress, he said.

"That is true!" said Mom. With my dad gone, she had finally found another man to scold me. "Today you will go with them to the mosque," she added. But while they were talking, I snuck out of the house to the movies. When I came back that evening, the guests were still there, eating meat and maize.

Omar scowled at me, but then he reached into his pocket,

pushed aside his beard comb and mirror, and pulled out five American dollar bills. After he was sure we could all see his money, he gave me one of the bills and said, "It is yours." It turned out Omar had a cousin in America who was sending him fifty dollars a month.

I was still confused why they were here and why they were giving me the money. But in Somali culture it is not appropriate to ask guests questions like that. I went to Nima who was making tea behind a curtain we used to separate our house from the kitchen. "Who are these people?" I whispered.

"I was about to ask you," she said.

From the kitchen we overheard them talking about a wedding, presents of goats, a silent Muslim ceremony with no dancing. Omar was explaining his plan for the wedding, saying it would happen on Thursday.

"Nima, come here," said Mom. Nima came running from the kitchen. "Look how gorgeous she looks!" Mom said to the men. "Nima, you are so lucky. Omar has come to marry you. And we accepted."

Nima had no words; I think she almost had a heart attack. Of course she knew she would someday be married, but she never expected to marry a man more than twice her age whom she had never met. I was in just as much shock, and I felt so betrayed that our mom would do this with no conversation, just for some money and goats.

Mom told us that Omar just got in from Baidoa and that he was Rahanweyn and a relative of ours, being the son of our dad's cousin. A Somali marriage is mostly considered kinship between clans and families. Family marriages are always considered more respectful, and therefore every mom wants her daughter to have an arranged marriage within the family. But Mom said it was actually our dad, through a messenger sent to Dhuha, who made the decision to marry Nima to Omar. The culture did not allow Mom to disagree. The wedding was happening next Thursday, and two goats would be slaughtered. Guests including Macalin Basbaas had been invited; there would be sheikhs present, which meant no music or fun at all. Just eating meat and praying.

Mom talked about how fortunate Nima was to marry a man who had memorized the Koran, who regularly went to the mosque, who never missed praying five times a day, and who received money from abroad. "Nima, look at you! You are so lucky!" Mom said.

Nima was still out of breath and could say nothing.

All I could think of to say was "Mom, no music?"

"Shut up!" she said. "Shame on you!"

The wedding day came, too soon. It would be Nima's last day in our house, leaving me home all alone with Mom. But I wasn't feeling sorry for myself, only for Nima. Unlike our mom, with her festive nomad marriage, Nima did not have other women around her who could teach her about the wedding techniques or ululate in joy. It was only our mom who whispered into her ear every time Nima cried because she was frightened about going into the house of a man she didn't know.

That morning I tied the goats by their legs and cut their throats while saying, *"Bismillah."* "I start in the name of Allah." If I had forgotten to say this, many people would not eat the meat, because it would not be halal. Then I skinned and gutted the goats with my sharp knife. We cut the meat into small cubes and put a huge pot of maize on the wood fire. By early Thursday morning, neighbors and religious leaders, including Macalin Basbaas, were sitting peacefully under the shade of a tree, murmuring the Koran and feasting on the meat, milk, and maize. I served them water to wash their hands. It was one of the rare encounters I had with Macalin Basbaas since graduating from the madrassa. I could not ignore him, because he was my former teacher, but I said only the most basic Islamic greeting. He did not bother to reply, but after gobbling down his meat and milk, he shouted out to me, "Bring some more!"

Outside in the street, Rahanweyn beggars had smelled the food. They sat in the heat of the sun, waiting for scraps. It was not possible for us to let all the Rahanweyn into the house; it was already filled with sheikhs, and there were only two goats. So Mom went out and told them to be patient. But they knew we were fellow Rahanweyn and would never shoot them, so they pushed their way into the house and started scavenging for food. Soon it was a chaotic scene. Mom insisted I get rid of them, so I grabbed a stick and started beating on some of the beggars, the same way Macalin Basbaas beat me. Order returned quickly, and the beggars left. The sheikhs went back to reciting the Koran and stuffing their faces.

The droning of the prayers and the eating went on for hours. Worse, because it was a strict religious wedding, Nima was forced to wear a heavy traditional dark hijab. She sat there baking in the sun, breathing heavily. I decided to stage a revolt. How could Abdi American, the great wedding dancer, let his own sister feel sad and bored at her wedding? I ran down the street and called a few of my friends. Minutes later we showed up with the boom box, ready to dance.

My friends were greeted with frowns by the women in hijabs and burkas and the men with long beards and in *kanzus,* but we didn't care. We put in a cassette of the New York rapper Ja Rule's remix of the Jennifer Lopez hit "I'm Real," and we turned it up loud. Then we started to dance.

Our mom was not impressed. Her jaw went slack, and she put both hands on her cheeks in a look of disgust. Macalin Basbaas and his followers quickly put on their sandals and left, grumbling that the devil had shown up at this wedding. Poor Nima did not know how to dance; she watched from her seat, sweating in the hot sun. But she was proud that I danced at her wedding; she did not care about the sheikhs. I made her happy for a few minutes. Her husband slipped out, and soon she had to leave as well. Mom and I walked Nima down to her new house, six blocks away. I hugged her good-bye. She cried. Mom gave her some final marriage advice: "Be obedient. Do everything he says."

I whispered in her ear some different advice: "Don't allow him to restrict you. Come home whenever you can."

With Nima married, Mom was lonely and decided to journey to Baidoa and search for my dad, who had been gone for a year. She set off on the Afgooye road by bus and arrived in Baidoa two days later.

Baidoa was very different from the last time she saw it, during our flight from Mogadishu. People streamed out of narrow alleys of the city, buying and selling goods. She walked through stall after stall in the market. Giant slabs of red meat were swinging in the sunlight. In other stalls people sold long strips of dried meat called *kalaankal,* which was chopped into small pieces and fried in ghee. In the grain market, women sold every variety of corn and seeds from sacks that attracted bees, wasps, and flies. Vegetables, watermelons, papayas, and bananas, all grown nearby, were everywhere. Men who were pushing wheelbarrows ran to Mom offering their services. Streets and open spaces were crammed with chickens, mattresses, shoes, and bright fabrics. And everyone spoke her Maay language.

Mom sat down on a rock near a kiosk that was selling freshly squeezed fruits and ordered a glass of mango juice to cool herself after walking in the hot sun. She scanned her eyes through the crowd to see if our dad was somewhere around there. She asked people if they knew Nur Dhere. No one knew. But then she remembered she needed to say Nur Dhere in Maay, which would be Nurey. She had lived in Mogadishu for so long she forgot to use her native tongue.

"Do you know Nurey, the tall guy?" she asked a woman.

The lady said yes. She said our dad could be found working in the charcoal market. Mom walked down to the charcoal market, a filthy place where the air was black with charcoal dust.

"Nurey!" she cried.

Within minutes he emerged from the dust like a ghost, covered head to toe in soot. They walked back to his battered tin kiosk, surrounded with bags of charcoal. A little boy, named Deeq, was sitting in the soot drinking camel milk. Dad explained that Deeq was one of his two children with his new wife. She was dark and thin, ten years younger than he, and she sold tea next to his charcoal business.

In Somali culture a man can marry up to four wives. Mom was respectful and told him that she missed his presence. He cursed Mogadishu as a place of the devil. Then she said good-bye.

9

Sin and Punishment

On the morning of October 3, 2005, I woke up to a loud clamor in the street. Everyone in the neighborhood was running in one direction, down our dusty road toward the sea. I didn't know what was happening, but I joined the crowd. Block after block, the crowd grew bigger. Were the marines coming back? Had someone brought in food? Nobody knew, but still we ran. The sky was darkening; people pointed at the sun. It was a total eclipse.

"Mahdi! Mahdi!"

The cry went up through the crowd. It was the arrival of the Mahdi! The Mahdi is the redeemer of Islam, the savior who will come before Judgment Day and vanquish evil before the world ends and we are all taken to heaven. The Hadith says a solar eclipse will announce the arrival of the Mahdi.

Soon everyone was chanting, "Mahdi! Mahdi!" and I joined them. Moms were frantically searching for their children, not wanting to lose them on the path to heaven. I found my mom and we ran together. Finally we arrived at the white sand of the Mogadishu beach, just as the moon was halfway across the sun. We looked around for the Mahdi, but what we saw, on a sand dune, was a pile of human skeletons. They had been dug up from a graveyard. There were skulls detached from bodies. One still had long, straight white hair that blew in the ocean breeze—not an African. A man was standing atop the pile of bones, yelling.

"Spit on them!" he said. "Curse them! These are the Christian bodies buried in Mogadishu!"

Christian bodies buried in Mogadishu? This was definitely the end of the world to me. I thought this man must be the Mahdi, he had come and was killing Christians as we had been taught would happen by Macalin Basbaas. I learned later these were the bodies of Italian soldiers who died during World War II in Somalia. A group of Islamists had dug them up, desecrated the graves, then built a tin-roof mosque on the spot. By now it was afternoon, and the sun had totally disappeared behind the moon. The crowd descended on the bones, happily kicking the skeletons to pieces. I grabbed one of the skulls and threw it to the ground.

But the sun came back; the sand again baked under our feet. The Mahdi had not arrived and the world had not ended. I went home. This was not the first time the world had almost ended in Somalia. Every day while I was growing up, the world was ending the next day when you would probably be shot. There was never any future. No Mahdi, no marines, would come to save us. But there was one prophetic sign on that day: the Islamists who madly dug up those graves would soon change the world as I knew it.

By early 2005, Somalia had a transitional government for the first time since the civil war started. But this government was based abroad, in Kenya, because the warlords with their thousands of militiamen were still in charge of Mogadishu. The new government had given the warlords ministerial positions in the hope they would back down, but the warlords had no intention of giving up control. They were making millions of dollars in ransom by pirating merchant ships off the coast. Then they found a source for even more money: the American taxpayer.

The U.S. government believed that some of the terrorists who had bombed the American embassy in Nairobi in 1998 were hiding in Somalia. And it knew that the warlords had the power to find and capture terrorists. Soon the warlords—the same groups that had brought down the two Black Hawk helicopters and dragged the bodies of U.S. troops through the streets of Mogadishu—were helping the U.S. government hunt down radical and foreign Islamists.

Of course the Americans didn't publicize this new partnership, but the warlords were happy to make it known, and in fact everyone could see that they were swimming in money while raiding mosques and grabbing radical sheikhs. This began a massive purge of not just potential terrorists but Islamic scholars and madrassa teachers, who were abducted, deported, and "disappeared." The warlords grew bolder by the day, turning the hunt for terrorists into a reign of terror—culminating in the shocking assassination of the chairman of the Ifka Halane Islamic Court.

At that time there were five Islamic courts in Mogadishu, each corresponding to a clan. In the absence of any government these courts settled routine cases and disagreements, everything from divorces to petty crimes. Mostly they ordered payments of animals or cash; there was no corporal punishment, and they had no armed enforcers. The Ifka Halane Court chairman was a popular man and a Hawiye, the same clan as the warlords and most residents of Mogadishu, which is what made his killing such a shock. In mosques across Mogadishu, the assassination inspired tirades against the warlords and their American supporters. Public opinion quickly turned against the warlords, and this shift became an opportunity for the courts to unite, despite their clan differences, against a common enemy. They soon gained the support of the Hawiye people, which made it even harder for the Hawiye warlords to claim leadership. People in Mogadishu were tired of lawlessness, tired of warlords, tired of attacks on their religion. The world's war on terrorism since 9/11 had become perceived in Mogadishu as a war on Islam. This in turn boosted public support for the Islamic courts and against the Western-backed warlords. When the courts banded together, calling themselves the Islamic Courts Union (ICU), the stage was set for a radical Islamic takeover.

The first chairman of the ICU was Sheikh Sharif Ahmed, a madrassa teacher who was able to bring together a group of his students and other young men to train for a war against the warlords. Even though he was Hawiye himself, he reached out to other tribes including my own, the Rahanweyn. Everything he said was based on the Koran and Sharia law, and every time he talked, he cursed the United States and its allies like Ethiopia. People in Mogadishu who were furious at the American war on Islam found a man they could listen to.

Soon the Islamic Courts Union established a unified Sharia legal system throughout Mogadishu, as opposed to the earlier courts, which were independent and unorganized. It trained its own well-disciplined magistrates, young men with shaved heads and long beards, to settle cases of theft, forgery, rape, and divorce, all based on the Koran. They also were secretly training young men as Islamic soldiers, practicing weaponry outside the city late at night. Out of these trainings emerged a religious army that could retaliate against the warlords. But first they began killing anyone who resisted Islamic law.

By now the wealthier members of the Hawiye clan were

contributing money to the ICU, which enabled the Islamists to buy more arms and attract more young soldiers. Soon they had taken over the important seaport of El Ma'an, just north of Mogadishu. Following that takeover, a series of clashes between the ICU militias and the warlord militias brought Islamic control over several neighborhoods right in Mogadishu. Besides Sharia law, the ICU restored security and provided social services and charitable works. People were happy to find freshwater available and police on the streets. This popular support for the ICU motivated the religious militias to face the warlords in other areas of Mogadishu, which started months of bitter battles across the city.

Those fights required more Islamist soldiers to battle the warlords, who had thousands of troops, so the ICU launched a massive recruitment effort. It held huge demonstrations all over town, where clever speakers preached of the holy mission and the rewards of the afterlife for Islamic martyrs. Young men in Mogadishu who had no jobs, no future, and nothing to do jostled to be first to sign up. Like young Americans who enlisted after 9/11, they were eager to make a difference and be heroes for their country. The ICU provided breakfast and dinner to its soldiers. Fresh goat meat, bread, and hot tea were offered daily, and also women they could marry—the dowry paid by the ICU, no problem if you're broke. But the best benefit was the promise of entering paradise if you die in the name of Allah. In that paradise you would encounter the *hoor al'ayn* (the beauty of the eye), a group of seventy-two virgins just for you whom no eyes have ever seen.

Long lines of young men queued for the sign-up. After just one day of training, the new recruits were thrown into the front lines of battle with the warlord militias, who had been fighting professionally for years. The Islamic soldiers were highly motivated by their afterlife in paradise and did not fear death; they chased down the heavily armed militias of the warlords on the streets, taking over positions and advancing. As the warlords began to flee, the ICU seized their heavy weaponry and took over strategic neighborhoods and even the airport. By April 2006, most of Mogadishu was under the control of the ICU and the warlords had scattered.

People started volunteering for civic duties such as clearing the rubbish from the streets, rebuilding houses, and opening the airport that had been closed for sixteen years. For the first time since the Americans left Mogadishu in 1994, I returned to the airport. This time it was being run by men with long beards and *kanzus,* not by U.S. Marines in their camouflage uniforms. I watched as the first airplane landed, bringing a group of Somali diaspora who were eager to return to the city and reclaim their houses destroyed or confiscated by the warlords. Along the tarmac the ICU militiamen sat in the beds of their trucks, wrapping their faces in turbans so only their angry eyes appeared. Unlike the marines, who showed their faces and even wore their names on their jackets, these soldiers didn't want you to know who they were. I waved at them like I did to the marines, but they did not wave back. They only held their fists up and shouted, *"Allahu akbar!"* I realized waving was now a sin, and all we should do is say, *"Allahu akbar!"* God is great.

The districts that divided clan warlord control were eliminated. Clans didn't matter anymore, only Allah. I was walking in places where I once dodged bullets, places gangs and militias had ruled, now without fear. The city was different. One flag, the color black with a white script that said "There is no god but God himself," was flying everywhere. The houses were still in ruins, but Mogadishu felt reborn. Instead of gunshots constantly, we heard Islamic chants blaring from huge speakers on the trucks of the ICU fighters. The chants were all *jihadi:* "Go to the war! Go to the war!" Mosques were filled with people who again felt the freedom to worship without fear of being abducted by warlords. After prayers the sheikhs would curse America and praise Osama bin Laden. *America is the enemy of Allah, God bless Osama inshallah.*

Among the people happy for the change was my mom, who had opened a kiosk in Bakara market where she sold maize, sorghum, and rice. To increase her sales, I scampered back and forth in the alleys, coaxing shoppers to come down and check out our food. But everyone else did the same thing, so the loudest voice got all the attention. Also it was so noisy there because right next door was the gun market called Cir Toogte (Sky Shooter), where customers tested the guns on the spot, all day long. Many times the shell casings fell on Mom and her maize. My mom and I were raising our voices so high all day long, trying to make money, until by sunset I was hoarse. When I sat next to my friends at the movies, they complained they could no longer hear my translation because of my scratchy voice.

The ICU had announced a curfew from dusk to dawn. Anyone seen on the street was assumed to be breaking the law and could be imprisoned or shot. This meant there was no chance of theft in Bakara market overnight, so Mom could leave her bags of corn, beans, and grain in her kiosk without lugging them back and forth from our house every day. Her load was lightened, but now my mom's clothes became a new weight. Like every woman in Mogadishu under the new rule, she had to wear heavy clothes and face cover under the hot sun. Everyone was either covered or bearded and listened to Islamic chants, so it was hard to tell who was a member of the Islamic Court fighters and who was just doing their bidding; you had to be careful what you said to anyone.

But with no fear of crime, the market was packed. Bearded men walked up and down the alleys, making change for large American bills. All this commerce had become the main source of revenue for the Islamists; they came and collected money they called charity, really a tax, from the small businesses including my mom. But she was happy. *"Alhamdulilah!"* Mom said every time I complained. Praise be to Allah!

"Who thought of this peace?" she would say. *"Alhamdulilah!"*

I knew what she meant. The Islamists were doing a good job by not allowing bullying or clan superiority and by kicking out the clan-affiliated militias. If anyone bullied anyone else under their rule, you could just call out for help and an enforcer would show up, like calling 911 in America. But to me, the Islamists were not in Mogadishu to serve and protect, they were here to deprive me of my freedoms. I was not sure what to do with the new changes in the city. Wearing my hat that said "Titanic" almost got me killed one day when a young Islamist thought it was the name of an American city. If he had known it was a Hollywood movie, he surely would have killed me. Pictures and names associated with America were crimes, not counting the pictures and names on the American dollar bills that they had in their pockets.

My mom regularly went to a three-hour workshop. An Islamic leader, a former Taliban fighter, and his wife stood under the shade of a tree. On the first day the subject was "How to force your kids to pray regularly." The second day was "The benefits of committing suicide in the name of Allah by killing Christians and Jews." And the workshops went on and on, nothing but death, killing, and Sharia law. Mom got an Islamic flag and flew it over our house. I could not remove it, because houses without the flag would be targeted.

One day Mom came to me and suggested I join the Islamists. "They are going to be rich," she said. "There is no other faith but

Islam; they will conquer the whole world! They are acting on the Sharia!"

"Mom, I want to be who I am. I can't carry guns and shoot at people."

Then she talked about all the good things the Islamists had done, her eyes getting bigger to show me how wrong I was. "If you want to get married to Faisa, have kids, and have money, this is your chance," she said.

She might have been right. If I joined the Islamist fighters, it would have been easy to visit Faisa's house with a long beard; her dad would have been so happy with the wedding. But I would probably be killed in battle soon after. At night, when the air cooled down, everyone was forced to go to former soccer fields and watch young Islamists train for battle. It was like U.S. Marines boot camp—strenuous fitness drills, tactical foot marching, situational training exercises, and weapons use—except these soldiers were all dressed in black and gray *kanzus.* I was bored and wanted to leave, but attendance was mandatory. When it finally ended, the soldiers prayed not for peace but for war with America and Europe: "God make us meet American troops, make us wipe them out. Give us the upper hand. We are your soldiers."

These events lured thousands more young men to sign up for what I always called "the one-way ticket." But they were too late to get me. I didn't want to die for them; I wanted to live in a beautiful American city with paved roads, gorgeous women, money, cars, and jobs. Every day I wondered if the world knew what was happening in Mogadishu. At times I was mad at America for leaving us behind in 1994. When I told my friends that America would come back and rescue me from this nightmare, or I told Faisa that America would be my future home, they all rolled their eyes, but I didn't care; I knew it was true. Now, under the Islamists, I wasn't so sure.

. . .

Every day my heart pounded with the fear of being recruited as a soldier for the Islamists. I knew that once you joined, there was no return. You could not decide to drop your gun and be a normal person again. Death was the only way out, and death was calling to everyone my age.

Friends who had played soccer with me abandoned the pitch and joined the Islamists. Guys I had laughed with at Eddie Murphy movies now signed up for the holy war. The training grounds in Mogadishu were thronged with these young men and women, all fighting for the title *jihadi,* or *shaheed,* martyr. Boys I had known on the streets of Mogadishu came back with new names, new wives, and new clothes after the training. They all nicknamed themselves after international jihadists like Abu Ayman, Hamza, Osama, Mullah Omar. They had been instructed to fight sin. And sin was not just the enemy troops, it included sports, movies, music, Western clothes, even the way we walked and talked.

One of the new recruits was a boy I had gone to madrassa with. His name was Mukhtar and he graduated after me, then became an assistant to Macalin Basbaas, who of course was happy with the Islamists. He and I played soccer together before the Islamists came, but now he had changed. Now his name was Abu Jihad, and he no longer cared about soccer. One day he showed up at my house dressed in a black *salwar khameez,* the knee-length shirt and loosely fitting pants worn by al-Qaeda, with a turban wrapped around his face revealing only his eyes. On his shoulder hung an AK-47. Abu Jihad had been told by his emir to go eliminate sin, so naturally he thought of me. He came to my room with another teenager, who also carried a gun. Abu Jihad must have heard I had a poster of Madonna in a bikini in my room, but when he came, it was long gone, my parents having thrown it away. There was just a blank wall. He was so disappointed, it was his first assignment to eliminate sin and he hadn't found any. He asked if I had a prayer mat in my room.

"No. But it is in my mom's room," I said.

He told me to pray regularly or else I would be in trouble. "No joke!" he said.

My biggest fear was that my mom would walk in and tell him that I was reluctant and not interested in jihad. Then he would take me out to his emir at the training ground and force me into the ICU. Looking around for anything sinful, he saw my jeans and cap, hanging on a peg. He ripped them off the wall and slashed them with his knife. He searched through the room and found my boom box. He knew I used it to play tapes and dance at weddings; he knew everything I did. He turned to his *jihadi* friend and said, "Look at this sin!" Using their gun butts, they smashed the boom box to pieces before my eyes.

"We will come to your house most often," said Abu Jihad. "We have our eyes on you!" Then he left. That same night, worried about all the threats in the city, Falis removed all the movie posters from the video shack. She hid the tiny television in her bedroom.

Through all of this turmoil life had to go on, and we soon got word that my sister, Nima, was pregnant with her first baby. I had not seen Nima in several months, but my mom and I heard that she was in much pain. I decided to go check on her, but first I needed her husband, Omar's, permission.

Omar spent his days with his friends at the pharmacy street in Bakara market. There they sold all sorts of drugs from a line of kiosks packed with counterfeit and expired medications in boxes and bottles imported from abroad, written in English and

Arabic. Women hidden under thick robes shopped for these cheap medications using U.S. dollars. Every kiosk had a name taken after the Prophet Muhammad's companions or Islamic scholars. I walked down the row of kiosks to see if I could find Omar. He was breaking large bills at the stand of the money changer, who sat on a big tin box with dollar signs painted on every side.

We said hello using the formal Islamic greeting. He told me that Nima was still in pain but that he had a group of sheikhs who read the Koran over a bowl of holy water for Nima to rub over her body and drink. "She will be fine," he said with a shrug. I told him I would come down on Friday to see her.

The home shared by Nima and Omar was just one room about eight feet square, in a house with other families in other rooms. Nima lay on a wooden bed next to a shelf lined with different medications. I looked at the containers: bottles of Hemoton syrup, boxes of aspirin, blister packs of colored capsules—it looked like a pharmacy. Before she let me in, Nima had put on her hijab, because that's what a Muslim woman must do when a man enters the house. I was disappointed to see that my own sister, whom I had cared for her entire life, was today treating me like every other man in the city. But those were the new rules.

She told me she had been in this bed, pregnant, for weeks. Her body was covered with rashes and pimples. Her skin was darker. She talked about how many times during the day she took the medications as instructed by a pharmacist in Bakara market who never went to school. I read one of the boxes of the syrup she was taking: it had expired two months earlier. Nima could not read and wouldn't have known. I told her but she said nothing. What could she do?

Even as sick as she was, carrying a baby, Nima had to cook for her husband so that he could be fed when he came home at sunset. It was hard for her with all the pain. I went back many times to help her cook, clean, and wash, each time seeking permission from Omar first. Nima had her baby, a healthy girl, but my sister never fully recovered.

At least I had some good news from my brother: Hassan had made it to Nairobi. It turned out the refugee camps were no paradise on earth—violent, filthy, and hopeless places where the same militias and gangs of Mogadishu terrorized people. Hassan paid a bus driver six hundred Kenyan shillings, about six dollars, for a ride to Nairobi and what he hoped would be a better life.

Through our e-mails Hassan was the only person left in my world who encouraged me to keep up my American dream. The Internet café in Bakara market had not been closed by the Islamists, because they also used it, especially the international *jihadis* staying in touch with their families. Into that shop came foreign fighters with their faces covered, speaking Urdu, Arabic, and other languages. Hassan e-mailed in English so the Islamists couldn't read his words. Of course that was dangerous too, because if anyone saw me reading English, he would surely find a way to translate and then execute me for praising America. So I always picked the computer at the corner of the room where no one would stand behind me. I read my brother's e-mails quickly and replied just as fast, then logged out of my account and got out of that place.

Abu Jihad kept his word, checking on me daily. When I saw him approach our gate, I would sneak out the back, avoiding him. I would spend time with my mom in the market, then after sunset I would sneak back into the house. Nights were so scary. I could hear the murmurs and conversations of the Islamist soldiers outside the mud walls of my room, and I could hear the screams of people they were beating for minor mistakes.

One night two bombs exploded in Falis's video shack. The first one pierced the roof; the second destroyed the television in her bedroom and the cassettes. When we all woke up in the morning, we learned Falis had been taken to prison by a group of Islamists. I ran to the shack. The ICU had brought in a bulldozer, which was clearing the rubble of the explosion. A group of young fighters gathered. They said the land had been found to be sinful and therefore the Islamists took it and would turn it into a preaching place where people would be taught Islamic lessons.

A crowd built up as I stood there watching my beloved video shack disappear before my eyes. This, not the dreaded madrassa, had been my real school. A fighter walked up to the crowd holding the Koran in his right hand, talking about how sinful it is to watch movies. "You see naked people in the movies, *women who have no clothes on!*" he shouted. "It is a Western culture that they want to impose on Muslims. It is *haram.* Wherever you see sin, you must destroy it with your hands!" He seemed like he had been given training in how to speak clearly about Islam. He was good at sending the message. The crowd cheered, *"Allahu akbar!"*

Falis had been sentenced to pay five hundred dollars, besides losing her property. The ICU put up huge speakers on the remaining walls, playing Islamic chants every day and encouraging jihad. In the same way and around the same time, our neighborhood soccer pitch was turned into a spot where people who were caught playing soccer were punished, usually by twenty or forty floggings.

Soccer, movies, music, dancing—these were all the things that had kept me going in Mogadishu. Now, with everything banned, my future was falling into a deep dark hole. I started writing to Hassan only once every two weeks, always in Somali. One day I e-mailed him, "I don't know if I will be able to e-mail you again, but, Hassan, in case you don't hear from me, I might be in the hands of the Terminators." That was our secret word for the Islamists.

"I think my world is going to end soon," I wrote. "Mom wants me to join the ICU. I am scared of carrying a gun. I want to leave."

Hassan wrote back, "Abdi, these Islamists will be like the Taliban. I think America will do air strikes against them. I am scared for you too. Let's think of a way for you to leave."

10

Trapped

One Thursday morning in June 2006, when I was about twenty-one, I was lying on the mattress in my room, looking up at the ceiling and thinking about my life, when a neighborhood boy came in.

"A girl who is outside wants to see you," he said.

I dashed out quickly, wondering who it was. She was wearing a heavy hijab and face cover, with gloves on her hands and socks on her feet. Even in the heat of that day, there was not a tiny part of her body visible. But whoever it was, she waved her gloved hand at me from the street corner. I stood there puzzled.

"Abdi, it is me!"

It was Faisa. I had not seen her for months, she was always holed up in her house, and I was afraid to go near it. I had never been welcome there, but now I would probably get shot. It was always crowded with young men who came to study the Koran with her dad, hoping to get great jobs in the Islamic government, or maybe even to marry Faisa or her sister. Sometimes at the mosque I would see her dad sitting in the front row, and I tried to hide from him.

But today Faisa had made a break from their house. She was

standing at my corner in the hot sun, dripping sweat through her hijab, afraid to come in.

The streets were clear. The enforcers had not been patrolling that day, probably out on briefings. Their black flags were still flying everywhere. Their prayer mats, jerry cans full of water, flip-flops, and uniforms were arranged around their sandbag outposts. But they were all gone.

Underneath Faisa's hijab I could see her bright orange *dirac* and a shawl. She looked me in the eyes and said, "I've missed you. Take us somewhere."

I did not know where to take her; the city had changed so much since she and I used to walk together. There were so many Islamist checkpoints in the city, and they couldn't all be off duty today. We both knew that men and women walking together was a crime, the Islamists said so on the radio and from huge speakers. But we didn't know the punishment. I took a moment to think about it. My heart was beating hard as I looked down the street in case the Islamists returned.

The only place I could think of was the beach.

Uruba beach, our old meeting place, was a couple miles away. Walking that far with an unrelated woman would be way too dangerous, but I decided we could take a minibus. When it pulled up, the driver immediately instructed Faisa to go to the backseat. Under the new moral code, women had to sit in the backseat of the bus while men sat in the front rows. No man and woman could sit next to each other. I knew that bus driver when the warlords were in the city, he used to play traditional Somali music in his bus that people enjoyed, but this day he was playing recitals of the Koran. If he played music, he would lose a hand or a leg. No one spoke to anyone else in the bus because there might be an Islamist spying on people. We all sat there very quiet and enjoyed the Koran.

Traveling through the city was peaceful of course, there were no gunshots or roadside bombs, but there were constant butterflies in my stomach. *When will they find out Faisa and I are dating?* My heart rate had increased drastically.

We got off the bus at the Hamarweyne junction in front of the Catholic cathedral. The roof of the church was completely gone, blasted and burned away, and the two bell towers had been destroyed except for one crumbling corner pointing up to heaven like an old man's crooked finger. Inside, high above the Gothic arches, the massive stone carving of Jesus on the cross was now bathed in sunlight and pockmarked by hundreds of bullets: target practice. Dozens of kids were climbing up on the rubble to throw rocks at Jesus. We moved on toward the beach, Faisa walking three steps behind me. We did not talk to each other, but I constantly looked behind to make sure she was okay. We got up to Bank Street, overlooking the green water of the Indian Ocean, and inhaled the fresh sea air. I wondered if Venice Beach in California smelled as good. From the movies I knew it looked very different: no one at Uruba beach was surfing, and the hotels along this beach were bombed-out ruins.

People were crowded on the beach but not for fun or relaxation. Many were washing their clothes with the seawater, smashing their garments against the rocks. Others were fishing in small boats, coming back with nets full of snapper, marlin, and tuna. From the boats men were carrying those huge fish on their shoulders like my dad used to do. They cut up the fish right on the beach and sold the meat in cubes for two American dollars. Women who weren't washing clothes just watched. All were wearing thick robes and face covers. None of them dared to get into the water. Except Faisa.

She stood in the sand and removed her face cover, gloves, sandals, then her socks and her heavy hijab. "I was choking to death in these clothes!" she said. Her soft orange *dirac* danced against the soft breeze, revealing her curvy body. This was as close as you could get to Venice Beach in Mogadishu.

"Isn't this what you dreamed of?" Faisa asked me. "Peace and a happy life?"

I smiled and told her about how people in Miami and California go to beaches just for fun, wearing bikinis and shorts. I told her that if we were in Miami, we would see white sailboats out across the water, more people having fun on those boats, also in bikinis and shorts.

"Bikini is madness," she said. "I would never do that." She started talking about how good things were under the rule of the ICU; even though she had to sweat under all those clothes, she was happy that she could walk around without fear of crime. I wanted to argue, but in Mogadishu you could not trust anyone, not even your girlfriend. I wanted our date to be free from discussions of the ICU or Sharia, but when I tried to talk about movies or songs, Faisa changed the topic to Islam.

I pointed at some fishermen. "Oh, look at that big fish they caught!"

"Thanks to the Islamic Courts," she said.

The day was so hot and the water looked so good. Faisa was still drenched in sweat from her hot clothes. I stripped down to my shorts and beckoned Faisa to the water with me, but she hesitated nervously. We looked around and could not see any Islamists close by. Finally she walked down to the surf holding hands with me, slowly letting the water move up her body. Whenever she felt her feet touch something, she threw herself on me. We teased each other like they do in Hollywood movies.

But this was Mogadishu. It didn't take long for the crowd to spot us and start complaining. Women yelled out to Faisa, "Hey, shame on you! Your breasts are visible!"

Faisa felt so humiliated. We quickly got out, but someone

had already run down the road and called the Islamists. Before we had even dried off, four angry teenage boys with covered faces, guns on their shoulders, and whips in their hands surrounded us. Without saying anything, they just started flogging us with their whips. One guy whipped Faisa; two others knocked me to the sand and pressed their rubber sandals against my face, while a third whipped me viciously. Faisa was screaming, "I will not do it again! I seek Allah's refuge from Satan, the accursed one!"

One of the enforcers pointed at her wet body, barely concealed under her clinging wet *dirac,* and yelled repeatedly, "What is this? *What is this?* Is this Europe? Or America? What are you wearing?"

Then he turned to me. "Who allowed you to walk with a girl holding hands?"

A crowd had gathered around to watch the episode unfold. I could hear people murmuring, "He's the *American* guy." They laughed and said I was stupid. Then Faisa and I, bleeding from our wounds, were marched down the next block into an old building next to the former National Bank of Somalia. This was a makeshift prison and court where people caught in different criminal activities were taken. Faisa was accused of breaking Sharia law. Two men led her into a room and closed the door.

Finally it was my turn. I was made to get on my knees before an interrogator, who asked me my name, where I lived, and what I did for a living. "My name is Abdi, I live in KM4, I don't do anything."

He scribbled my information in Arabic on a sheet of paper, walked away, and came back with the magistrate, who was scowling. He opened a Koran and read, "Tell the believing men to lower their gaze, and protect their private parts . . . and tell the believing women to lower their gaze, and protect their private parts."

Of course I knew that verse, I knew the whole Koran by heart, but today for the first time I was seeing it used directly against me. My punishment was twenty lashes and "counseling." I wasn't sure what "counseling" meant. I knew what twenty lashes meant.

A man whose face was obscured under a thick beard, his forehead dark with dirt from constant prayer, came before me with a huge leather whip. He started flogging me as he counted down the lashes: "Twenty . . . nineteen . . . eighteen . . ." When the lash hit my skin, it was like a dozen needles stabbing me.

After the whipping, my counseling began. Same guy, he just set down his whip and quizzed me on the Koran. "What are the names of the prophets? Recite the ninety-nine names of Allah!" On and on.

I answered all his questions no problem. During this time people kept pouring into the building, all of them accused of crimes against Sharia law such as smoking cigarettes, not praying on time, stealing, or not wearing clothes of a certain length and thickness. Our counseling came to an end when the call for evening prayers rang from the nearby Marwaaz mosque. I was never so happy to hear the call to prayer.

Of course I had to go to the mosque. I was sitting in the back, away from the scary face of the magistrate who had sentenced me. But when the prayer ended, the magistrate approached me, led me outside, and started asking me questions about my life.

"Do you ever listen to music?"

"No."

"Are you obedient to your parents?"

"My dad is gone."

"Where is your dad?"

"In Baidoa with his other wife."

He let me go home but told me to report in the morning for more counseling. I came the next day, other young men were there and we all crammed into a minibus. They drove us to a soccer stadium they were using to perform Sharia punishments. There was a metal table in the center of the pitch. As we stood around nervously, four men appeared from the other end of the pitch, dragging a man who was blindfolded. The prisoner's hand was placed on the metal table as two guys held him tight. Another pulled out a machete and swung it down hard on the man's wrist; his machete must have been quite dull because it took four blows to remove the hand. As the prisoner screamed in agony, they dipped the stump of his wrist into water to wash off the blood, then wrapped it with a bandage. An emir stood in front of us. "See, everyone! Take this as an example!" Then they let us go, warning us we would receive more counseling later at the mosque.

Faisa was lashed as well, then sent home with a warning that if they saw her going to the beach again, she would regret it for the rest of her life. I never showed up at the mosque. Friday prayers were a time of massive recruitment for the holy war, and I suspected my counseling would be a trap to enlist me. On that Friday alone they recruited over three hundred men.

I knew that if I were to avoid the recruiters, I had to blend in. My jeans and cap had already been slashed by my old soccer pal Mukhtar. Now I stopped speaking English, dancing, and playing soccer. Falis's video shack was gone; the movies were gone. Everything fun was done. Even my meager source of income was lost, because it was no longer safe to teach English. I canceled classes.

Many young Somalis had been crossing the Gulf of Aden on rickety boats into Yemen, then registering as refugees. Hundreds of men, women, and whole families were doing this, and some were lucky to be resettled in Europe or America. Others crossed into Saudi Arabia and found jobs cleaning houses, working in day care, or herding goats. I decided to try. I knew I might die trying, but I would surely die staying.

But leaving Somalia was not easy. First I needed money for ground transport to Bosaso, the northern Somali port on the Gulf of Aden, some nine hundred miles from Mogadishu. Once there I would need to pay the smugglers for the dangerous overnight passage to Yemen. Other people who left had been given money by family members abroad, but of course I had no one to help me overseas. Hassan could barely feed himself in Nairobi, much less give me money, because illegal refugees could not work.

I went to see my mom in Bakara market. When I told her about my plan to leave, she scoffed. "Hassan is suffering in Kenya," she said. "He can't work, has nowhere to go, nothing to do."

"I have no work here."

"At least you could join the Islamists; you would get things for free. And maybe you will be able to find a good job in the Islamist government in the future."

It's what she always said. I asked her if she could help me with some cash, at least to get to Bosaso town.

"I pay *zakkah,*" she said, referring to the religious tax. "After that is only money for food."

Her *zakkah* was going to support the Islamist army, exactly what I was trying to escape. It all seemed so hopeless, rigged against me. In desperation I went to Bakara's regional transport section and wandered over to the line of brightly decorated minibuses leaving for the north of Somalia. I had no money in my pockets, and no driver would take me. I saw other young men in the depot working as "conductors"—basically touts who round up passengers for the buses and try to collect tips from the drivers, as well as from passengers for carrying belongings.

I started going to the depot every day, from early in the morning until sunset, working for tips. It was not an easy job, I had to run down the alleys grabbing people by the hand and leading them to the buses. At times people got angry and threw rocks at me. It was so noisy—loud calls, jostling around. Sometimes the drivers ignored me and never handed me cash, even when I helped fill their buses, but other times they gave me some money. I helped passengers carry heavy things like mattresses and furniture from the market to the bus depot, and sometimes they threw some cash at me. In this way I saved fifty dollars.

On a July morning in 2006, I was off on the road to Bosaso. The bus was crowded with people, women in the back, men in the front. We would need to pass checkpoints manned by the Islamists, so it was important to maintain Sharia law. I sat in the middle seat, next to a bagful of carrots, onions, and potatoes. The bus smelled like a produce market, but at least I wasn't riding with a goat like Hassan. A few hours out of Mogadishu we came to the first checkpoint. A boy jumped onto the bus, his angry eyes scanning the passengers. His head was wrapped in a scarf that said "There Is No God but Allah." Luckily, he was only checking that women were seated separate from men, and he waved us to go. At the second checkpoint, armed enforcers removed four men from the bus whose hair was considered too long. I was one of them. A young man ordered us to our knees. One by one they cut our hair roughly with scissors. I got back on the bus with the worst haircut of my life—whole chunks of hair missing on top. It was embarrassing, but at least I still had my head.

After five hundred miles, deep into central Somalia, we reached the junction town of Galkayo, a strategic place where many roads meet and the Islamic Courts were still battling with clan militias. We heard gunshots, rockets, and shells landing in the distance. I was not scared of the sound of battle; in fact it felt good to know we were entering an area that wasn't totally controlled by the Islamists. Women and men on the bus started talking to each other, and soon everyone was moving around to sit together like normal adults. People started telling their stories of life under the Islamist rule. Everyone had a story. I shared mine about the terrible day on the beach with Faisa.

Our bus was only going to a depot just north of Galkayo, where I found another bus on to Bosaso. On it I sat next to two men named Ahmed and Abaas, both from Mogadishu, who just like me were escaping the Islamist rule. The three of us became friends in a few minutes, laughing at stories we told about Mogadishu and our old neighborhoods.

At four in the morning our bus pulled in to the desert seaport of Bosaso. We were eager to find the place where people catch the boats to Yemen, but it was still dark. We sat at the side of the street, waiting for the morning sun. After a while we walked around town for an hour. As dawn broke, we headed in the direction of the water, which we could smell. Along the way we came across militiamen who were preparing for a war with the Islamists, who they said were on their way to Bosaso. Probably they wanted to control the port, a source of money. Finally we saw the water. It looked just like the wide sea off Mogadishu, but this was the Gulf of Aden. Not far beyond that horizon were Yemen and Saudi Arabia.

As we got closer to the harbor, we heard the commotion of men, women, and children. They were all leaving Somalia to be refugees in Yemen. The port was protected by a long jetty of concrete blocks and rubble; rows of wooden boats were tied up along the inside of the quay. Militiamen with guns were walking up and down the quay, and the smugglers were collecting boat fare. Then I heard how much it cost: *eighty dollars.*

I had only forty dollars left after taking the bus. I had to figure out what to do. My new friends, Ahmed and Abaas, had the money; they paid eighty dollars each and got onto a boat. The smugglers filled this small boat, meant for maybe twenty-five people, with more than a hundred, pushing and cramming bodies into every space like a slave ship. Now I could see why so many of these boats capsized, though I'd heard many passengers also died from suffocation, dehydration, or beatings by the smugglers. The crew had to keep the people from moving or the boat could capsize, but passengers were so crammed in that they would be in agony without stretching an arm or a leg. As soon as they tried, they were whipped and beaten. Women were sometimes raped. Some crews robbed the passengers and then threw them overboard to the sharks. In Yemen they had to swim from deep water to the beach because the smugglers were avoiding the Yemeni patrol boats. Many died within sight of Yemen because they could not swim or were eaten by sharks. Someone said on the beaches of Yemen were mass Somali graveyards.

There was a lot of jostling, and the militias fired shots into the air to control the crowd. Finally the boat was ready to leave, the passengers hidden under a heavy tarp. They were off to Yemen. I wanted to be on that boat with my friends. I didn't care how dangerous it was, I did not want to go back to Mogadishu. I wedged into the line for the next boat. When it was my turn to pay, I handed the smuggler my forty American dollars.

"Where is the other forty?" he shouted. "The boat is eighty dollars!"

I started telling him I didn't have the rest, but he didn't want to hear my story. He threw the cash back in my face and said, "Fuck you!" and moved on to the next person. In a few minutes that boat was off, me still on the pier, miserable beyond belief.

Evening was settling in Bosaso, and the crowd waiting to get on boats grew larger. I needed forty more dollars. I did not know what to do, so I walked back into town to see if there were any jobs available. I found nothing. There was no big market like Bakara where you could find odd jobs as a tout or porter. And I knew that the more time I spent in Bosaso, the less money I would have, because sooner or later I would need to eat. I skipped dinner, but I had to get breakfast. Locals figured the migrants came with a lot of money, so they were gouging prices on everything. Bread and tea that would have cost twenty cents in Mogadishu were a dollar.

That night I lay on the beach, next to a crowd of migrants waiting for the sun to rise, a few hundred feet from the pier. In the morning I went back to the pier and saw a familiar face. It was Abdullahi Madowe, a man from my neighborhood in Mogadishu. His wife and two kids were with him, all trying to get to Yemen. When he saw me, he ran over. We chatted a bit, I told him I had financial issues but that I too was hoping to go to Yemen. He wished me good luck. I watched as he and his family boarded a boat and slowly disappeared over the horizon.

By afternoon we heard that Abaas and Ahmed's boat had made it to Yemen safely. I was happy for them, but all I could think about was my own sad situation. I paced up and down the beach for hours. Mostly I didn't want to admit to myself the obvious: I would be going back to Mogadishu. Then came terrible news: Abdullahi Madowe's boat had capsized a few hours off the Somali coast. More than seventy people drowned. Abdullahi and his family did not return. Had I been on their boat, I probably would have died with them; had I been on Abaas and Ahmed's boat, I would have lived. As I trudged back to the bus depot, I felt my whole life was like that; every day that I could remember was a matter of life and death.

11

No Number

Hassan was right. By July 2006, while I was trying to escape, the Ethiopian army, supported by the United States, was amassing along the border and preparing to drive out the Islamists. Finally they crossed over and slowly advanced toward Mogadishu—tens of thousands of well-trained soldiers, backed by tanks and airplanes.

Abu Jihad was so happy. My old soccer pal could not stop talking about the *istishhad,* martyrdom death. "If the Christians kill us, we are going directly to heaven!" he kept chanting. On December 20, 2006, the full-scale war broke out. Abu Jihad was on the front lines and among the first to die. A week after the war broke out, Ethiopian troops marched into Mogadishu. Now it was my turn to be happy. I walked through the streets for hours with no signs of an Islamist. All that remained were their black flags, snapping in the fresh breeze.

On New Year's Day 2007, the sun rose above the blue flag of Somalia, flying for the first time in years. I woke up to find two uniformed soldiers standing in the middle of our courtyard. One was Ethiopian and the other Somali. They had come to search for weapons because the entire city was being disarmed. The Somali soldier was Rahanweyn, so my mom and Dhuha happily explained to him in Maay that we had no weapons. Satisfied, he leaned his gun against the neem tree and asked for a cup of tea. The Ethiopian was busy searching rooms; when he came outside and saw his Somali partner sipping tea, gun against a tree, he grew enraged and started yelling in Amharic. Of course none of us could understand him, not even the Somali soldier, but from his body language it was clear that he did not believe this was teatime. The Ethiopian didn't understand that Rahanweyn families in Mogadishu weren't allowed to have guns. The Somali soldier knew my mom was telling the truth.

A little tea party, a foreign soldier's tirade—not much to speak of, but it symbolized a larger problem and foretold the catastrophe to come. The foreign peacekeeping troops that poured into Mogadishu from Ethiopia and the African Union did not understand the complex history of Somalia's clan rivalries. They didn't realize how the majority Hawiye clan of the city would resent the new Darod president and fear all the Darod soldiers now swarming into Mogadishu. When the civil war started in 1991 the Hawiye militias had killed thousands of Darods and then invaded the Rahanweyn land. Would these Darod and Rahanweyn soldiers now take revenge on Hawiye civilians? When the order came down to disarm the city, the Hawiye felt threatened and vulnerable.

It didn't take long for the Hawiye elders to declare Ethiopia an occupying army. "We kicked America out!" they said. "It won't take us long to defeat you!"

The call from the elders became an opportunity for the Islamists to regroup and launch a holy war. This time, with the enemy right in their midst, it became guerrilla warfare. Suicide bombers targeted government buildings. Masked assassins killed anyone even remotely suspected of helping the Ethiopians and the new government. Market women who happened to sell some tea or qat to government soldiers were murdered in their homes. These newly radicalized Islamists massed in heavily guarded camps on the outskirts of town; at night they brazenly marched forth on murderous missions. They called themselves al-Shabaab, "the Youth."

With the clash of international armies and suicide bombings, the world was again paying attention to Somalia. But very few international journalists would risk coming. One who did was Paul Salopek, a Pulitzer Prize–winning reporter then with the *Chicago Tribune*.

One day I was walking through town, hopping over the smoking rubble from a fresh shelling, when I heard the click and whir of a motorized camera from a building across the street. Cameras were not normal sounds in Mogadishu. Up on the balcony of a guesthouse was an Asian photographer and a white man. They disappeared into the walls of the guesthouse, but I stood there, watching and waiting. Finally they reappeared. The white guy waved. I waved back. Then his bodyguards, some hired Somali militiamen at the gate of the house, thought I was making trouble for them. They pointed their AK-47s at my head.

"Go away!" said one. "Leave *now*." The white guy was still watching from above.

I was so afraid I would be shot, but I summoned all my courage and yelled up at the white guy. "I want to talk to you!" I said in my best English.

The man again disappeared inside. The militiamen were getting angrier, shaking their guns. "You can't communicate with the white man!" one said.

"You stupid man!" said another. *"Leave!"*

"He is okay. Let him come." The voice from the courtyard

was in English. It was the white man, now at the gate. His guards didn't understand his words, but of course I was the movie translator of Mogadishu.

"He says let me in to meet him," I told the guards in Somali. They thought I was tricking them; what twenty-two-year-old Somali man could speak English? And after all, they were getting paid to protect this guy. But the white man used hand gestures to let them know it was okay. They searched me thoroughly before I walked into the building. Finally Paul Salopek and I shook hands.

"Hi," I said. "It is good to meet you, sir. I am very excited!"

When he heard me speak English, his eyebrows went up. "Wow! Come on up, man.

"What do you drink, hot or cold?" Paul asked.

We were on his balcony. He had a Pepsi in one hand, and a kettle of tea was on the table. I never had Pepsi in my life, I only saw it in movies.

"That one," I said, pointing to the Pepsi.

"What's your name?"

"My name is Abdi."

"Abdi. Are you from this area?"

"Yes, I live down that road, toward the big tree over there." I pointed down in the direction of our house. I took a sip of the Pepsi. I had never tasted anything so delicious in my life. "Wow, I like this!" I told Paul. He brought out two more cans of Pepsi for me to take home, but I finished them all on the spot.

Paul asked me a lot of questions about life in Mogadishu, and I told him my story up on that balcony as we looked down on the ruined city. He and Kuni Takahashi, his Japanese-born photographer, were surprised that I had learned English just from watching movies. I told them there were no more movies in Mogadishu. I said most guys my age had been recruited by the Islamists, and I felt my luck was running out. "It sucks to be here, man," I said, using my best Hollywood slang.

Then I started bombarding Paul with questions about America. I asked him about New York, California, the cars, the food, what snow is like. He could not restrain me. Paul soon realized how much I loved America, and he said something that gave me hope.

"Abdi, I am sure that one day you will live in America." We spoke for three hours. When I left, Paul handed me his business card. Then he reached into his pocket and pulled out fifty dollars.

"Here, buy a cell phone so I can call you. What's left, give to your family." By now cheap cell phones were becoming widely available in Somalia, and for a few dollars you could buy scratch cards from a kiosk that gave you enough minutes to talk to family abroad. For even less money you could send text messages, if you knew how to write. Every few days you'd need to pay someone with a generator, like the cybercafe, to recharge your phone because no one had electricity.

We hugged and waved good-bye.

"Abdi," said Paul from the gate. "Make sure you e-mail me your phone number."

Walking out of that building was a return to the apocalypse. No more English, no more Pepsi. I might have been killed for meeting a white man; I could have lost my head just for hugging him. Thankfully nobody had seen us, so I tucked the fifty dollars underneath my belt and headed directly to the cell phone store.

Just before I reached the store, a bomb went off in front of it. As I ducked for cover, another exploded nearby. Suicide bombers were hitting Ethiopian troops right on that road. The bodies of soldiers lay in the streets. Gunfire erupted all over, and I ran. Night fell, and the hellfire rained down all over town. I had never seen Mogadishu's sky turn red like that before. The Ethiopians were using Russian BM-21 truck-mounted rocket launchers against al-Shabaab. The Russian name for this weapon is *grad,* which means "hail," and it was a hail of death coming from the sky. They could launch it from one corner of the city, and the rocket would pass over our heads with a sharp whistling sound; by the time it hit the target, it felt like the entire earth was cracking in half. We called this fearful thing *Fooriyaaye.* The whistler.

When the bombing stopped the next day, life returned on the streets. I walked into the nearby cybercafe and e-mailed Paul: "Dear Paul. I hope you are okay. I just came out of hiding from the shelling and the bombing. I am safe and will buy a phone soon so that we can communicate. Best wishes. Abdi."

Paul e-mailed me back a minute later: "Hey Abdi. My friend, you are such a strong man. I am glad I met you. Let's continue talking. Meanwhile, stay safe. P."

That was getting harder and harder. By now the citizens of Mogadishu were trapped between al-Shabaab and the government forces. When my mom walked to her market stall, dodging bullets the whole way, she passed through a government checkpoint where the soldiers tore off her hijab and forced her to show her face. Then, inside the market, al-Shabaab threatened her for daring to show her face, demanding she cover it and also give them money for "taxes." Then the government troops would steal her food.

Mom and I went to her stall the morning after the big attack to find that her small business had been reduced to a smoking pile of incinerated grain bags. Probably one of the Ethiopian rockets had hit it during the night. Before we could leave, the battle erupted again, with the sniper fire of al-Shabaab followed by the deafening tank mortars and then the dreaded BM-21. Its whistling sent us flat on the shaking ground.

Mom pointed to the nearby mosque and yelled that we should get into it. She didn't think it would be any safer, only that if we died in there it would be our ticket to heaven. Almost a hundred people had already squeezed inside the brick sanctuary, reading the Koran, crying, and calling out names of family members who were missing. Some people had cell phones and were calling relatives. Of course mosques have minarets, which make good sniper posts, and soon al-Shabaab soldiers were climbing the towers and shooting from the high windows at the advancing Ethiopians. When the foreign tanks found their way to the mosque, the first hit destroyed one of the minarets, sending bricks and rubble raining down. Before the second round could come, Mom and I decided against dying in the mosque and dashed out, holding hands. We ran and ran, not sure where we were going, but we followed a crowd that was heading south toward the Thirty Road.

Rockets fired from the tanks landed all around us. Bullets whistled. One time I looked behind me, and the building we had just passed was flattened. The tanks, like the angel of death, were gaining on us, so we ran faster. But in front of us were al-Shabaab fighters, primed for their glorious death and wrapped in suicide bombs, battling their way toward the tanks. With the advancing Ethiopians stalled by the suicide fighters, we had a narrow window to escape. Finally we reached the Thirty Road, miles from Bakara market. *Now what?* We could not go home. All roads going that way were blocked by the shelling.

"This way," I said, pointing down a road with no explosions. But before we got more than a few steps, an Ethiopian helicopter gunship swooped down like a space alien and opened fire. I could see dust flying off the ground, people falling, blood spilling. But as the helicopter banked for another round of firing, a rocket fired from an al-Shabaab bazooka knocked it down in a ball of fire. The fleeing people all cheered, *"Allahu akbar!"* Al-Shabaab brought down a helicopter! It was like Black Hawk Down all over again.

We hurried down a narrow alley that led out to a street and from there to an open space of small hills and sand dunes. We were five miles out of the city. Behind us the shells were still landing; in front of us was just a vast bush dotted with thorn trees. More people joined us, shocked and frightened, and we all just kept walking away from the city and the bombs. After a mile we came upon a building in the middle of the bush that looked occupied. As we got closer, I could see inside, where al-Shabaab fighters were pouring ball bearings into pipes; others were wiring detonators. It was a bomb-making factory in the desert. Thankfully, the fighters were too busy working to bother with us. We kept moving.

We were now walking deep into al-Shabaab territory. Mom and I joined hundreds of other displaced people who were building huts from sticks and cardboard. It must have been an old graveyard because I came across bones and a skull as I set to work building a hut. I used what I could find of trash and sticks to make a shelter that was barely big enough to protect my mom from blowing dust. She slept in there that night, me just outside.

By the next day this camp was crowded with makeshift huts. Sunrise revealed the faces of hundreds that had been walking all night long, tired faces and hungry mouths. Mom found a baby girl crying, no parents around, about a year old and wasted thin from hunger. She took this child and yelled for her mom. Finally the mom showed up. Almost unbelievably, it was my sister Nima. The baby was my niece, Munira. The last time I had seen Munira she was a few weeks old with a smiling face; today she was nothing but a reminder of our sister Sadia, dying of malnutrition. During the night Nima had built her own hut near Mom's, just by luck. So this was our family reunion. Nima's husband, Omar, was nowhere to be seen. He had disappeared into the city, maybe dead or alive, we didn't know. Within another day every inch of open space in the camp was taken.

The new camp was named Eelasha, which means "water." During the days of the Somali government this place had wells that had provided water throughout Mogadishu. In the civil war everything was looted and the wells were buried. Now there was only the name to torment thirsty people.

Within a week business activities had sprung up in the camp. Everything that was in Bakara market moved to Eelasha. The money-transfer agencies, telephone companies, mosques, everything. Macalin Basbaas built a hut for his new madrassa. Dhuha and her kids also moved in. It had become its own city. New friends, new neighbors, new Koranic teachers, and a new administration, the Harakat al-Shabaab al-Mujahedeen. There were Sharia weddings, with the most beautiful girls going to al-Shabaab fighters. Women must cover up, men must grow beards. Al-Shabaab fighters called on all men to gather at the mosque five times a day. One day the bodies of government troops were brought to Eelasha. We were told to spit on them and kick them. The dead al-Shabaab martyrs were never seen. They were buried quickly.

We were told that the Mujahedeen needed more men to fight for them. My heart was in my throat. Many times I had been able to avoid recruitment by slipping off and losing myself in the streets of Mogadishu. Out here in the camp there was no place to hide, and I was soon ordered to report for training.

. . .

We gathered under a tree, new recruits. We were told to call the government the *Murtadeen,* the apostates. "The president, the prime minister, cabinet members, and everyone else involved are all non-Muslims, enemies of Allah," said a young teenager who still had a boy's voice and face. "They should be killed the same way we should kill Americans and Europeans."

A man dressed in a military vest with a long *kanzu* and beard started our training—how to wear an explosive vest, how to approach the enemy, then how to shoot people. "Aim at the heart, aim at the head," he said.

Another man stood up and talked about how he had assassinated a government official a few days earlier. "I approached him; I did not fear, because there are infidels in our country. We don't fear killing them," he said. "Just open fire! Make sure they are dead!" I felt sick.

That night I whispered to my mom, "Mom, I have to go back to Mogadishu. I'm leaving now." In the paper huts of Eelasha, al-Shabaab could hear even whispers, so Mom said nothing but just brushed her hands on mine. I walked in the dark up over the Kaxda hills and across the open bush, trying to avoid the trails where al-Shabaab had planted land mines in case of attack. By three in the morning I had made it back to our neighborhood. There was no one around, the only sounds were snipers shooting randomly. I crept into what was left of our house.

Home felt good even with the roof, doors, and windows gone. Everything else had been looted. I found a shovel, went into my old bedroom, and dug a hole six feet deep that I could jump in at night when the shelling started. In there every night, like a grave, I hummed songs and closed my eyes to make myself forget about the whistling rockets and thudding explosions. I was always surprised to wake up in the morning alive. Outside, every morning, was more destruction and dead bodies, blood and bullet casings. But those like me who stayed behind also came out, chatted, and prayed together. I walked around the neighborhood checking on people. All the faces I knew were gone. Falis was gone. Faisa and her family had left for Ethiopia; we never said good-bye. I wondered if I would ever see her again.

Al-Shabaab released a new order: "People living in the government areas must leave immediately, or they will be considered enemies and killed." The government issued a contradicting order hours later: "Any civilian who moves to the al-Shabaab areas will be considered a member of al-Shabaab."

I was completely trapped. Days passed without seeing my mom, but I heard that people in Eelasha were dying of hunger and thirst. Then came a few days of quiet. The fighters must have been exhausted or out of ammo, who knows? I came out to the KM4 circle and saw that a few businesses had reopened. Next to the Fathi restaurant was a phone store called al-Imra Electronic. I went in and asked for a cheap phone with a memory chip. The man suggested a used Nokia 3110 Classic, thirty-five dollars. It came with a SIM card service that could let me send e-mails. I sent my first that night to Paul, giving him my phone number. It had been a month since we met. He called me an hour later. We talked until the shelling started and I had to jump into my hole. "I have to go, Paul. Bye!"

Then I figured out how I could download songs and even photos of beautiful women to my little phone. Before long I was listening to Jennifer Lopez, Ja Rule, Michael Jackson, and 50 Cent while hunkered down in my hole. The music made me forget about the shelling and helped me fall asleep. In the morning I left the memory chip with all the songs and photos in the hole, buried under the earth. If al-Shabaab caught me with that, I would surely be killed.

A few NGOs had started working at the government bases in Mogadishu, with funds from UN agencies based in Kenya.

Because of this, more Somalis became interested in learning English so they could work with the aid staff. One day I got called to teach English at a house in the neighborhood, to a Somali woman and her kids. I taught her basic lessons on how to communicate with foreigners. On a small blackboard with white chalk I wrote down lessons:

Asha: Welcome to Mogadishu!
Paul: Thank you. It is beautiful here. Blue sky, sunny, and warm.
Asha: Yes, it is. Also we have the warm Indian Ocean.
Paul: Good. I see it.
Asha: Okay, Paul, talk to you again.
Paul: Talk to you again too, Asha.

And another lesson:

Asha: Where are you from, Paul?
Paul: Asha, I come from California, U.S.A.
Asha: How is California?
Paul: Warm, sunny, and pretty like Mogadishu. But it has tall buildings and highways.
Asha: Okay, Paul, see you later.
Paul: See you later, Asha.

Once I made some money from this teaching, I decided it might be safe enough to renew my old English classes—this time along KM4 Street, now filled with other businesses. I found an empty space and moved in. Somewhere I scavenged a thin wooden panel that someone had painted black, and some chalk. I wrote the first lesson on my blackboard, hoping some students would show up. To be safe, I decided the instruction should focus on the Koran in English.

A: Can you tell me the Five Pillars of Islam?
B: Yes. They are fasting, prayers, the pilgrimage, the faith, and charity.
A: Have you been to the pilgrimage?
B: No. But I hope to go someday if Allah wills.

Then I waited. After a few days, some students started showing up. Typical of them was Abshir, a teenage boy who lived in Waberi, near Faisa's old house. He showed up every day with a pencil stub and a notebook, into which he copied everything from the blackboard. By the next lesson he had memorized all that dialogue. I knew nothing about him or his family, only that he believed in the future of Somalia, and he believed English would someday help him get a good job. Unlike me, he and the other students had no interest in American culture, no interest in leaving. I did not share their optimism for Somalia's future, but I was still happy to teach them English.

They liked the lessons about Islam, so I put together more:

A: Who created you?
B: Allah created me.
A: Why did Allah create you?
B: Allah created me to warship him.

I meant "worship," of course, but it was close.

The next day as I was preparing for the lesson, a bomb exploded just down the street. Abshir was on his way to class; the explosion killed him instantly. I decided it was too dangerous to hold school in a public place, and from that day I never went back to teach there. Instead, I went from house to house, teaching people who lived in the government area and who could afford to pay me. I was saving some money.

But in Mogadishu your presence never goes unnoticed. One

morning my phone rang. The caller ID displayed, "NO NUMBER." I answered. "Hello?"

"Is this the one they call Abdi American?" said a man's voice.

"Yes," I said, thinking it must be someone I knew. "Who is this?"

"You must drop that wicked nickname. We know who you are; we know where you live."

"Sorry. Okay. But that's not my nickname anymore. It is an old name."

"You are lucky I called. I have warned you." And then he hung up.

12

Messages from Mogadishu

By 2008, Somalia had been at war for seventeen years, but calling this living hell a "war" was too polite. It was really just endless gory terrorism on starving civilians who didn't care which side won. A million people had been killed, and a million and a half forced from their homes. Half a million had now evacuated the city for the camp in Eelasha, where my mom and sister lived. But some remained, like me, and some form of life was still going on inside the city despite the constant slaughter. There were cybercafes, shops, restaurants, and even colleges. I paid five dollars and enrolled in the Somali Institute of Management and Administration, which promised to teach math, English, computer programs, Arabic, Sharia law, Tarbiyah (Islamic education), administration, and management. I was asked to take an English placement test and answered all the questions, which were easy for me, unlike the other students who either failed or barely passed. I started in a class with twenty-five students, learning English and computer. Our teacher, Mr. Wewe, was surprised at how well I answered the English questions. Soon he put me in charge of the English class on days when he was late because the roads were blocked. I would stand in front of the class and repeat the lessons in my American accent.

Other students asked me how I learned this English. I couldn't say I learned from movies, because someone in the class could be al-Shabaab, so I said I learned it from reading the class books.

Classes were always fun, but getting to school was not. One day I was in a bus behind another bus that drove over a roadside bomb, killing most of the passengers, some of them students I knew well. Another day a rocket hit the college itself, killing students and teachers. None of this closed the school or stopped us from going. When the shelling led to the cancellation of all bus service, I had to walk the six miles to school. There were always two or three al-Shabaab soldiers at the entrance of the college, checking our books, hair, and clothes. One time they whipped a girl for wearing a skirt. Windows were broken and doors were missing, though that was a godsend one day when Ethiopian troops entered the college after they had pushed al-Shabaab out of the area. We all managed to escape through the open windows.

One afternoon in early 2009, after classes I went into a cybercafe and saw an e-mail from Paul:

> Keep your head down, Abdi. [Somalia] is getting a lot of international news. By the way, how old are you now? I'd like to write a short piece about how you and others who have been sending news emails—I won't use your full name, if that is a security problem, but I would like readers to know your age. And are you still teaching?

Not long after that, Paul wrote again with a link to his story in *The Atlantic*. It was titled "The War Is Bitter and Nasty," which was a quote from one of the e-mails I had sent him. A week or so later, around five o'clock, just before sunset, I was walking home when my phone rang with a strange number. I answered even though I was shaking, thinking it was al-Shabaab again. *Maybe they found out about my communications with Paul! This could be the death call.* My heart was beating so fast I did not say anything, I just waited for the person on the other end to say he would kill me now.

"Hi, is this Abdi?"

It was a female voice, in American English. She sounded like a movie actress.

My heart was still pounding, but now from excitement. *Maybe Paul had used his connections! Maybe this is someone from the U.S. government who wants to get me out of Somalia!*

"Yes, this is Abdi." Speaking English on a phone in public could mean death, so I was looking around in case anyone was watching. The woman on the phone said she was Cori Princell, a producer for an American public radio show called *The Story,* which was hosted by Dick Gordon. They hired local people on the ground in places around the world and had them talk about their lives for American listeners. She had read Paul's article in *The Atlantic* and wanted to discuss a diary recording project with me.

"Could you call me back in fifteen minutes?" I said. "I am walking on the street now. I can't talk."

I raced home just before Cori called me back. We spoke for twenty minutes until my battery died. I told her my frustration in the city, how I wanted to live a life like everyone else in the world. How I was trying to make something out of my life by going to college.

"I don't have a future here," I said. "I could die anytime; it can be tomorrow, or this evening, who knows? Everything I enjoy has been taken from me. I live in a world isolated from the rest of the world. I dream of going to America. I know I belong in that country."

Just before my battery died, she said, "Abdi, we would love to share your voice with our listeners. Please let me know, and stay safe."

Of course while Cori and I were on the phone, all the people in her studio were listening. I was later told they had been so surprised at the way I spoke—not just my English, but my confidence. I know that not many people in Mogadishu would have risked meeting Paul or picking up a phone call from America while walking on the street. But I did all of this for two reasons: First, I had nothing to lose in Somalia; I would be killed anyway. Second, I wanted to break the barrier and connect myself to the world. I wanted to tell my story.

But part of me said no. *What if al-Shabaab is listening to American radio or reading the website? They know me: I'm the one they call American. They will easily find me and behead me.*

The other part of me said I would be crazy not to try. *This is finally my chance to be who I want to be! My voice would be known in America, like the Hollywood stars!*

I e-mailed Hassan. He wrote back:

> Do it. Do it. This is a chance. Don't waste it. Al-Shabaab don't read the website of *The Story*. Your audience will be in America not in Somalia. This is not the BBC. So say yes.

So I said yes. I did not tell my mom, who would have had a heart attack. America by now was the most hated country in Somalia. America had sponsored the Ethiopian troops in Somalia and led air strikes that took many lives. America was fighting Islam across the Middle East.

In the black stillness of a November night in 2009, I crawled six feet under the ground in my bedroom hidey-hole, pushed the record button on my cell phone, and started speaking to America:

> It is midnight. Pitch-dark. I can hear gunshots ringing. Heavy shelling landing. This might be my last night on earth. Or I might survive.

I talked about my mom, my sister, Faisa, and the movies—all the good things that happened before.

> I am a schoolteacher in the most dangerous city, Mogadishu. Before things got as bad as they are now, we at least had something to entertain us. Every night we would go to cinemas and come home late at night. I used to watch American Hollywood films. I couldn't miss one. I was a movie buff. Most of my friends and my girlfriend would call me the American. It's a name they gave me after seeing how I speak American English. I always like to keep my hair long and styled, and I always like to dress in an elegant way. And I have taught myself to walk, pump iron, and speak English like the carefree stars I have watched more often in Hollywood movies.

Every night I would record a diary. At the cybercafe I visited the website of *The Story* and heard my reports; they had a photo of me, taken by my friend Hussein with his phone, from behind; we had agreed not to show my face. My stories were titled "Messages from Mogadishu" and were introduced by Dick Gordon, the show's host. He called me "our reporter" and "our man in Mogadishu."

The producers liked my stories, but the audio quality was

poor from my cheap cell phone, and it took a long time to upload the recordings. So the producers connected me to a BBC reporter in Mogadishu who was also a Somali, also taking a huge risk like me by broadcasting to the outside world. He had a computer, and his equipment was much better for recording. So once every week I would collect in my mind all the events around me, walk to his house, and tell my story.

After I filed a report called "Surviving Mogadishu," e-mails flooded into *The Story*. One came from a doctor at Dartmouth College named Sharon McDonnell. The only Sharon I knew was Ariel Sharon of Israel, so I assumed this was a man. The e-mail carried the subject line "Gorgeous, Exquisite and Painful." Sharon wrote,

> I worked in Afghanistan and various parts of Africa and the Middle East. Every element of the story was brought to life by Dick Gordon and the understated way that Abdi tells his story.

I wrote back,

> Hi Sharon,
> This is Abdi from Mogadishu. I got a forward of your e-mail to *The Story with Dick Gordon*. I wanted to thank you for your kind feeling and appreciation. Mogadishu had been this way and worse for twenty years, without central government. I had never seen peace for my life. I had been experiencing the worst through my life. Al-Shabaab and the government are fighting for the third day of constant firing and shelling. I didn't go out to my teaching these three days. I earn living by teaching

English. I would like to flee but there is no way I can do that with no money. My mom is in the camps.

And then came an e-mail from Sharon that took a whole week to absorb. The first surprise was the line "As the mom of a son . . ." So this Sharon was a woman! The second was when she wrote, "Is there any way I can help?"

I felt my American dream was cracking open slowly. Every e-mail from Sharon after that was full of hope. She introduced me to winter, attaching photos of her house in Maine with snow covering the ground. She sent a Christmas card to my family as an e-mail attachment, with a picture of her family. Then we started speaking on the phone. Sharon was asking about ways I could leave. But where to go? For Christmas she wanted to send me some money, so I told her how to do it safely through Hassan in Kenya, who could then send it to me in the *hawala* wire transfers. That way no one would know it was coming from an American. *The Story* was also sending me payments for my reports; between *The Story* and Sharon, Hassan and I were receiving money from people who weren't related to us and didn't even look like us. Five hundred dollars from *The Story,* $300 from Sharon, $200, $100. One day I handed my mom $150. She had her mouth wide open and did not believe it.

"How did you get this much money?" she asked.

It was time to break the secret to her. I told her about the radio work, meeting Sharon, everything. I told her that some good human beings, Americans, non-Muslim, sent all this money not only to me but to my family.

"Mom, eat well. That's all your money."

I told her that through this generosity of Americans, Hassan also had enough money to survive and pay rent. Mom was able to hire three men to build a nice hut that could fit her, Nima, and my niece. Thick enough to protect them from the sun and the dust and cook out of the wind. They could buy food and water. Overnight my family joined the "upper class" of Eelasha, but accepting that money was hard for my mom. She and Nima needed food and shelter, but she worried that if she died, she would be banished to hell for taking infidel dollars.

Back in the city I kept going to college, with dollars hidden in my clothes. I communicated with Sharon every day. When our Internet was down, Hassan would e-mail her on my behalf. The discussions about leaving Somalia continued; Kenya seemed the best option. But leaving my mom behind was my biggest worry. If something happened to her, if she got injured, I would want to be there to help. Then I thought, "If I stay here, I will surely die and she will have no help anyway."

Sharon organized a group she called Team Abdi. It included Ben Bellows, an American former student of hers working as a doctor in Kenya, Cori Princell and Dick Gordon from *The Story,* Paul Salopek, Hassan, and Sharon's family. Their mission was to get me out of Somalia. Plan A was getting me a visa to Kenya. But the immigration official in Nairobi just laughed when Ben asked. He said they don't grant visas to Somalis, ever. Somalis in Kenya are classified as refugees and are not allowed to work. They are supposed to be confined to those desperate camps near the border, where (theoretically) international agencies feed and shelter them. Somali refugees in Nairobi, like Hassan, lived in limbo—not allowed to work but with no access to refugee services. They were forced to survive by their wits and to avoid the police. Yet hundreds of thousands of Somalis lived in Nairobi; they owned shops, restaurants, and services. Somalis bought food and clothes and paid rent. They were responsible for roughly a third of all economic activity in the city, yet the Kenyan authorities pretended they did not exist, perhaps out of fear that acknowledging them would encourage more migration. So much for Plan A.

Plan B was an overland trip using smugglers, as Hassan had done years earlier. But that had become impossibly dangerous under al-Shabaab. You would be killed at the first roadblock.

More than a year passed as I continued to file reports for *The Story*. We kept discussing safe ways to get me out. Then, on a Saturday evening in March 2011, two explosions completely destroyed our house. Luckily, I was on my way home, still a few minutes away, when the bombs went off. I don't know if I was targeted or if it was random, but either way I would have been definitely killed if I was at home. My hidey-hole wouldn't have saved me; it was buried under debris and pieces of the tin roof. Breathless with fear, I called Hassan as I was standing there in the dust.

"There was a bomb in the house," I told my brother. "I can still smell the powder. Everything is destroyed. I have nowhere to sleep. Tell Team Abdi it is a scary night."

That night I slept at the corner of the street, in a dusty space behind a neem tree. When I woke up in the morning, I learned that Team Abdi had put together five hundred dollars to buy me a plane ticket out of Somalia. I did not yet know where I would fly to, but I would need to get a passport.

I went to the government immigration office downtown. The guard at the gate sneered at me.

"A passport costs eighty dollars," he said.

I fished a hundred-dollar bill out from my pants and unfolded it in front of him. His look of disdain changed to respect as he opened the gate. The clerk inside took my picture. I filled out some forms. Within an hour I was clutching my new Somali passport. That was the easy part. Where was I going? What country would give me an entry visa?

While I was getting my passport, Team Abdi learned that

I could fly directly from Mogadishu to Kampala and get a one-day Ugandan visa upon landing. That would give me twenty-four hours to find a way from there into neighboring Kenya. I went to the airline agency at KM4, showed my passport, and bought a ticket to Kampala. The clerk didn't have to ask if it was one-way.

My flight was in three days. The safe thing would have been to lie low in Mogadishu until then, but I could not leave without saying good-bye to my mom. So the day before my flight, I stashed my plane ticket and phone under the debris of our house and made the dangerous minibus journey one last time to the miserable Eelasha camp.

The first roadblock was manned by government soldiers and was easy enough, they just asked where people were going and checked to see no one had long beards. After that we entered al-Shabaab territory, and the road was blocked by about ten checkpoints. At every one the bearded fighters would board the bus and make sure all the women were sitting in the back and not touching any men. Then they looked around at the men, checking their haircuts and their teeth for brown qat stains, which would indicate a non-Islamist and possibly a government spy. Anyone who looked suspicious was dragged off the bus. Someone suspected of working for the government might get beheaded on the spot. Men with hair too long might only be forced to endure a rough haircut. I was glad I did not have my plane ticket, that would have surely spelled death. I forced myself to show no fear on my face. I just acted like a regular guy who lived in the camps, liked al-Shabaab, and had gone to run errands in the city. But inside I was trembling that someone would recognize me as the recruit who had deserted after just one day.

Mom was cooking over a fire outside her new hut when I arrived. I whispered to her that I was leaving the next day on an airplane, and she stopped stirring her pot. She could think of nothing to say. Finally she told me she was happy and that this was a good thing. I said good-bye to Nima and told them both not to tell anyone of my plans.

"Wherever we end up, I'll see you when I see you," I said. Then I shook hands with my mom; under al-Shabaab it was forbidden even for a mom and grown son to hug, and there was no point in risking attention.

The bus back to Mogadishu was scary because the fighters didn't like to see people leaving the camps. I was pulled out and interviewed three times. I made up so many stories—*I was going to protect our house from burglars, I was going to fetch clothes for my mom,* whatever I could think of. Every time they let me go. That night I slept for the last time in my hidey-hole, which I had cleared of enough debris in order to crawl in.

The next morning my mom showed up. She had taken a bus from the camp.

"Mom, why are you here?" I was worried her presence would attract attention.

"I wanted to say good-bye to you," she said.

We walked together to the airport. I had no bag, no extra clothes, nothing that would look like I was going on a journey—just a guy taking a walk. Carefully hidden in my clothes were my plane ticket, my passport, my freshly charged phone, and seventy dollars.

The airport terminal entrance was guarded by Ugandan troops from the African Union mission. A soldier barked at us: "Only passengers allowed!"

I fished out my ticket. He inspected it warily.

"You may enter," he said. "Not her."

I turned to Mom. "So this is finally good-bye," I said.

"Good-bye, my son. I am so happy for you and I will pray for you."

It was all I could do not to cry in front of that soldier. I felt so sad, but my mom's blessing made me feel okay.

The airport was like a military base. Al-Shabaab had been targeting the airport every day with shelling, and I could feel the building shudder from nearby explosions. A Somali soldier laughed when I flinched. "This is the safest place in Mogadishu!" he said. More Ugandan soldiers searched all the passengers before we boarded the plane, then marched us through the terminal.

The plane's engines were running, it was ready for a takeoff. There were not many people on the flight. I took a window seat, my phone ringing with calls from Paul, Cori, and Sharon. "I am on the plane," I told them. "I will check with you when we land." As the plane backed away from the terminal, I looked out and saw my mom standing there in the sun, waiting for us to take off. She passed from my view, and I could no longer hold back my tears. I wept in silence for a long time. Then I saw other passengers were crying too.

When the plane lifted off, everyone prayed to Allah for a safe flight. To avoid al-Shabaab rockets, the plane banked rapidly and turned out over the Indian Ocean. African Union gunships sped across the water, leaving white foamy trails. The plane climbed so fast I was surprised how quickly we were high above the city. The hot sun was glinting sharply off the tin roofs of the buildings of Mogadishu. I had seen the movie *Escape from Alcatraz,* and I felt like I had broken out of a prison. My future was a mystery, but at least I was leaving hell forever.

I was surprised to learn that our plane would first stop briefly in Nairobi, which made me excited and anxious. Excited because my brother lived there, and soon I hoped to be there myself, even though I knew I could not leave the airport that day. Anxious because some other passengers were telling stories of Somalis being taken off their flights in Nairobi and interrogated inside the airport. Some disappeared forever. To be young and from Somalia was like being a drug dealer who is being watched constantly by law enforcement.

After two hours we landed in Nairobi. I could tell this airport was very different from Mogadishu. It was much bigger, and there were airplanes from all over the world—Air France, British Airways, EgyptAir, Ethiopian Airlines, many others. The runway was not pocked with bomb holes. From the windows of the transit hall I could see airport shops and men dressed in suits hurrying to flights. "Maybe someday I would wear a suit," I thought. I could not wait to get to this city.

I tried making some calls to Team Abdi, but my Somalia SIM card turned out to be useless in Kenya, and soon I was back on the plane, headed for Kampala. I found out later that the team was extremely worried. Al-Shabaab had recently targeted Kampala with twin bombings that killed nearly a hundred people at a soccer match. The attacks were revenge for the Ugandan military presence in Somalia, and Uganda had been on the alert since then. While I was flying, Team Abdi was working behind the scenes to ensure I would not be arrested at Entebbe Airport or turned away from the Kenyan border, but no official in either country seemed able to guarantee my passage.

The sun was just dipping below the horizon as the plane banked over Lake Victoria and descended to Entebbe Airport. Below me was the source of the Nile, the river that flowed all the way to the Mediterranean—the gateway to Europe and beyond. Somehow this was comforting and made me feel closer to safety and freedom. In fact I was a long way from either.

All the Somalis on the flight were directed to go into one of the waiting halls. There were no seats. Pregnant women, crying children, elderly people who seemed sick and weak, we all sat on the hard airport floor. Again my phone had no service. I paced back and forth wondering what was happening. Every now and then an officer would walk up to me and say, "You! Sit down."

Hours passed. No one came. Other passengers, wearing nice clothes and transiting to other countries in Europe and North America, walked past us. None of us cared, we were Somalis and used to this. At least we were lying on a floor made of tiles, not a dusty road with dogs and graves. I was so tired I fell asleep on the floor with a bunch of other Somalis. It was past midnight when an officer with a cell phone in his hand stood above us and spoke. I was only half awake and thought I was dreaming when he said, "Who is Abdi Iftin?"

Everyone woke up. And every man raised his hand. Everyone was Abdi Iftin. It was like the movie *Spartacus.* Of course I raised my hand too. But the officer, who didn't much care who was Abdi Iftin, turned to someone else. "Are you Abdi Iftin? Come with me."

The young man and the officer were leaving when I dashed after them.

"Excuse me," I said. "I am Abdi Iftin."

The officer scowled, then demanded to see our tickets and passports. When he determined I was the right one, I followed him into a tiny room. Without saying anything, he handed me a phone.

"Hey, Abdi. How are you?"

It was Ben Bellows in Nairobi. He had called the airport to assure the authorities that I had a place to stay for the night and that I had a bus ticket for Kenya in the morning. Somalis were being held at the airport because the Ugandan government could not determine if they were leaving Uganda within twenty-four hours; indeed, many of my fellow passengers had told me they had no intention of leaving Uganda. They were essentially being imprisoned at the airport. Ben said Team Abdi had made me a reservation to spend the night at a Kampala hotel, and my bus ticket to Nairobi was waiting for me there. Someone from the hotel had been waiting for hours outside the airport, holding a sign with my name on it. She had finally left, said Ben.

"Fifty dollars, please!" the officer said to me.

I paid for the visa, which probably included a bribe to the officer. At one in the morning, my passport stamped for a twenty-four-hour visit, I walked out of the airport into the dark night. I shivered in the strange cold, something I had never felt; even though Entebbe Airport lies almost exactly on the equator, it is four thousand feet above sea level. Immediately, I was surrounded by a scrum of taxi drivers shouting at me in Swahili and English. I was so cold and hungry I just felt frozen in place.

Then came another piece of good luck. At that moment a middle-aged man shoved his way through the crowd of drivers and spoke to me in Somali.

"Are you Abdi Iftin?"

"Yes!"

He grabbed my hand and dragged me out, yelling to the drivers in Swahili, "Get away from him! He's my friend!"

I had never met this friend, but he was Somali and also spoke Swahili, so I went along as he whispered in my ear: "They will charge you a lot of money. Don't listen to them. They want to rip you off."

"How do you know my name?"

"There was a beautiful woman who was standing here with your name on a sign. She left. I figured it must be you." He kept talking as we walked to his own taxi. "What do you do? Are you a businessman?"

I didn't know what to say. Apparently, he had never seen a Somali with his name on a sign held by a beautiful woman at the airport. He thought I was someone with a lot of money. We got in his car and he pushed a cassette tape into the player—Somali music! I had not heard it in so long. He told me his name was Aleey and he had left Somalia ten years earlier. He had crossed into Kenya, then moved to Kampala, where life was more hospitable for Somalis, though that was changing with the recent al-Shabaab attacks.

"Are you hungry?" he asked.

"Yes!"

"Let's eat here."

He pulled over at a small late-night kiosk and ordered a soda and a *mandazi,* a type of fried bread. I ordered the same thing. He asked me to pay for it. I pulled out my last ten-dollar bill.

"Oh, you have to change the money," he said. He took me to a nearby exchange center where I converted the American bill into Ugandan shillings.

"I need a SIM card," I told him as we ate. "Do you know a place where I can buy one?"

"I will take you there."

As we drove to the Somali neighborhood in Kampala called Kisenyi, he put on some brand-new Somali music: Farhia Fiska's "Desire for Love." Farhia was a former Somali refugee who had made it to London and started recording songs that Somalis loved. Aleey turned it up loud; there were no Islamists to cut off his hand.

All the shops were closed, and the streets were empty. I was afraid there would be no place to buy a SIM card. But Aleey pulled up in front of a darkened store and banged on the door. A sleepy Somali opened the gate and started yelling at him.

"Why are you waking me up after midnight? I just went to sleep, man!"

It was Aleey's brother and this was his shop, so it was okay.

Minutes later I had a Uganda SIM card that would also work in Kenya, and five dollars of talk time. "Now you can call your friends," he said. "Where are you staying?"

"It's called the Shalom Guest House."

"Oh! What? No, no, that is not possible! What do you do, my friend?"

He explained that he had driven many rich white people to this hotel but never a Somali. Then again he had never heard a Somali speak English like me. He felt sure I must have just flown in from London, and he refused to believe my story. I understood. I could hardly believe it myself.

On the way to the hotel I called Hassan, then Ben, Sharon, Cori, Paul, and Dick. Everyone was so relieved that I had made it safely to Uganda. Aleey dropped me at the guesthouse, and we exchanged phone numbers. He waved good-bye. "I will come for you tomorrow to show you around town," he said.

I walked up to the receptionist, who handed me the key to my room. She said they had been expecting me much earlier. She knew nothing about my struggles. My room had big glass windows and a huge TV screen. There was a freshly made king-size bed, bigger than my mom's entire hut in the camp. And a shower. On a desk was a sealed envelope with my name on it. Inside was a bus ticket to Nairobi and three hundred dollars in cash. Ben had a friend in Kampala who had dropped it at the hotel.

I was so tired, but I felt I needed to get clean before I could sleep. I stood there in the shower wondering why there was no bucket, and what all the knobs did. I turned one and was surprised when water dropped from a nozzle like a stream, cold and scary. I went down to ask the receptionist for a bucket. She laughed. "You don't need a bucket," she said. "I will show you."

Back in the room, the lady showed me how to work the knobs and make the water come out nice and warm. Hot water without starting a fire! I felt kind of stupid but I thanked her and she left. Then I stripped and stood under that water and turned the knob until it was steaming hot. I stood there for a long time, in a trance, washing away the dirt and blood and pain of Mogadishu. I stood there until all that hot water was gone.

13

Little Mogadishu

I woke up late with the TV remote still in my hand. I must have fallen asleep watching movies. There were many missed calls on my phone from Team Abdi. Time was running short. I had to leave Uganda that night for Kenya. Everyone was still worried.

I called Aleey, the taxi driver. He said he was already waiting for me at the hotel reception. I threw on my clothes—no bag to pack—and went downstairs. There were several white people getting ready for their day of tourism in Uganda. They had fancy backpacks, and they were stuffing them with hats, sunscreen, lunches, and water bottles. We got into Aleey's taxi, and I told him to take me to the bus station. He looked at me like I was crazy.

"Don't take the bus!" he said. "It's a trap! They will find you at the border and send you back to Uganda, and then Uganda will put you on a flight to Mogadishu. They have done this to so many people I know."

By now I felt I could trust Aleey, but I said I had no other options.

"I know a better way," he said. "You can catch a ride on a tanker truck to the border. There after nightfall you can take a *boda-boda* across the bush into Kenya and meet the truckers on the other side."

A *boda-boda* was a motorcycle taxi. Aleey told me that along the Uganda-Kenya border young men earned money by smuggling Somalis into Kenya on their motorcycles, avoiding the road crossings.

"It's the best way," said Aleey.

I called Hassan.

"I think he's right," said my brother. "If they check for visas on the bus, you will not be allowed into Kenya."

We drove back to Kisenyi and parked at a gas station where a tanker truck was filling up. The two Ugandan drivers were eating *mandazi* and drinking tea. Aleey spoke to them. They approached me and said it would cost a hundred dollars for the ride. I handed them the cash, and they waved me into the cab. I said good-bye to my new friend, Aleey, wondering if I would ever see him again.

"Hide here," one of the men said in English, pointing to the tiny sleeper bunk behind the seats. "Don't make any move. Stay still."

"Don't worry, my friend," said the other. "You will be in Kenya soon."

We lurched off down the road. Soon darkness fell, but it mattered little from where I was curled up in the bunk because I could see nothing anyway. "Turn off your phone," said one of the men. "We don't want any attention. There are police everywhere."

The road was bad and I kept banging around in that bunk. Hours passed, and we were still in Uganda. The two men played rap music all the way. Finally, at four o'clock in the morning, we were a few miles from the border. The tanker truck pulled slowly in to a side street, parked, and opened the doors.

"Come. Come. Come," one whispered to me. "Go there, catch a *boda-boda*."

I hopped out of the truck and ran across the street into a dark narrow alley. I could not see anything except the dim light of a motorcycle.

"Lete," the motorbike man said in Swahili. Let's go.

"How much?"

"Ten dollars."

"No. Five dollars," I replied. I was getting better at bargaining for my various forms of illegal transport.

"Okay. *Lete.*"

I handed him the cash and climbed onto the bike behind him. We took off through the forest and in five minutes were in Kenya. The truck was there waiting for me. It was still dark when we rolled into Kisumu, a big junction town on the Kenyan side of Lake Victoria. It was still more than 150 miles to Nairobi. We pulled in to a parking lot; the drivers said they were too tired to go on. "Let's sleep here and proceed in the morning," one said. They spread a piece of a cloth under the truck to sleep on. The night was dead quiet. I quickly fell asleep while the two men were smoking a cigarette. When the sun rose, I woke up under the truck to the sound of Kenyans coming to work. The place we had parked was an outdoor repair shop with many junk cars and components sitting everywhere. The two drivers were gone.

"Wewe amka!" A shirtless man was telling me to move on in Swahili. He needed to work on the truck and I was under it. I asked where the drivers were, but no one knew. I waited for an hour, two hours, three hours, but they never returned. I called Hassan; he was worried and so was everyone else on the team. By now it was obvious the drivers had betrayed me. I had paid them for a ride all the way to Nairobi, but I was hours away and

on my own. I checked my pockets and was glad to find I still had money hidden in my pants. I was going to need it.

I walked around the muddy streets of town, past market stalls where traders were selling hay, long spikes of sugarcane, and pyramids of fruits. Women carried huge baskets on their heads, and people were running to catch *matatus.* Street kids in filthy alleys were sniffing glue from plastic bottles. I did not know where to go. Then I heard a voice calling: "Nairobi, Nairobi, Nairobi!"

It was a *matatu* conductor shouting out to passengers. I hopped on. The bus had fourteen seats, but by the time we left for Nairobi, the conductor had jammed more than twenty people on board. Passengers were literally on top of each other. Someone was sitting on my shoulders, while I leaned on someone's back. The stereo was blasting Bob Marley when the conductor in the front passenger seat stretched out his hand to collect the fare. "Five hundred shillings," he said in English.

I knew that was about five dollars. I had no Kenyan money so I handed him my last twenty-dollar bill. He gave me back some change in Kenyan shillings but not nearly enough. When I argued with him in English, he replied angrily in a native dialect I couldn't understand, so I let it go.

"My friend, are you Somali?" asked a man sitting next to me, in English. He was middle-aged and wore eyeglasses, and he smiled all the time despite the discomfort of the journey.

"I am," I said.

"Oh, I love the Somali people! But I hate al-Shabaab. I have seen them on TV. Very bad."

We became instant friends, and he acted like a tour guide. I kept asking him the names of towns we were passing. Everything was very green like I had never seen; corn and hay grew everywhere. The road to Nairobi was so clean and smooth. Sleek cars, their tinted windows rolled up, sped past us. We stopped at a police checkpoint and my heart was beating fast, but the officer said something to the conductor and waved us on. It was not Mogadishu, they didn't care where women sat or if we had beards. The afternoon turned to dusk, and as we came around a final turn into the city, the setting sun reflected off the skyscrapers of downtown Nairobi. It was so beautiful! The streetlights were switching on everywhere. I had never seen so many lights. I felt like a caveman dropped into the modern world. People outside were standing in groups talking, laughing, enjoying the evening. I texted Hassan, my heart pounding with excitement. Our bus inched through traffic, passing market stalls, banks, government buildings, and Christian churches. Everything was a wonder to me, but I thought we would never arrive. Passengers in a hurry were jumping out of the bus as it slowed down. Finally we pulled in to the chaotic Accra Road *matatu* station, and I descended in a daze.

The station was so busy, people shouting and bumping into each other. It was like watching bees. I strained to see Hassan in the crowd. Then someone tapped my shoulder.

"Abdi!" he said in a deep voice I did not recognize. I turned and felt I was looking into a mirror. It was my brother, Hassan, but in adulthood he had become just like me—tall, thin, the same long face and wide brow. *When did we become twins?* We hugged and held each other for several minutes. Both our phones were ringing from Team Abdi trying to find out if we had met. We ignored the phones and just hugged.

"Let's go eat," Hassan said. We turned a corner from the bus depot and entered a restaurant. The sign, with a white man in glasses and a white beard, said "KFC." "It is American owned," Hassan said, knowing how much I liked anything American. The fried chicken, French fries, and Coca-Cola tasted amazing to me.

"Do you eat here every day?" I asked my brother.

"No! This place is only for rich people. But we are celebrating."

After dinner we jumped into a *matatu* headed for Eastleigh, the neighborhood also known as Little Mogadishu. We arrived around nine at night, but the place was as bright and busy as day. Every stall, every kiosk, and every shop was run by Somalis. Somali music and American rap were blasting from everywhere. The streets were filthy like Mogadishu, smelling of shit and piss. As we got off the bus, we had to jump over rank water onto a small patch of dry earth. I didn't care about the filth. I just stood there and marveled at all the stuff for sale—shoes, clothes, belts, milk, candy, chewing gum, soccer balls. Anything you wanted. I smelled fried samosas and saw steam rising from teapots. Restaurants were selling goat, camel, and cow meat with rice. It was like being in Mogadishu but with merchandise and no bombs.

My joy was interrupted by a sudden clamor from the crowd, followed by panic and running in all directions, like frightened cattle. I had not heard any explosion, so I couldn't understand why all the Somalis were running. Hassan grabbed me by the hand.

"This way!" he yelled. We ran, turned down an alley, and ran again. We ran for a quarter mile. "What is going on?" I asked between my panting breaths.

"The police," said my brother. "They come like this every night to rob the Somalis."

After a few minutes the police were gone and everyone was back on the street, business as usual. Tea shops filled up, and conversations went on, just like nothing happened. I was starting to think maybe life in Nairobi was no paradise.

Hassan had reserved a room for both of us at the Hotel Medina for one night. This was one of the best hotels in Eastleigh, with running water and a restaurant, owned by Somalis, but he chose it because it had the same name as our mom. We went to our room and talked for hours. I told Hassan about my adventures, and he told me about his own long journey to Nairobi, which he had only hinted at in his e-mails.

The green Mercedes had broken down in the bush, he said. The one-armed driver was picked up by another driver, along with the two women and the goat. There was no room for Hassan, so they left him in the desert; the goat was more valuable. He walked for days across the barren red land with no water, at times drinking his own urine. He encountered many human skeletons as well as lions and hyenas, which terrified him and reminded him of our mom's stories.

He did not know the direction to Kenya, but eventually he caught up with other families walking toward the refugee camps. After eight days of walking, they were met at the border by aid agencies, then quickly registered as refugees with fingerprints and photos. With their new refugee IDs in hand they waited for transportation to the camps in Dadaab, their new home. When the truck that was carrying them pulled in to Dadaab, they were all told to descend and wait. But after the truck left, there was no one else. Slowly people who had walked with Hassan were met by family members or friends. Hassan found himself sitting under an acacia tree waiting and waiting. Two days went by, and no one came to help him, no food or water.

Finally, he hitched a ride on a dump truck carrying sand to the other side of Dadaab, ten miles away. There he saw people queued for food. He had not eaten in days, but Hassan was told he could not get food; first he had to get a coupon to apply for food. The food coupons were distributed along clan lines, and this area of the camp seemed to be controlled by the Marehan tribe from Kismayo. With hundreds of women and children from their own tribe arriving daily, no one was interested in helping a teenager with a strong Mogadishu accent. He was not even given a space to build his own hut. Whenever he finally got to the front of a line, the response was always the same: "Leave here!" Everyone was just trying to survive, and there was no room for pity.

Someone told Hassan to go and see a Rahanweyn man who lived about twenty miles deep in the camp. He went there and the man said he was not in fact Rahanweyn. But unlike everyone else he took pity on Hassan and handed him six hundred Kenyan shillings for a bus to Nairobi. "Nairobi has some chances for you," said the man. "Don't show the police your refugee ID, or they will send you back here. Tell them you are a kid and don't have one."

He caught the first bus out. When the police stopped them for checks at the border, Hassan hid his refugee ID. Finally his English, which we had practiced so many nights in our bedroom, was a lifeline to Hassan. In plain and simple English he told the Kenyan police that he was seventeen years old and had no ID. They let him go. When the bus dropped him in downtown Nairobi, Hassan followed other Somalis and ended up in Eastleigh, where he had been living ever since.

Hassan soon learned how to survive on the streets of Little Mogadishu. He picked up some Swahili phrases and was able to make some good friends, including his roommate, Siyad. The two of them were also business partners—hawking socks, sneakers, and belts on the streets of Eastleigh. They would buy in bulk from the shops; a bundle of socks cost about twenty dollars and could be sold on the street, by the pair, for a total of thirty dollars. This was illegal because the Kenyan police did not allow street vendors, especially refugees, who are not allowed to work. But like street vendors in cities around the world, Hassan and Siyad developed a sort of radar for the police, and they would snatch up their merchandise and dash away before trouble. In this way they could save enough money to buy dinner, pay rent, and pay off the police on the occasional times they got caught.

We talked until three o'clock in the morning, when we both fell asleep. I awoke at sunrise to the cries of the conductors calling out the destinations of their *matatus*. Eastleigh in the morning was a noisy place, filled with seemingly crazy people. I looked out the window. Young Somali men, dressed and shaved like American gangster rappers, wearing headphones, walked along jamming to music I could not hear. I saw beautiful Somali women in colorful dresses and exotic-looking Kenyan women of the Kikuyu tribe. Music was everywhere, people laughing and dancing. This place was lit!

We checked out of the hotel. Hassan and I had a list of things to do on that Sunday; first was buying me some new clothes and a haircut, then visiting Ben Bellows. I bought a pair of jeans for five dollars and a T-shirt with the American flag for three dollars. Then I walked into a Somali barbershop. There were portraits of soccer players, rappers, and actors all over the walls. You could choose your hairstyle from the celebrities on the walls! When it was my turn, I pointed to Usher, the American singer. "Like that," I said. Sides trimmed down to skin, top and back growing wild. So cool.

Next I bought a necklace, a wristband, and some sneakers. I was sure no one looked more American than me. Hassan laughed, I changed so much in one day, but freedom from al-Shabaab felt like the best gift in the entire world.

Later that day Hassan and I jumped onto a *matatu* and headed to a nice restaurant across town to meet Ben Bellows and his wife, Nicole. They were so happy to see me and proud that they had helped Hassan and me reunite. The menu was confusing, we didn't know what to choose, but burgers seemed like the most American dish, so we both ordered one. After the meal we went to Ben and Nicole's house for a visit. They handed us a hundred dollars of their own money to help with getting me settled. After a few hours we were back in Eastleigh, but not to the hotel. Now I would be staying in Hassan's room on Eighth Street.

The building where Hassan lived was home to dozens of Somalis, each family squeezing into one tiny room. The stairs, pitch-black even by day, creaked and swayed so much I felt they would collapse anytime. Jerry cans of water and sacks of charcoal sat everywhere. People washed clothes in buckets and hung them on their balconies, dripping down on the street below and adding to the pool of mud in front of the house. Cockroaches crawled on the walls. Of course this is the way tens of millions of Africans live, in cities across the continent, so residents of Little Mogadishu were just grateful to be out of a war zone.

Hassan lived on the third floor. Siyad had gotten married and moved back to the refugee camps with his wife, so I was the new roommate. The room was small but at least had two windows facing the street. There was no furniture, no bathroom, no kitchen. Basically Hassan lived outside and used his room only to sleep. Rolled up in the corner was a single foam mattress and a pillow; we used some of the money from Ben and Nicole to buy another set for me. None of this mattered or bothered me once I saw the main attraction in his room: a Toshiba laptop and piles of DVDs of Hollywood movies. Hassan told me there were thousands of DVDs sold on the streets of Nairobi. "You could never even watch them all in your lifetime," he said. I decided I might try.

The next day was Monday, and all the offices would be open. That morning after bread and tea we jumped into a *matatu* to the office of the United Nations High Commissioner for Refugees (UNHCR). Because I had been smuggled into Kenya, I was not yet registered as a refugee, which was the first step in getting to the United States. I was carrying all the letters sent by Team Abdi. We arrived and saw to our dismay that hundreds of other people had the same idea that morning. The line stretched around the building. After four hours we finally got inside, and I was seated with a hundred other people in a waiting room. Six hours after that, a Kenyan man in a dark suit came out.

"Time out today!" he yelled. "Come back tomorrow."

We came back the next day. Same long line in the chilly morning, me in my American flag T-shirt. Same long wait inside.

"Computer problems," said the man this time. "Come back tomorrow."

Frustrated, we called Ben Bellows. He e-mailed someone at the office who got back to him: "I will see Abdi tomorrow."

On Wednesday I got up very early and took the *matatu* by myself to the UNHCR office. Four security guards were pushing Somalis away from the gate. I jostled through the crowd and approached one of the guards.

"My name is Abdi Iftin. Someone who works here is expecting me."

The guard put his arms on my chest and pushed me. "Go away!"

No one ever came out calling my name.

Thursday Hassan and I went back together, armed with a new strategy. We approached one of the security guards, and Hassan spoke to him in Swahili: "I will pay you."

The guard took Hassan to a place where the camera could not catch him, and we handed him two thousand shillings—about twenty dollars. He let me into the waiting room. At three o'clock in the afternoon a man walked up and called my name.

In another room he took my picture and fingerprints, then led me to a desk for the paperwork. I was officially registered as a refugee living in Kenya! Now I could seek protection and resettlement in the West.

Every day after that, Hassan and I went to the UNHCR, hoping for a protection interview. Since coming to Nairobi, Hassan had been interviewed more than ten times. On the wall of the building they posted names of people selected for protection and resettlement. Hassan had been checking the list for years. He was never picked. But now, with all the letters of support from our American friends, we thought our chances were high. Still it was always the same: the officials wrote down our phone numbers but never called for an interview. We watched other Somalis whose names were posted who could not control their happiness, tears running down their faces. It was hard to watch; we could not share their joy. Life as a refugee in Nairobi was permanent for those whose names were never picked. Real life only began for those who were selected. The UNHCR was the switch between happiness and misery.

I continued to file radio reports for *The Story,* now from the BBC studio in downtown Nairobi. Instead of life in a war zone I told Americans about life as a refugee in Little Mogadishu. One big difference between Little Mogadishu and real Mogadishu: in the Nairobi version you didn't wake up every morning wondering if this would be your last day on earth. So that was a definite plus. But Little Mogadishu was still a daily test. You were on your own, and survival depended on your strength, wits, and good luck. The Kenyan government and the UNHCR offered no help to the hundreds of thousands of Somali refugees living there, it was like we didn't exist. Everyone had to fetch food, clothing, and shelter for himself, but refugee documents were not work permits, so there was no official way to earn money for those things. Your documents did not protect you from police harassment either.

You felt trapped in Little Mogadishu. To the east is Moi Air Base, a former British RAF base and the headquarters of the Kenya Air Force. Naturally, it is completely fenced off, a dead end. To the west, between Little Mogadishu and the skyscrapers of downtown, is the feared Pangani police station, from which corrupt officers fan out every night in search of bribes from refugees. And to the north is the vast and notorious Mathare slum, one of the worst in all Africa. Compared with the tin shacks of Mathare, Little Mogadishu appears as organized as midtown Manhattan, with straight numbered avenues, real buildings, and services.

But within Little Mogadishu was an armed Somali youth gang who called themselves the Super Powers. Those gang members realized the Kenyan police did nothing to protect people in Little Mogadishu; refugees ran from the police and would never dare to report a crime. So the gang members terrorized residents, snatching cell phones and cash at gunpoint. One night two Super Power guys held Hassan by the neck right in front of our building. They took his cell phone and some cash, then let him go. Another night they chased me down an alley. Luckily, I outran them.

Fortunately, there were a lot of places to blend in with the crowd. The two main north-south roads in Little Mogadishu are First Avenue and Second Avenue, both of them so packed with people day and night that you can hardly walk. The cross streets are lined up between them, starting with First Street in the north and all the way down to Twelfth Street. On just about every one of those streets you will find a mosque, a *hawala* money-wiring shop, a small shopping mall, tea shops, photo studios, barbershops, and tall apartment complexes crammed with people. Even Kenyans do their weekly food shopping in Little Mogadishu. People come from as far away as Uganda, Burundi, Rwanda, and West Africa to shop for black market and often counterfeit electronics, which are cheaper in Little Mogadishu than anywhere on the continent.

The neighborhood is organized by the names Somalis have given to smaller communities within it—like the zone on Twelfth Street called California Estate because refugees who lived there mostly moved to the United States after a long wait of screening and interviews.

One resident of California Estate was a well-dressed young woman named Muna. She was short, of light complexion, and not as skinny as most Somalis, probably because she had grown up in Little Mogadishu, eating a lot of chicken. She was living with some roommates and was very independent. New refugees could tell she knew so much more about the world than they did. Watching her walk down First Avenue was like watching a confident American woman on the streets of New York. She feared nothing and was not the least bit shy like most Somali girls. People looked up to her, especially the neighborhood men, whom she completely ignored. Muna was mad about America and determined to marry a man who could bring her there. Naturally, I felt we had much in common, and I decided to pursue her.

My first love, Faisa, now living in the refugee camps in Ethiopia, had a phone and we still texted each other. One day she told me she was engaged to marry a man in Sweden. This was not love; like Muna she was only looking for a way out of her miserable fate of being a refugee. I understood, but it reminded me of my sister, Nima's, marriage. Two goats or a ticket to Sweden, what's the difference? I knew Faisa and I would probably never see each other again.

In the afternoon Muna liked to hang out at the Obama Studio, a sort of social club where they played American music and you could also rent minutes to use the Internet. One day I watched her on the computer, texting with a Somali man in Minnesota and another in Seattle at the same time. While doing this, she was also checking out other U.S. men on her Facebook account. A few days later I ran into her at the Balanbaalis Studio, another social club where young Somalis would dress up, dance to loud American music, and drink Cokes. These were mostly people who received money from family members in the United States, so if you were on the hunt for an American husband, it was a good place to hang. I walked up to Muna and told her in Somali that I wanted to date her.

She laughed. "You have no money. Why would I date you?"

"Because they call me Abdi American," I said. I knew this was a thin argument, but it was my only card to play.

She stared at me, taking in my accent. "Are you from Mogadishu?"

"Yes."

"What's it like?"

"You have never been?"

"No," she said. "My family was displaced from the south. I grew up in the camps. Anyway you are wasting your time. I don't date men in Africa. Especially refugees."

Meanwhile, Hassan and I kept trying to land resettlement interviews, with no luck. Sharon called from Maine. A friend of hers, a teacher at the University of Massachusetts named Margaret Caudill, was leading a group of American nursing students to Kenya to improve cardiovascular and metabolic health in rural areas. The project was called Afya Njema, "Good Health." Hassan and I were invited to volunteer for them. With nothing else to do and tired of waiting for something to change, we gladly accepted.

One afternoon in May 2012, we stuffed some clothes in a backpack and jumped onto a *matatu* bound for the Methodist Guest House in Lavington, Nairobi. This would be our home for two weeks, and we couldn't believe it had a swimming pool! We arrived just as dinner was being served, and when we walked into the dining room, the whole group of twenty-two American students and three teachers rose in applause. They had heard my stories on NPR, and to them we were celebrities. To us they were a dream come true. After the cheers, Hassan and I sat down at the dinner table as everyone listened to our stories. We were hardly able to eat, they had so many questions. I took selfies with everyone and posted them on Facebook. The first person to comment was Muna.

"Are you in the U.S.?" she wrote.

In the morning we got up early and rode a bus to the work site along with a group of Kenyan nursing students. As the bus sped out of Nairobi for the two-hour drive to Nyeri town, the American students put on their headphones. Some were reading books. Some took naps. I wanted to know everyone's name and all about their American stuff.

"What is this?"

"This moisturizes your lips."

"What do you use this for?"

"This is for your skin."

When we got off the bus, we were surrounded by hundreds of Kenyans who were curiously waiting for the nursing students. They shook hands with all of us one by one. The Kenyans thought Hassan and I were African Americans.

I was assigned to register the patients, then measure their weights and heights. Hassan, who by now spoke fluent Swahili, had to translate for the elderly Kenyans who didn't speak English. I was wearing a T-shirt that said "Chicago," and a Kenyan student asked me if I was from there.

"Yes," I said, walking away quickly to end the conversation. I was ashamed at having lied, but I was so happy to be around all those Americans that I couldn't bear to admit to him that I was in fact one of life's losers—a lowly Somali refugee. Or admit to myself that I would have to return to Little Mogadishu when the project ended.

By the second day, the Kenyan students figured out that Hassan and I were refugees. On the bus I heard some of them snickering and muttering, "Al-Shabaab," but I tried to ignore them and made friends with an American woman named Shannon from Bangor, Maine.

At the end of our last day of work we threw a party at the guesthouse. Everyone danced and sang songs; the Americans drank beer. I grabbed a can of soda and danced like I'd seen cool stars do in movies, with a drink in their hand. The next morning we checked out of the guesthouse and said good-bye to our new friends. They said they would miss Kenya and would come back next year.

Margaret had brought some cash from Sharon for Hassan and me. It was enough for us to set up a street business selling socks and shoes. We worked seventeen hours a day to make enough to buy food and pay rent, waking up at five in the morning to grab the best spot on the side of the road and not going home until midnight. But it felt good to pay our own way and not constantly need money from Sharon.

After weeks of hard work and with a little cash in my pocket, I texted Muna and asked if she could meet for a hangout. She agreed, and we met at one of the restaurants in Little Mogadishu. She got right to the point.

"Abdi, you are wasting your time, bro. I am not going to

date a man in Little Mogadishu. How can I date someone who is broke like me?"

Still, it was nice to sit with her. Later I came up with an idea. I went to the Obama Studio and had them Photoshop my picture standing next to the Empire State Building, the White House, and other famous places in the United States. I went on Facebook and updated my residence to California. I posted all the photos, along with the ones I took with the American students. When Muna saw it, she said she broke out laughing. It was worth it for that.

Al-Shabaab already had a presence in the refugee camps in northeast Kenya, and they were getting more aggressive in the country. In October 2011 they kidnapped two Spanish aid workers from Doctors Without Borders, taking them into Somalia as hostages. In response the Kenyan government declared war on al-Shabaab and sent troops, tanks, helicopters, and artillery to battle the terrorists deep inside Somalia.

It was called Operation Linda Nchi, "To Protect the Nation," but the residents of Little Mogadishu had a pretty good idea we were not going to be protected. As the troops marched across the Somali border, police encircled Little Mogadishu, assuming that residents there would heed the call of al-Shabaab to retaliate against Kenya. Soon the streets were cleared, and businesses were closed. Everyone went home and turned on the TV. Hassan and I locked our door and sat quietly. Outside we heard sporadic shots.

Life changed overnight in Little Mogadishu. Police night raids increased, especially in mosques. Men with beards were taken out. Executive orders were announced: all refugees must leave Nairobi and go to the camps. This was the beginning of the hide-and-seek games between us and the police. I managed to sneak out early one morning, catch a *matatu* downtown, and file a report for *The Story* about a friend who got taken to jail overnight:

> He told me [the police] threatened him because, they said, "you know the sympathizers of al-Shabaab here, you need to tell us. If you are not al-Shabaab, then you know the sympathizers." And he was like "I don't know!" He cried out that he doesn't know anything, he doesn't have any idea about al-Shabaab or al-Shabaab sympathizers or anything like that.

Soon after that, Hassan and I were on our way out of our apartment when two men in civilian clothes walked up quickly behind us.

"Show me your IDs or passports, please," one of them said.

We stopped and looked at them. They brought out handcuffs.

"Where are your Kenyan IDs or passports?"

"We don't have Kenyan IDs," Hassan said. "We have refugee documents."

As I reached into my pocket for my refugee document, the man handcuffed me and told me to follow him.

"Where are you taking me?" I asked. "Please show me your police ID."

From his leather jacket he pulled out an ID; I couldn't tell if it was real or fake. I tried to protest the arrest, and he pulled out a gun. He led me to a corner of the street where fewer people walked. Hassan was brought by the other man.

"I will take you to the Pangani station!" the man holding me shouted. My heart froze, but then the negotiation started. "How much do you have?" he asked. "Give me a thousand shillings!"

"I don't have it," I said.

"Seven hundred!"

"I only have one hundred."

He pulled my wallet out of my pocket, shuffled through it, and took the hundred-shilling note with the picture of Jomo Kenyatta, the first president of Kenya. He smiled, tucked away his pistol, and left, no doubt to find another refugee he could tap as an ATM. That's what the police started calling us. Hassan also negotiated his way out of the other man's threat. We walked away realizing this would be our new danger every night.

Nairobi was a roofless prison for me and my brother, and for the thousands of other Somalis. There was no future besides more police harassment and the terrifying fear of being deported to Somalia. The dim light at the end of our dark tunnel was the hope that someday our American friends might help us escape.

The police raids in Little Mogadishu and the Kenyan troops in Somalia were all good news to al-Shabaab, it was exactly the chaos they craved. The terrorists soon escalated the fight. There was a hand grenade thrown into a church in Nairobi, a *matatu* attack, a bombing in a Mombasa bar. Metal detectors and heavily armed police were stationed at hotels, restaurants, bars, and bus stations. The Kenyans blamed all Somalis. "Get Them out of Our Country!" the newspaper headlines shouted.

After several unexploded bombs were retrieved from an apartment in Little Mogadishu, more young men in the neighborhood were dragged off to jail. Often they never returned. There was no way to identify terrorists—they had the same refugee papers we did—so any young man was a suspect. Hassan and I kept our heads down, with our hearts in our throats. When Hassan and I had to be separated, we would text each other more than a hundred times every day, making sure we were okay. Women were no safer; they were being raped by the police. All of the people who lived in our building exchanged phone numbers. When the police were coming, we would all text each other: "They are coming down 6th, run toward 5th." Refugees would lock down their stores, hide in the bathrooms, under the beds.

Meanwhile, the Kenyan citizens had stopped coming to shop in Little Mogadishu. The neighborhood was sealed off and surrounded by police checkpoints at all exits. The local media did not report what was happening in Little Mogadishu, but I did. Dick Gordon, the host of *The Story,* was growing more worried for our safety. He mentioned that his daughter Pamela was working for the Red Cross of Canada in Nairobi. She invited us for coffee on the rich side of town at a fancy shopping center called the Westgate Mall. Hassan and I managed to evade the police checks and get on a *matatu.* The mall was like something I had seen in movies of California or Florida: huge, clean, with gardens and moving stairs and shops full of people—white people, Kenyans, Asians. Everything was so expensive. We had a nice talk with Pam. She gave us her mobile number. "In case something happens to you, call me," she said.

Because we had no luck getting resettlement interviews, Team Abdi's next plan was to get us American student visas. To improve our chances and give us some college experience, Hassan and I began taking online English classes with one of our fans in America, an English professor at Lyndon State College in Vermont named Nene Riley. She assigned us to read literature and essays and write reports summarizing the main points of the pieces, our reaction to them, and how they applied to our own society. We had exchanges with several students from Lyndon State College, and it felt like we were studying in the United States. My writing steadily improved.

With Sharon's help we applied to Southern Maine Community College as international exchange students. Sharon and her family sent a letter to the college confirming that she would support us financially and that they were our American family in Maine. Hassan and I had to take something called the Test of English as a Foreign Language, which took half a day. We both passed the test, and soon after that DHL Nairobi delivered official acceptance letters from the school.

We were going to college in America! The next step was getting our student visas, which required interviews at the U.S. embassy in Nairobi. To support our requests, Team Abdi had gathered letters of recommendation from seven U.S. senators: Susan Collins and Olympia Snowe of Maine; Bernie Sanders of Vermont; Kay Hagan and Richard Burr of North Carolina; and Carl Levin and Debbie Stabenow of Michigan. With everything ready, we paid our interview fees and waited for the appointments.

My interview was a week before Hassan's. That morning I woke up at five, so nervous, and got on a *matatu* before the police would start searching for refugees. The interview was at eight. I got there at six. After intensive security screening I proceeded inside the embassy and joined a waiting room of people who looked just as excited and nervous. My feet were actually sweating. As I sat there, I thought of my mom and my sister back in Mogadishu. If I got the visa and went to the United States, I would go to college, get a good job, and send them money every week. Life would be great for all of us.

"B-20, proceed to Window Eight."

That was me. B-20. I stood up and walked to Window Eight. The man behind the counter was a middle-aged, bald-headed white American.

"How are you today?" he asked.

"I am fine, sir. How about yourself?" I used my best American accent, trying not to faint from my nerves.

"Not bad. Have you ever traveled to the U.S.?"

"No."

"Have you ever traveled to any other country besides Kenya and Somalia?"

"No. But I passed through Uganda on my way to Kenya."

"What do you do now in Nairobi?"

"I am a refugee here, sir."

"Did you ever go to college in Nairobi?"

"No."

"And Somalia?"

"Yes, I went to a college in Mogadishu but it collapsed before I finished."

"What are those letters in your hand?"

"These are letters of support from senators and other supporters. Do you want to see them?"

"Sure."

He glanced quickly at the letters, looked up at me, and said, "I am sorry. You don't qualify for the visa this time. Good luck wherever you end up." Then he handed everything back to me.

I was frozen. I could not leave his window. He turned to his computer and started typing.

"Sir," I said with tears in my eyes. But he ignored me and called the next person, B-21.

I walked out of the embassy like my dad when he returned to Mogadishu, crippled and wobbling. Like his, my dream had been destroyed. I felt I did not belong to this world and that I must have been created to have a permanent broken heart. I was so shaky that I was afraid of getting hit by a car, so I had to sit down and breathe. I texted Hassan. Soon everyone on Team Abdi was sending me condolences. Hassan got denied a week later.

We tried one more time, after Ben and Paul e-mailed people they knew who worked at the embassy. Again we were denied. One of the requirements of student visas is that you must have strong family ties in your home country so you aren't tempted to stay in the United States after school. Of course staying in the United States was absolutely our goal, and the embassy officers probably knew that.

We decided to try to go to school in Kenya. It wouldn't change our refugee status or help us get to America on student visas, but at least we would be improving our lives. And the police were less likely to harass a refugee with an official student ID. With the financial support of Sharon and her family, we had nothing to lose. First we applied to the best universities in Kenya, University of Nairobi and United States International University. We got turned down. We had no school transcripts from Somalia, and anyway Macalin Basbaas's madrassa was unlikely to impress them.

We set our sights lower and finally gained admissions in October—Hassan to Methodist University, me to Africa Nazarene University. So without too much trouble we were both official college students, with student IDs. Classes would start in April 2013.

Excited to share my good news, I walked down to our favorite tea shop on Sixth Street and met my friends Yonis, Farah, and Zakariye. We were drinking tea and talking about the usual things—life, girls, and sports—when something caught my eye across the street. There, on the door of the Internet café, was a new sign: "Notice: Apply Now for the American Green Card Lottery."

The green card lottery? I had never heard of it, but Yonis said it was a way to get a visa just by being lucky. You applied online and waited to see if you were picked. It was all about luck, not the people you knew or the skills you had. The Internet café owner was charging twenty cents to make the application, so he was encouraging people to try.

"Let's do it," I said.

"Oh forget it," said Farah. "It's a waste of time."

"You never know," I said. "It's only twenty cents!"

I dragged my friends across the street, and we sat down and googled the lottery. It was officially called the Diversity Immigrant Visa Program and was meant to give people from poor countries a fair shot at U.S. immigration. Every October, some eight to fifteen million people around the world apply, and only fifty thousand get visas—a fraction of 1 percent. It would be much easier to get into Harvard. Nobody in the café knew any Somali who had ever won.

I am sure that if the application fee had been fifty cents, I would not have bothered. But for twenty cents, which we all assumed we were just throwing away, my friends and I took the chance and applied that day. So did Hassan. All we could do after that was wait seven months for the results in May.

The New Year arrived and Kenya was consumed by its upcoming presidential election. On March 4, 2013, the country voted for Uhuru Kenyatta, son of Jomo Kenyatta, whose face was on the money that the police stole from us every day. The son ran on a platform of national security, vowing to wipe out al-Shabaab, which of course meant even more al-Shabaab attacks. Somalis expected more police raids in Little Mogadishu, and on election night we all stayed locked behind our doors, praying there would be no bombs or shots. For months after the election, tensions were high everywhere in the city.

School started in April. My course of study was mass communication, the school's version of journalism, and I was excited to be in classes every day. The hard part was getting there because the campus was fifteen miles away in the Ongata Rongai neighborhood, requiring two *matatu* rides. Anywhere along the route you could be hit by a suicide terrorist or a roadside bomb or grabbed by the police; anything could happen. One day I was in a *matatu* coming home from an exam when the passengers, noticing I was Somali, got worried that I was al-Shabaab and carrying a bomb in my backpack. They started yelling at the driver.

"Why is he here?"

"Kick him out!"

The driver pulled over to the side of the road and ordered me off. Unfortunately, he had stopped right in front of the Pangani police station. Al-Shabaab had bombed that station a few weeks earlier, and security was very tight. If I got off the bus there, I would be arrested at best, and maybe shot on sight. You could not offer bribes in that spot, because the station had cameras there. I begged the driver as the passengers kept shouting, "Kick him out!"

"I am a student!" I cried. "I am not a terrorist!" Finally I turned my backpack upside down and emptied out all my books, pencils, and pens onto the floor of the bus. I held up my student ID for everyone to see. This argument went on for five minutes until the driver sped off, then dropped me away from the police station. I stopped carrying a backpack and wore only a T-shirt in public so I could not be concealing a bomb.

Finally, May came, time for the lottery winners to be announced. My friends had forgotten about it, but not me. I had been thinking about it every day, waiting for the moment. I texted my friends to meet one afternoon at the Internet café.

We had to wait for a computer terminal, it was so packed with people checking the results. They had been coming since the morning, Kenyans, Ethiopians, Somalis, all of them walking out glum-faced.

"See, this thing is fake," said Yonis.

When we got a computer, Farah went first. No luck. Zakariye. No. Yonis. Same. I went last. As I entered my application number and date of birth, I thought about all the good luck I had received in my life. There was the time my family escaped execution on our flight from Mogadishu when that fighter recognized my dad; the time I met Paul by chance that day in Mogadishu, setting me on a path as a radio correspondent; Sharon hearing me on the radio in Maine one evening; Aleey, the Somali cabdriver in Kampala who rescued me from Entebbe Airport. So much good luck. I clicked Submit, on the luckiest day of my life.

14

Long Odds

I thought it was a mistake. Nobody wins the green card lottery. I reentered my information, twice. Both times it said the same thing: "You have been randomly selected . . ."

People in the café went crazy, slapping me on the back and cheering. The owner was so happy, now he could brag about having a lucky café. "You're an American now!" he shouted. "You're going to the land of opportunity! Remember us back here!"

It went on and on, the handshakes and congratulations. I was in a state of bliss. When things calmed down, I finally had the chance to read further. The website did indeed say "You have been randomly selected . . . ," but that wasn't the whole sentence. The rest of it said, ". . . for further processing."

You have been randomly selected for further processing.

What did that mean? I read on. It turns out that winning the green card lottery does not actually win you a green card. It wins you the chance to *apply* for a green card. Not everyone who applies will actually get a green card, so the lottery draws three times as many "winners" as there are actual green cards to give out. In 2013, I was one of 155,000 people chosen around the world to apply for just fifty-five thousand green cards to be issued in 2014. About one chance in three.

That didn't seem too bad. In my life I had beaten much worse odds. But that wasn't all. The lottery winners are numbered, and the people with the smallest numbers get the first crack at applying for a green card. When some of those early winners fail to pass for whatever reason, the next numbers in line are invited to apply. When all the green cards are issued, the process ends for that year. If your number has not been called, it's all over. You lose your chance. And even if your number finally gets called, the cutoff date for diversity green cards is September 30 of the issuing year—2014 in my case. On that date no more green cards would be issued, even if not all fifty-five thousand had been awarded yet. So the clock was ticking for everyone.

The first name chosen from the Africa region received case number 2014AF00000001. Number one. My case number was 2014AF00047441. I had to read it carefully several times to figure out it meant there were more than forty-seven thousand people ahead of me. In Africa. Not counting other winners all over the world, trying for the same visas. It seemed like impossible odds. For me to get to America, I had to hope tens of thousands of other desperate people around the world lost out.

The math was bad, but the paperwork seemed even more daunting. If I ever did get an interview to apply for a visa, I would need all sorts of documentation about who I was, and what I've been doing all my life. But the U.S. government didn't recognize any civil documents from Somalia. No Somali passports, birth certificates, divorce papers, or marriage licenses were accepted. In other words I needed to produce civil records to escape a country so broken that we had no civil records. Years later I learned about the term "catch-22." That's what it was.

The one hope was that Somalis could sometimes get a waiver on those documents. But other paperwork was always required, starting with a medical certificate to determine that I was healthy. I didn't think that would be too hard, but I'd never been to a doctor in my life, so I really didn't know. Then you had to get school transcripts, but with all the police raids I could not get to school every day, and my attendance was poor despite my best efforts. The worst requirement, the one that filled me with dread, was obtaining something called a Letter of Good Conduct, certifying I was not a criminal. Of course I was no criminal and had no record, but getting proof of that required walking into Nairobi police headquarters and getting fingerprinted. The same police who were harassing us daily.

Hassan did not win the lottery. I think I was more upset than he was.

Over the summer of 2013 we lay low while plotting ways to gather my paperwork if I did get the notification to apply. We made barbells out of empty milk cans filled with rocks and sand, and we took turns working out in our room. I thought maybe if I looked ripped like Arnold Schwarzenegger, it would help me pass my physical exam to become an American like he did.

I reported on my lottery win for *The Story,* and then *The Huffington Post* did a story about me. I became the most famous green card lottery winner in the world, even though I had not even been selected for an application interview. Every day I checked my e-mail for news from the State Department, but nothing came for weeks and months.

On September 21 a group of al-Shabaab terrorists attacked the Westgate Mall—the same place Hassan and I had met Dick Gordon's daughter Pamela for coffee. They pulled up around noon on a Saturday and began lobbing hand grenades everywhere. Inside, the mall's video surveillance cameras showed terrorists walking up and down, randomly shooting Kenyans and foreigners out for a day of shopping. They let go those who looked like Muslims, or those who could recite the Koran, or even just name Muhammad's mom. (Aminah, good to know.) Before then, their attacks were mostly around the slums, but now they had targeted the rich part of town. Over the two-day standoff, sixty-seven people were killed and many more injured.

Five miles to the east, Little Mogadishu was turning into a ghost town. People closed businesses; streets were cleared. Inside, every apartment was packed with people watching their televisions and waiting for reprisals. Many other people jammed into the mosques and prayed for peace. Within days, police in red hats invaded the neighborhood. This was the General Service Unit, a highly trained paramilitary wing. "Refugees must go back to the camps!" said a Kenya police spokesman on TV. "They must show themselves to the police officers!" Then they went straight to the mosques and started dragging everyone out.

Police trucks were sent into every block of Little Mogadishu. Outside our building, cops were loading Somalis into a truck like sacks of maize, just throwing them in on top of one another. Women screamed, and children cried. When the trucks filled, they drove off to the big soccer stadium at Kasarani, which had been turned into a concentration camp, and when there were no more trucks, they marched people on foot, ten miles, to the stadium.

Around midnight we heard screams from downstairs, then banging at our door.

"Open the door, you terrorists, or we will break it down and kill you!"

Hassan and I knew our latch would give easily, so we

decided there was no choice but to open. On the other side stood two policemen in red hats, but mainly what I saw was the fist of one, thundering against my face. He hit me so hard I was blinded. Then the two of them started kicking and punching both of us. The next thing I remember was one of the cops dragging me downstairs by my collar, like they do in movies. I was screaming for my life. Hassan was right behind me. They lined us up outside in front of the police vehicle so they could see our faces in the truck lights. It was chilly and rainy, and I was shivering. My shirt was torn. I had not eaten since that morning. In my head I was going back to Somalia.

One by one they asked us to show IDs. When I pulled out my refugee ID, the officer threw it back in my face. He held my neck and told me to jump into the back of the truck. It was already packed with Somali refugees, there was no space, but I squeezed in and waited for the truck to move. "My American dream is dead forever," I thought.

But then some good luck. The red hats started negotiating for money. In the end, those big-shot paramilitary cops were all about the bribe, just like the regular street cops. Anyone who could bail himself out with cash could go back to his apartment. Hassan and I bought our way to freedom with eighty dollars that we still had from Sharon. We felt bad for the people who had no money for bribes.

The roundups and deportations went on for months, into the spring of 2014. In January, I had received a call from a BBC Radio reporter in London named Leo Hornak. He had read a blog post I wrote for a Kenyan charity about winning the lottery. He was doing a story about people who won all sorts of lotteries and wanted to interview me. So on February 4, I snuck downtown to the BBC studios and recorded an interview with Leo in London. In April, Leo decided to do a radio series based on my story, with me recording our Skype calls using a small digital device. But first I had to get the device—another trip downtown.

It was a Marantz 620, about the size of a deck of cards. I could upload the recordings on our laptop; fortunately, we still had Wi-Fi, which had been installed illegally by a Somali guy before the Westgate attack for one hundred shillings a month, and somehow we still had electricity. My first recording, on April 18, made Leo feel guilty for having me come downtown:

> I'm in my room here in Little Mogadishu. The streets are under siege. The most wanted thing here is a Somali face. In the meantime I ventured out of Little Mogadishu for the first time today. My friends, my brother, and everybody who knows me can't still believe it. On my first step out of my door, I felt butterflies in my stomach. My brother was at the door telling me not to go. It's dangerous. But I have to do an audio diary for the BBC. But the equipment to record my stories is at the BBC bureau at downtown Nairobi. But between that audio recorder and me is a treacherous difficult journey. My travel out of Little Mogadishu was like crossing the border into another country, with heavy border patrol. I walked along the walls of the buildings and avoided the streets. But due to heavy rains in the morning, the streets are ankle deep in mud. I carefully stepped; any car moving sends chills down my spine. I saw bus number six headed downtown; my eyes scanned through the passengers. There's no single Somali here. All eyes were fixed on a Somali face. The bus was rocking with a Jamaican music that was more than my ears could hold. The throbbing beat was unbearable. But it's not my ears I care about, but my life.

Hassan and I became totally afraid to leave our room, even to use the bathroom downstairs. The building was by now almost empty. As the days went by, our food began to run short. We pooled our supplies with another Somali family still on the ground floor of our building—two women, one a single mom with two small boys. They had also paid bribes to stay in their place. Soon we were down to tea and some bread that was still being delivered by a Kenyan on a bicycle. One night I told Leo over Skype that we were getting desperate.

"I'm starting to feel like maybe we won't make it. Our eyes are turning red and our hair is running out. We're looking like pretty skinny."

I wondered if a skeleton could pass the medical exam for a green card.

The family on the first floor ran out of money and decided to go back to Somalia. I told Leo,

> This really broke the heart of my brother and I because that means we are going to be alone. What they are telling me, "Abdi, what are you doing here? C'mon move, you're dreaming about an America that doesn't exist! This is a dream, c'mon, boy, you're wrong." That's what they're telling me, Leo. At some point I'm thinking like it would be okay to go with them. This is totally no life.

But the road home to Somalia had no promise of life. In the Kenyan countryside, gangs of robbers and rapists preyed on the returning refugees. And once they crossed the border, refugees were in the hands of al-Shabaab. That mom downstairs was more worried for her two little boys than for herself because she knew al-Shabaab would probably kidnap them for indoctrination. But what else could she do? Starve them to death in her apartment?

I told Leo that the Somali refugees were like the migrating wildebeests that face crocodiles one way and hyenas the other way. Either path is deadly and many will perish on the way, but some will make it. I chose the path of staying in Kenya, hoping for a miracle.

With everyone else in our building gone, Hassan and I stopped leaving our apartment for anything. Classes had started, but we were not able to get to school. We covered our window and turned off all the lights after dark. We tried not to even move. We were down to a kilo of tea, some sugar, and a loaf of stale bread. Our stomachs felt like they were eating themselves inside out, and our eyes grew sticky. It was like the famine of our youth in Mogadishu, except we were in a modern African city with shops and restaurants full of people. In my hunger I salivated at the thought of the KFC, with that delicious chicken and Cokes, at the bus depot where we ate on the first day I arrived in Nairobi. It seemed a million miles from the ghost town of Eastleigh.

The police were always outside our building, leaning on their trucks, eating *mandazi,* the Kenyan version of doughnuts, and making jokes. When we dared to sneak downstairs to the bathroom, we could never flush the toilet, because the police would hear it. A bucket shower was out of the question; we did not bathe for months. One night the police came up and banged on our door. Terrified, we stayed dead still. Finally they left.

Days felt like years. Weeks passed excruciatingly. Near starvation, we decided someone must venture out for supplies or die. Not only that—Ben and his family were moving to Zambia;

the terror attacks in Nairobi were even chasing away Westerners. Before he left, we needed to get some cash from Sharon, through him. So one morning before daybreak, I crept out of our building for the first time in weeks. I carried my student ID, the last cash that we had, and my refugee document. I walked past Ninth, Tenth, and Eleventh Streets. All were empty and looking spooky. The lights of the police trucks flashed down at First Avenue. I ran in a zigzag like a soldier in a movie, ducking behind signs and empty kiosks. When I reached Twelfth Street, I jumped on a *matatu* and was off toward downtown.

Bad luck: We hit a roadblock a mile from Little Mogadishu. The police were checking for Somali refugees. My heart was in my throat as the officer boarded the bus and waved his flashlight across the passengers. He noticed me right away.

"You!" he said, waving his light. "Come down!"

I descended as the bus drove away.

When I showed him my refugee document, he slapped my face and told me to sit on the side of the road. He kept checking other buses and found two more Somalis, who joined me where I was sitting. Finally the officer told me to stand, then he pushed me to the side and began the usual negotiation.

"Ngapi?" I said in Swahili. How much?

We argued back and forth until I handed him thirty dollars. He freed me and I caught another bus. Every minute Hassan was texting me to make sure I was fine. More roadblocks and I would run out of money.

Life in downtown Nairobi was carrying on as normal; there were no police in sight. As I walked up the busy Tom Mboya Street, some pedestrians veered away from me. They could tell I was Somali, but no one hassled me. Ben took me to a restaurant near his office. For the first time in weeks I had fresh food and cold lemonade; it was heaven. He handed me six hundred dollars for food and bribes. On my way back, I bought gallons of clean water, red beans, corn, some fruits, milk, and rice. I made it back with no trouble because the police didn't care about buses going into Little Mogadishu, only coming out.

I had been building up the courage to get my Letter of Good Conduct from the police. I had no idea if my lottery number would even be called for a visa interview, but I wanted to be prepared. On May 12, a Monday, I got up early and made several calls to everyone who cared about me. I asked people to act quickly in case I got arrested. Paul sent a letter to journalists based in Kenya, including Tom Rhodes, the East Africa representative of the Committee to Protect Journalists, and Peter Greste, a reporter for Al Jazeera. Leo e-mailed the Ministry of Internal Affairs. It felt good to know people were fighting for me, but I also knew I would be on my own at the police station.

I got together every letter of recommendation that I had, the U.S. senators', the journalists'. I took all my refugee papers, in duplicate, and folded cash into my pockets. I said good-bye to Hassan, walked downstairs, and opened the front door a crack. No police. It had been raining all night; maybe the rains had kept the police off the streets that morning. I ran quickly down the muddy lanes of Little Mogadishu and hopped on a bus bound north for Kiambu Road.

The Criminal Investigation Department (CID) is a huge complex of low white buildings on the other side of the Mathare slum, beyond the A2 highway that divides rich from poor. It borders the elite Muthaiga Golf Club and the Karura Forest, sort of like the Central Park of Nairobi. I was in no mood to appreciate the scenery as the bus dropped me in front of the main gate.

It had started raining again. Three officers were standing guard. Kenyans came, were searched with metal detectors, and went in. A few Somalis stood around in the rain, getting soaked. When I approached the guards, I was trembling with fear. One immediately walked toward me and yelled.

"Do not come any closer!" he said. "Wait over there." He pointed to the other Somalis and made it clear we were not allowed inside. We stood in the rain for four hours. Finally a man in a dark suit came out. He addressed the Somalis one by one. When it was my turn, he said, "Show me your identification."

When I pulled out my UNHCR refugee papers, he pushed me aside and moved on to the next person. I chased after him.

"Sir, please, I need the police fingerprints for my visa interview."

He turned and scowled at me. "What country are you going to?"

"United States."

He turned and moved on. I followed him down the line. Finally he turned around and said, "There's nothing I can do but take your paper and send it to UNHCR; then I have to wait for them to come back to me. It will take more than five months." In other words, he needed to verify that my documents were real. He took the duplicate of my refugee ID and ordered me to leave.

On the bus back to Eastleigh I was almost in tears. I didn't have five months; the 2014 visa period expired in four and a half months on September 30. Besides, I didn't believe him anyway. Not that it mattered—my number had not even come up for a visa interview.

Everything changed two days later, when good luck came to my in-box. It was an e-mail from the State Department:

> Dear DV applicant. An appointment had been scheduled for you at the U.S. embassy in Nairobi on July 22, 2014 07:30 AM. You will be required to submit sufficient proof of identity upon arrival. If you fail to obtain a DV-2014 visa by September 30, 2014, your registration will expire.

So this was it. I was on the list! I had sixty-nine days to round up my paperwork. Sixty-nine days to arrange a medical exam and get transcripts from a school I could no longer safely attend. Sixty-nine days to somehow get that police background check. I texted all my Somali friends with the news. They did not encourage me.

"Shit, you are crazy," wrote Yonis. "Forget about America and the lottery thing. That's not happening."

Even Hassan thought I was deceiving myself at this point. "I think it is time to give up, Abdi," he said.

But I would not give up on my American dream until America slammed its door shut. So my brother and I made a pact that day: If I did not get my visa after the July 22 interview, we would join the refugees migrating north across Sudan and into Libya, hoping for the dangerous sea passage to Italy. We would not go back to Somalia, but we were done with Kenya.

First, the easy part. Africa Nazarene e-mailed my official transcript. The university was sympathetic to my plight and knew how hard it would be for me to travel to the school. If only it could be that simple to get my police report.

May 16, a Friday, sixty-seven days until my interview. Al-Shabaab blew up two *matatus* in Nairobi's huge Gikomba market. At least ten died; more than seventy were injured. The police as usual came in floods to Little Mogadishu, what was left of the population there. They swept buildings floor by floor. These new police would not take bribes, they had orders to arrest refugees and even shoot them if they tried to escape. So gunshots were ringing everywhere. Hassan and I sat next to each other trembling in our room. We heard the voices of the cops coming up the stairs. Boots kicked at our door, but they left thinking no one was there. After a few days the police got tired of raiding. We looked out the window and saw them sitting in their trucks, eating and talking. I crept slowly downstairs to use the bathroom. Hassan was watching out the window for police and would text me if they came in the building. Then it was his turn for the bathroom while I watched. I checked Facebook on my phone; my friend Zakariye, who did not win the lottery, was taking pictures of himself in Mogadishu. He had been deported from Kenya.

When we could sneak out, Hassan and I bought cheap used books from hawkers on the street, always looking to improve our English. We liked the books by successful Americans who could inspire us: scientists, inventors, and businessmen. Bill Gates was one. Another book we liked was called *The Art of the Deal* by Donald J. Trump. Hassan and I read that whole book hiding in our room. We teased each other, saying someday we would be as rich and successful as this guy Trump.

I went back to the CID headquarters a few times, despite the risk, fighting my fear, to see if maybe I would get a different answer. Every time it was the same scowling guy in the dark suit, and he did not appreciate me.

"I recognize your face," he said one time. "You are terrible! Did I not tell you to wait until I hear from the UNHCR?"

Time was running out. Thousands of lottery visas had already been approved for 2014. So many people were going for their interviews well prepared, less worried. The U.S. embassy in Nairobi was already doing extreme vetting of Somali visa applicants. A young man traveling alone, with no family in the United States, was highly suspect. Everywhere my hope was shrinking. I wished the embassy would read my heart instead of all these bullshit pieces of paper.

May 29, Thursday. Fifty-four days until my interview. I

received a phone call from Pamela Gordon. She had been reading the e-mail strings with Team Abdi about my troubles getting the police certificate. She said her Kenyan driver knew an officer inside the Criminal Investigation Department and maybe he could help. At least with her driver at the wheel I could probably get inside the complex. She asked when I would want to try and I said right now.

That afternoon I snuck out of our room to catch a *matatu* downtown. The police were off in the distance and didn't notice me. I hailed a bus, but the driver sped past me; he did not want a Somali on board. Several more buses ignored me. I was freaking out, watching for cops. Finally one bus stopped. I got off downtown and met up with Pamela and her Kenyan driver. On the way to the CID, Pamela handed me two hundred dollars to bail myself out if something happened. We easily went through the gate because of the white lady and the Kenyan driver.

At the main desk we mentioned the name of the driver's friend, and I was taken by myself into his office. On his desk was the copy of my UNHCR document. The other guy had never sent it, no surprise. The man stood up from his desk. "Follow me," he said.

We turned in to a hallway of the building, a place with no surveillance cameras. "Give me eight hundred dollars," the officer said, looking around nervously.

"I don't have that much money."

"What do you have?"

I reached into my pocket and took out the two hundred dollars Pamela had given me. He snatched it from my hand and took me back into his office.

Thump! The stamp came down on my refugee document, music to my ears.

"Proceed down the hall for your fingerprints," he said.

I waited in line for a few minutes in another room. When my name was called, a lady pressed all ten of my fingers onto a pad of black ink, then onto a white sheet that said:

DIRECTORATE OF CRIMINAL INVESTIGATIONS
POLICE CLEARANCE CERTIFICATE
REMARKS IN CASE OF PREVIOUS RECORD, NIL

"NIL." No record. That was it! I couldn't believe it. I talked to Leo that night from our room:

> My police clearance is done! I'm looking at my ten fingers. They're all black from black ink from fingerprints. This was the only problem, I dealt with it, it's done!

June 6, Friday. Forty-six days until my interview. I had scheduled my medical exam, which was at the Migration Health Assessment Center in northwest Nairobi, near the U.S. embassy. Another scary dash for a *matatu.* This time when I left our building, I found a police officer standing in front. He was older and had a big belly, with lots of stars on his shoulder and a billy club under his arm. He took me by surprise, and I think I scared him more than he scared me. I could tell he was a high-level officer, not one of the usual beat cops who roughed up Somalis. Maybe he was out investigating some actual crime. When he saw me, he took out his walkie-talkie and called for backup, like he didn't want to deal with me by himself. Soon two more cops joined him. The new ones tried to take me down to the ground for a beating, but the older officer stopped them. Maybe he felt sorry for me, I don't know.

"Stand up!" he said to me. "Who else is in there?"

"No one." I was lying because Hassan was upstairs.

The officer did not bother asking to see my ID; he just demanded some money. Minutes later I was on my way.

The guard at the gate of the Migration Health Assessment Center searched me with a metal detector, then let me in. I had all the required documents. First came a blood test; then they checked my weight and height, then a quick physical. In twenty minutes it was done. "You are all good," said the lady. "We'll send the results to the embassy. Good luck on your interview!"

June 15, a Sunday, thirty-seven days to go. Thirty masked al-Shabaab gunmen bombed a police station in the coastal Kenyan town of Malindi, stole its weapons, and went on a rampage, killing at least forty-eight people in the small village of Mpeketoni. Many of the victims were watching a World Cup match in a video hall. An al-Shabaab spokesman bragged about the attack and said they were planning more. We braced for more police raids.

July 7, Monday afternoon. Fifteen days and counting. I was walking down Eighth Street when a gang of about fifty young men from the Mathare slum, armed with machetes and clubs, appeared from around the corner. Because I was a young man and certainly al-Shabaab, I was a perfect target of their anger. They chased me down the street, throwing rocks and swinging their machetes and clubs. I ran as fast as I could and threw myself headfirst into the mosque, then slammed the door shut, bolting it behind me. They knocked and kicked as I joined the other Somalis in the evening prayers. Finally they left. I am sure they would have hacked me to death because many other Somalis were killed by these vigilante gangs. The murders never made the news.

July 21, the day before my interview. I washed my shirt and pants under the faucet in the bathroom downstairs. I carefully laid the shirt under my mattress to press it overnight. Leo called. "I'm not going to bed anymore," I told him.

> I'm not going to sleep, I'm sure about that. Tomorrow's going to change my life. It's going to change my life to be the happiest person, or else it's going to change my life to be the most devastated man on earth, so it's these two. Tomorrow night I'm coming back to this room, breaking everything, smashing everything right here because I'm happy or I'm angry. In both situations I will break everything I know; I will just give a punch into my laptop.

I couldn't sleep out of anticipation, but also pure fear. What if the police raided our room that night? What if I was taken out to prison or to the airport for a deportation back to Somalia? Once you miss your interview at the embassy, it's finished. No more chances. My heart was racing.

At four thirty I headed downstairs carrying an envelope containing my Letter of Good Conduct, the letters of support from senators and journalists, Sharon's sponsorship letter, and a printout of the e-mailed transcript from Africa Nazarene University. I reached the embassy gate by five. I sat on the side of the street next to the embassy building, which opened at seven. By six o'clock, a line of people arriving for their visa interviews trailed around the building. Many of them were Kenyans who had won the lottery like myself. At seven fifteen I went through the security check, proceeded inside, and paid the $330 fee for the interview. As I waited, I saw people walking out grinning. Their visas had been approved. Others had been denied and were crying. Seeing these different emotions made me even more nervous.

My number was called to Window Nine. An African American woman with a huge smile greeted me. "Hi!"

"Good morning, ma'am," I said. So far so good, this woman was black like me and seemed nice.

"Please, can you raise your right hand and swear that everything that you will say is the truth?"

I did.

"Where did you go to college?" she asked.

I told her and indicated the transcript.

"This transcript does not have a signature. Did you know that?"

I looked at it. She was right. The e-mailed transcript had no signature. She took out a pink piece of paper and on the bottom wrote two words, "Missing transcript." She handed it to me and said, "Sorry, I can't give you the visa. Send it to us if you can get one with a signature. And don't come back here. Just send it through DHL."

Send it through DHL?

I was speechless, frozen. All I could do was look into her eyes and beg with my own eyes for mercy. "Please change your mind," I was praying. "Please I need some luck today."

But the lady didn't change her mind. She picked up her microphone and called the next number.

Dazed, I walked outside and collapsed under a tree. I was holding my head in my hands, wishing this was a nightmare I could wake up from. But the pink slip in my hand felt too real. I texted all my friends: "This is the worst day of my life." I sat there for a few more minutes, rubbing the pink slip between my hands. Then I stuffed it in my pocket, got up, and headed for the *matatu* station. The university was far and traffic was bad. As we sat stalled behind other *matatus* coughing black smoke, my heart raced and my right knee bounced. Please move, please move. It was four o'clock when I ran into the student affairs office. The woman behind the window said, "I'm sorry, we are closed."

"Please!" I said. "Please help me!" The lady saw my face and realized I was on fire. She signed my transcript. I dashed back downtown on another bus, crawling through heavy rush-hour traffic, arriving at the DHL office at six.

"We are closed," said the man in the office. "We close at six."

I begged and pleaded just like at the school. He let me drop the package. Within a day the U.S. embassy would receive it, he said.

Nine days passed. I was calling the embassy every day, and every time they said, "No. We have not received the transcript."

On August 1, Leo called the U.S. embassy. He identified himself and said he was on deadline for his story and wanted to know when a decision would be made on my application. The embassy staff member had no information for him. But two hours later I got an e-mail from the State Department: "Your document has been received and your visa will be sent by tomorrow."

15

White Rooms

On the phone that night, Leo asked me what I did when I got the e-mail. "Oh my God," I said, "I jumped off the bed and hit my head on the ceiling!"

> It's issued! I've never had such a big smile, never ever ever. It feels like the dream has just become real. I feel like I am not a refugee. This is not a refugee that is hiding from the police. I'm an American citizen.

Well, not exactly. But I had won the right to live and work in America. Not won. I had *earned* it. Years of practicing English, a lifetime of dodging bullets and bombs, risking death by refusing to join the Islamists, hiding from crooked cops, and above all never giving up. Leo asked Hassan if he had any jealousy that only I had won. He replied,

> Actually, Leo, I tell you I don't have the least jealousy at all. If two of us get visas to get out of here, it would be even better. But if someone told me right now, "There is one visa, which one of you will take it?" I would say Abdi. Because he's new to this country and

> I know how we are so fearful at night. And I know how he can't sleep at night. For him to get a visa is my biggest pleasure. Yeah, there's luck there, but luck can be fair.

Leo asked the State Department if his phone call had made the final difference. They replied, "The journalist call played no role in the timing of the visa issuance. Any visa process coinciding with a press inquiry is merely a coincidence."

Maybe, maybe not. I didn't care. Abdi American was finally going to America.

On August 8, I got a call from DHL that it had my visa and I could come collect it. By noon I walked out of that building carrying my amazing, beautiful American visa. It was Friday in downtown Nairobi, and the streets were packed with thousands of people happy that the workweek was ending. But no one was skipping like me. I had to be the happiest man in Nairobi that day.

With my visa in hand Sharon and Ben quickly bought me a plane ticket for Boston. My flight was on Monday at five in the morning, connecting through Addis Ababa and Frankfurt. With all of this confirmed, Leo flew into Nairobi that weekend to meet me and finish the radio documentary we were doing together. Sunday evening, my last day in Little Mogadishu, Hassan and I snuck past the police and caught a *matatu* decorated with photos of President Obama. The driver was playing Michael Jackson songs. It was perfect. Before meeting Leo at his hotel, we made a quick shopping trip. I needed luggage for my stuff—all I had were plastic shopping bags—and some clean clothes.

At nine o'clock that evening, a small Mazda car hired by the BBC staff showed up in front of the hotel. I don't remember breathing during the twenty-minute drive to the airport. *What if a terrorist attack happens, or a bomb is thrown somewhere? They could lock down the airport and I would never be able to leave!* Leo had his microphone in my face asking me what I was feeling like. I told him I felt like the clock was ticking. I was so nervous about the airport and if the immigration people would arrest me for being a refugee. Meanwhile, I was thinking Hassan would have to go back to that room, alone, in the dark with no company, just the brutal police.

At the airport entrance we were stopped by the police, they peeked into the car, Leo said hi, and the Kenyan driver waved. They let us go. We all got out and entered the airport departure terminal. Leo took some pictures of Hassan and me. We hugged and said good-bye. I was so choked up I couldn't say anything to my brother. Hassan told me to stay strong. His last words were "Remember to support Mom!"

With that, I proceeded inside. The Kenya immigration officer looked at my visa, stamped my refugee documents, and waved me through. So easy with the right piece of paper. It was ten o'clock when I sat down at the gate for the long wait until my flight. I was the first passenger there.

Hassan and Leo decided to wait at a cafeteria inside the airport until the flight took off, to make sure I departed without being arrested. I sat there looking around the airport, watching people come and go. In a few hours many other people joined me in the wait. Finally our boarding was announced. I had a window seat. When we took off, the sun was just rising above the horizon. My American dream was now becoming real life, and it seemed like everything in my past life was becoming a dream that I needed to wake up from.

After a stop in Ethiopia we landed in Frankfurt, where I had to change planes. That airport was so huge I freaked out for a moment trying to connect with my flight to Boston. We had to take a bus to the departure gate on the other side. Again I boarded Lufthansa, the biggest airplane I ever saw. Again I had a window seat. An American lady with her teenage daughter sat next to me. After takeoff they shut their eyes and acted like the flight was boring. I was awake; I could not take my eyes off the window and the screen in front of me that showed where we were. At some point we were flying over the United Kingdom; I looked down, and I could see water and what seemed like a city. Then all was blue for hours and hours.

My heart was beating fast as the plane banked over downtown Boston and descended to Logan Airport. My face was glued to the window as I looked at the skyscrapers of America, then the blue waters of the Atlantic. Even though we were going down, I felt like I was going up to heaven. When the wheels bumped on the runway, I couldn't control myself. "I am in America!" I shouted.

Even the bored lady next to me found a way to smile. "Welcome!" she said.

As we taxied to the gate, I thought of my brother in Kenya, my mom on the dusty streets of Mogadishu waiting for the good news, my friends in the tea shop in Little Mogadishu who applied for the visa lottery when I forced them, all the while assuring me it was hogwash. But I had no thought of saying "I told you so." I was overwhelmed with joy, with tears melting down my cheeks.

Exiting the plane felt like a historic moment, like when the first man walked on the moon. I wondered if gravity felt different in America, but it seemed about the same as in Africa. People poured out of the flight; they were in some sort of a hurry. It seemed like everyone knew what to do and they knew where they were going. I just felt like standing there and watching everything. I looked around the immigration hall. So far no

Hollywood, no Disney World, no Statue of Liberty or Harvard University, not even Walmart or KFC. I saw people who looked a little like Bruce Willis, Sylvester Stallone, Eddie Murphy, Oprah, or Tom Cruise, and I couldn't take my eyes off them. But I was not the only stranger there. A group of Asians speaking a strange language were lined up in front of me. People of other colors were everywhere. A black man right behind me in the line was glued to his phone.

"Hi!" I said.

"Hello." To my surprise he had a thick African accent.

"I'm from Somalia. Where are you from?"

"Nigeria," he replied, barely looking up from his phone.

It was the first time in my entire life I saw a Nigerian. He told me he had lived in America for ten years.

So many different kinds of people in America! I expected big, muscly white guys to be in charge at the airport, like the marines I knew from Mogadishu. But lots of the airport staff were Asian, short with round faces. As the line moved on slowly, I gazed up at the huge television screens flashing the news:

. . . actor Robin Williams has committed suicide . . .

. . . violent protests erupted in Ferguson, Missouri, after the killing of a black man . . .

It was a police officer who shot the man, but people were protesting, taking to the streets. Although many Americans might not be happy with things in the United States, to me the protests were just a sign of freedom that people can get out onto the streets and show their unhappiness. Kenyan police would have killed Somalis who dared to protest in Little Mogadishu.

When it was my turn, an officer asked me some questions and handed me a form to fill out. I had to choose between being African, African American, Hispanic, or Caucasian. This threw me at first because I had never thought of myself as African. In Somalia we identify ourselves by our tribes.

An officer led me into a room where a nice American lady took my fingerprints and photo. She had blue eyes and blond hair, and she said my official green card would arrive at my address in Maine. "Welcome to the United States!" she said warmly. Everything was very quiet, official, and businesslike in the airport, not like all the chaos and shouting in African airports, and I wondered if all of America was this serious. But when I finally walked through the doors from the immigration hall into the terminal, I flinched from the sudden rush of activity. People were everywhere, holding signs, wheeling suitcases, hugging relatives. Now I was really in America! Somewhere out there in the crowd were Sharon McDonnell and her daughter, Natalya, both trying to catch sight of me. Then I saw them; they were holding a sign that said "Abdi Iftin." Sharon had straight shoulder-length blond hair, and Natalya a dark ponytail. We met and I stooped to hug them. Both were so much shorter than I imagined, not like Americans in the movies or the marines in Mogadishu. They looked up at me with huge smiles. "Welcome!" said Sharon. "Let's take you to your new home."

We left through a huge revolving door to the curbside. My first moment breathing the fresh air of America! Except it smelled like diesel fumes right there, not much different from Africa. I ducked down and kept my eyes fixed on Sharon, this small person who had changed my life forever. I was looking at her like she was superhuman—not superhuman like the comic-book heroes I saw in movies but in some other way that was maybe even stronger. We took some pictures; I bounced from place to place asking for shots.

In truth I was also a little scared. A Somali living with a white family could be known as a converted person, someone who left the culture and Islam. What would my family and friends think? What if Sharon had a dog? What if the dog licks and sniffs me? How would I behave?

We got into the car. I sat in the backseat, still curious about the gleaming city of Boston, when Sharon said, "You need to put on your seat belt."

I couldn't figure out how to do it. Sharon and Natalya laughed and showed me how to buckle up. "You need to do this every time you get in a car," said Sharon. "It's the law." I couldn't believe I was in a place where people actually obey laws. Also I had never seen a female driver in my life, except in movies.

We left the airport on a busy divided road out of Boston heading up to Maine. I saw lots of big stores and restaurants. I saw a restaurant called Kowloon shaped like some kind of South Pacific island hut, but it was like no hut in Somalia; it looked larger than the huge Isbaheysiga mosque in Mogadishu. Next came some kind of cowboy place with a neon cactus sign as tall as buildings in Nairobi. I kept thinking, "Here I am in a car in America with friends who helped me and my family even though we are not in their tribe or even the same religion." This was an aspect of humanity very new to me. I sat quietly as we drove and tried to make sense of it.

Night fell slowly and late, it was past eight o'clock and still some light. We kept driving through the twilight, zooming by more huge shops and parking lots, now blazing under blue lights. Soon there were fewer lights and buildings, more trees. I rolled down my window to get a better flavor of America, the cool late-summer wind slapping my face. When we pulled off the highway for gas and some food, I ordered a cheeseburger for my first American dinner. With a full tank we were off on the road again, this time Natalya driving. Sharon talked about the weather, how the trees will change colors, how snow will fall, Thanksgiving, Christmas. They already had plans for all these events.

Finally we pulled up in their driveway. Sure enough, at the door we were greeted by their dog, named Lacy. She jumped all over me, licking. Dog saliva is considered impure to Muslims, so now I was definitely getting butterflies in my stomach. I froze with fear.

"She's friendly," said Natalya. "She's just excited."

The two cats, Tigger and Jasmin, did not even bother waking up from their naps. But the dog followed me upstairs to my room and jumped on the bed. When Sharon and Natalya said good night, I wondered if the dog would leave me. She stayed there. I couldn't sleep with a dog in my room, it was too scary, so finally I got her out and shut the door.

I was too excited to sleep, but fortunately the morning came soon: five o'clock and it was already light. America seemed quiet, not like the streets of Mogadishu or Little Mogadishu. I watched the morning light filter into my room from the large window overlooking the driveway and then got up to look outside. A herd of deer grazed like camels just beyond the cars. As they moved on across the lawn and vanished into the tall trees, the sun appeared between the branches where squirrels were playing. So the window faced east; now I knew which way to pray. The walls of my room were painted white and blue, strange colors for walls, which are always the color of mud in Africa. The ceiling was so flat and perfect; how do they do that? The house was built in the nineteenth century, but to me it looked brand new. There was a dial on the wall to adjust the heat. The room was obsessively neat: somebody's clothes hung perfectly in the closet, not draped over a frayed clothesline like in an African hut, and pictures of birds and flowers in gold frames hung on the wall. A sculpture of Buddha sat quietly on the floor. I didn't know who Buddha was, but I soon learned Sharon and her family believed in Buddhism.

Outside, tiny fast hummingbirds dove from a tree to a bird feeder for a quick drink of nectar. They were no bigger than African bugs, and I watched them for a while, wondering if they were ever killed by cats. The only sound coming from outside was a chime softly ringing in the gentle wind. This room seemed way too big for just me, probably double the size of the room my brother and I shared in Nairobi.

I got dressed and went down to see the family.

"Let's help you fix your first American breakfast," said Sharon. The breakfast would be milk, eggs, and toast. They had lots of eggs from their chickens. "And also there's lots of leftovers in the refrigerator," she said. I did not know Americans ate leftovers. The refrigerator was packed with leftover soup, rice, eggs, pasta, juice, sauce, everything. Drawers were full of food. There were crackers, granola, dog food, and cat food. There was food everywhere in the kitchen. The living room was full of books and magazines. There was a big red couch to sit on and read. A nice porch and a big Apple computer. I went on and updated my Facebook posts. This time I didn't need Photoshopped pictures of me in America: I used actual pictures we took at Logan the night before. My friends commented with questions like "Are u living with a Christian family?" "Are you going to convert?"

My orientation started with using the oven and the toaster. I had seen kitchens in movies, but I never thought I would use such things. I learned how to warm things from the "fridge" using the microwave. Soon I learned about the dishwasher, the clothes washer, the dryer, which food goes where in the refrigerator. I learned how to measure things in inches and pounds, not meters and kilograms. I learned to leave tips at restaurants. And I was learning new English words every day, starting with "closet," "vacuum," "the vet," "chicken coop," "the barn," "mowing," and all different types of food.

I met Gib, Sharon's husband, the most easygoing person I have ever come across. He is short and thin, and his deep blue eyes miss nothing. He seems to think very carefully before he says anything, and he likes things to be in order. Gib teaches postgraduate epidemiology at the University of New Hampshire in Manchester. Before he went out to "run errands," he asked me, "Is there anything you want me to get you from the grocery store?" He spent his leisure time doing things around the house. He would disappear into the basement and work on electric wires, or out to the yard putting up a fence.

In Africa it is unusual for a man to know how to cook, but Gib cooked great meals—fried rice, guacamole, and the most delicious cakes. When we went together to buy groceries, we stopped at a drive-up window for coffee takeout. Gib explained how the speaker box worked. "There is a real person talking, even though we can't see them," he explained. It seemed like ordering food on a mobile phone, which I learned you could also do.

I could not get a job in the United States until my Social Security card and green card arrived. While I waited, the McDonnell-Parrish family offered me a job in their house. I would cut and stack firewood for the winter. I fed the horse, cleaned the stall and the chicken coop, watered plants, cleared fallen branches from the driveway. I spent all day working outside and came in only for a quick break for lunch of a sandwich and some orange juice. They paid me ten dollars an hour. I worked every day of the week and earned over six hundred dollars, but it went fast. After buying a bike, some new clothes, work gloves, and goggles for splitting firewood, I had enough left for my daily treat of doughnuts and coffee at Dunkin' Donuts. At night I would relax by browsing on Netflix and watching movies.

I woke up every day enjoying work, and there was always something to do; even clearing spiderwebs from the barn was a job the family had long wanted to do. Natalya was scared of spiders, but years earlier I had cleared spiderwebs for Falis in her video shack, so I was prepared.

Natalya was a senior at Yarmouth High School, but this was still summer break, so she and I walked miles every day through town. As we walked, I waved to drivers passing by, and they waved back or smiled. Natalya told me some people in America are racists. I was not sure what racism was; all I knew was hatred and bigotry from Kenya, and that was not about skin color. She took me around to meet the neighbors so everyone would know me and not dial 911 when I walked around. We played soccer and video games and went on shopping trips to L.L.Bean in Freeport. Natalya described me as her adopted brother to everyone. She had not had someone at home to hang out with since her older brother, Morgan, moved to California; now she again enjoyed doing things with a brother. One day she posted a photo of me on social media holding my favorite chocolate chip vanilla ice cream, describing me as her older brother. My Somali friends started calling me on the phone, in shock. One said, "Have you lost your mind? You can't make her a sister unless she is Muslim."

Weeks passed. Fall came. The sun was setting and rising more like in Somalia around six, but it was getting much colder than it ever does in Somalia. The leaves on the trees were turning golden and red; I had never seen such colors on trees. In the house people talked about the weather, food, vacations, books, and movies. There was always something going on. But today we were talking about Halloween, which was in two days, and the huge pumpkin was at the doorstep. I got oriented about tricks and treats and wearing costumes. Sharon gave me a list of funny characters I could choose to be. I picked Spider-Man because I knew him from the DVDs I had watched in Africa, but other characters on the list were strange to me. Me in my Spider-Man costume and Natalya in her Victorian ghost costume, we visited neighbors' houses for trick-or-treating. It felt a little weird because not many adults were dressed in costumes, but the neighbors filled my small bag with sweets.

I never heard of changing the time on clocks—I thought the time is what it is—but one Sunday morning everybody went around the house setting the clocks an hour back, and suddenly it was getting dark really early. Soon Thanksgiving was coming. When the day finally arrived, we had ten people around the table, mostly relatives. Everyone wanted to meet me, the new member of the McDonnell-Parrish family. We had turkey, sweet potato soufflé, apple pie, ice cream—so much food. I almost forget what it was like to be so hungry you are in physical agony. Almost. I couldn't believe I was sitting at a large table surrounded by white people with glasses of beer in their hands, and I was like one of them. They talked about American football, TV shows they had seen, and hiking and other trips they did. They talked about their animals, their families. I watched and learned. I talked about my life, my story, and my new life in Maine.

I watched from across the street as the mailman dropped envelopes into the box every day. The idea of mail was so strange; even stranger was that it would be delivered to your house instead of your waiting in a line somewhere and paying a bribe, but I was getting used to it. I ran to grab the mail as soon as the mailman came, checking to see if my name was on anything. Mostly it was shopping catalogs, funny to look through and see all the things you could buy without even going to a store. I didn't want to shop. I was waiting for my green card.

When it finally arrived, I wanted to just tear open the envelope, but I was careful not to rip the card inside. It turned out the card was hard plastic and not so easy to rip. The card had a computer image of me, the picture they took at Logan Airport, next to a picture of the Statue of Liberty. It said "UNITED STATES OF AMERICA" and "PERMANENT RESIDENT." Me and the Statue of Liberty, permanent residents.

My Social Security card came soon after, which meant I could work and buy a car. Most important, it was the first step to my goal of becoming a citizen of the United States of America.

Meanwhile, back in Somalia, neighbors poured into my mom's shack in the Eelasha camp to congratulate her on my arrival in the United States. They treated her like she'd hit the jackpot. Distant relatives who had always avoided Mom were practically moving in, waiting for her to promise them something. But she had not received a penny from me. She expected money the day after I arrived, but weeks passed and I had not sent a dollar, because I could not find a job, and I had already spent the money I earned from housework. Sharon and Gib were so generous in giving me a place to stay and free meals, but once I had cleaned everything around their property, there wasn't much more work I could do for them. I had my green card, but I was short on "green*backs,*" another new word.

No one in Africa believed me. When I spoke to my mom on the phone, she was deaf to my complaints about the lack of work in America, where money grows on trees. She thought I had become arrogant, that my newfound wealth had changed me. I had no way to convince her that life could also be hard in America. But her problems were bigger than mine; she and Nima needed money to survive and buy food. I stayed up all night browsing through JobsinMaine.com and other websites, applying for any work that I thought I could do. I tried warehouses, laundries, bakeries, bathroom cleaning, floor mopping, and many other jobs. Most of them ended up being too far away from Yarmouth, and I had no car or even a driver's license. So I had to limit my search to jobs within walking or biking distance.

I walked around town, visiting neighbors, asking if they needed someone to work in their yard or help with anything. I visited local farms to see if they wanted help. Some of the online applications for warehouse jobs got back to me for interviews. The bosses smiled, and I felt good talking to them. I said how hard I would work. I filled out so many forms, signed papers, and answered questions. They all turned me down. Was it my English? I knew it wasn't as good as most Americans'. Maybe they turned me down because I was new to the country. I did not have previous work experience here in the United States, something they always asked about. I had no résumé or references.

My fears of unemployment grew stronger after every interview. I was really struggling to understand how America works. *What if I never find a job?* I was ready to do any kind of work, the dirtiest jobs, but still I could find nothing. Gib and I put up a sign in the front yard of the house. Sharon helped me write a few lines: "I am a young man from Africa. Healthy, no drugs. I need a job. Any job. If you know of any please call this number."

Maine is home to about fifty thousand Somali immigrants, most of them living in Lewiston, an old textile mill town in central Maine and the home of Bates College. Many others live in Portland, the state's largest city. The Somali refugees get help from resettling agencies like Catholic Charities that give them money for the first eight months and assign caseworkers who help them assimilate and find jobs. But I was not technically a refugee. And while Sharon and Gib were doctors who traveled the world helping to fight diseases, they were not social workers trained to help an African immigrant navigate America.

Also there were no Somalis in Yarmouth, a bedroom community ten miles north of Portland with fewer than nine thousand people. In Lewiston and Portland, Somalis can ride buses around town. In Yarmouth at the time there were no buses, so I rode a bike around, asking every business on Main Street if it had any jobs. People would stare at me like they had never seen a black neighbor. Children looked startled; they would hide behind their parents' legs and point. It felt strange to be so different. Somalis don't look like Kenyans, but it's a matter of degrees. Here I was like a space alien. I stopped by the Dunkin' Donuts, Romeos pizza, several horse farms, the laundry, even the transfer station. But no one had a job. I thought maybe I could hawk socks on the sidewalk like in Nairobi, until I remembered that everyone was driving in cars and probably bought socks online or at L.L.Bean just up the highway.

After weeks of futile job searching around Yarmouth, we decided I should go down to Portland and ask around in the Somali community about jobs. As we waited for the day to come, at dinnertime one evening in November the house phone rang. It was Christine, one of Sharon's friends who lived in Yarmouth and had seen the sign in our yard. She told Sharon that a local home insulation company was seeking men who could do tough work. Winter was coming and the demand for insulation was growing. I e-mailed the manager, and we arranged an interview that week.

The leaves of the trees were turning dull brown and falling as I walked to the interview. It was getting dark even earlier and getting even colder. The manager looked at my green card. "What is your name?" he asked. It was on the card, but I guess he couldn't tell my first name from my last name.

"Abdi," I said.

"Forgive me if I pronounce your name wrong," he said. "You look good, strong and energetic; we need guys like you, *Abbi.* This job is dealing with heavy material and climbing roofs. Are you okay with heights?"

I told him I didn't have a problem with heights and that I really needed the job.

"We pay eleven dollars an hour," he said. "We might increase the pay if your work is good." He seemed like he was apologizing for the pay, but to me it was great, the most I had ever earned in my life. He asked if I could work on weekends. I said I could work anytime day or night. I walked out of that building on air.

Monday morning, November 17, was my first day on the job. When my alarm went off at four o'clock, I dressed warm, in layers of silk and wool. I had my usual breakfast of eggs, milk, and toast. Everyone else in the house was asleep. It was a forty-five-minute walk to work and I headed out, with my new craft knife tucked in my belt, my staple gun in my back pocket, and my hard hat on. I walked through the woods; all was quiet and silent except the scared deer that dashed when they heard me coming.

"Welcome on board," said the manager when I arrived. He introduced me to the guys I would be working with. They were all big, muscular Maine guys in dirty clothes and big construction boots. Whenever they talked, they cursed. *Fuck, shit, bitch, ass.* They wrestled and punched each other. Except for being white, they reminded me of Somali militiamen, but I was so happy to have the job that I ignored my fear.

The crew boss, Joey, told the workers my name, but they all struggled with it. *Eddy, Abey, Abbdey.* I told them whatever was fine. I could barely understand their thick Maine accents anyway. Until now I was proud of my English, but they kept correcting my mistakes and laughing at my accent, so I felt humiliated and different. To them I was a strange African man, not the American I wanted to be.

The sun was coming up as we gathered for the daily safety meeting. The workers talked about a couple of employees who had fallen off a roof and hurt themselves, someone else's ladder broke, someone tripped and got hurt on his stilts. Every week there were stories of broken bones. I was told that I could go to a hospital for free if I got injured, which surprised me. I didn't know it was the law, I just thought the company was being nice.

Joey assigned me to work with Milton and Sean, experienced workers who had been with the company for more than ten years. Milton read the instructions for the day's job. It was a commercial building, six floors, we would "batt" the walls and the ceilings with fiberglass insulation. We were called the batting squad. Both Milton and Sean were big, strong guys with tattoos all over their bodies. Sean had piercings in his nose and lower lip; Milton was missing some front teeth.

I loaded the heavy rolls of insulation into the big delivery truck from "the shop," which is what we called the Yarmouth warehouse. Heavy bundles of fiberglass sat everywhere. Milton used one hand rolling the whole bundle to the truck. I struggled with two hands. While I loaded one, he loaded three. The tiny strands of fiberglass got all over my clothes; even with gloves, a face mask, and goggles I was itching. The three of us, the batting squad, climbed into the cab and drove off, Milton behind the wheel. Before the truck left, Joey shouted out from his office, "Remember, everyone, don't forget your hard hats and goggles! It's the law!"

As soon as the truck left the shop, both men reached into their duffel bags and took out marijuana. "Do you smoke the shit, dude?" Milton asked me.

"No," I said. I had never smoked marijuana or even seen it. I'd never even smoked a cigarette. As they puffed their weed, the smoke filled the cabin. "It smells bad," I said. They just laughed, looked at me, and said something I couldn't understand. They spoke so quickly and with sarcasm that was new to me. They talked about their wives, going to clubs, drinking beer, smoking weed, cars, winning the lottery, pizza, and professional wrestling. I sat next to them in silence, trying to absorb and learn their culture, looking out at the trees and buildings.

Milton got a call from his wife. He called her "the old lady." At first I thought he was talking about his mom, but he said his mom was dead. "Hey, today we have a new guy, *Abbi*," he said to his wife, then put her on speakerphone and signaled me to say something. I didn't know what to say.

We talked about Africa. To them, Africa was one big country of naked people who eat snakes. More monkeys and lions than people. I told them that we have highways, airplanes, and cars, which surprised them.

Milton had barely any space for another tattoo, so I was surprised to hear him plan to dedicate a new tattoo to his late mom on his neck, which he said would cost him over five hundred dollars. I could never understand that, or the piercings, but one thing we shared was that these guys all loved their families. Milton hung photos of his wife and kids everywhere, on his hat, in the truck, and at the shop.

The walls of the building were made of metal studs, not mud or blocks. It didn't seem very sturdy to me. While Milton and Sean smoked cigarettes and drank Red Bull outside the building, I started unloading the fiberglass batts and carrying them to the upper floors on an unfinished staircase. I was breathing heavy and my goggles fogged up, so I could barely see the stairs. Finally Milton and Sean put on their favorite rock-and-roll music blasting all over the building and got to work. They showed me how to cut open the bundles of insulation, then how to put on stilts so we could batt the ceiling. I saw the rafters above and now understood how Americans got such flat ceilings. Sean and Milton didn't bother to wear masks or goggles, but they told me I should wear them because I was new and not used to the fiberglass. "You'll take those off after a while," Milton said, laughing. They were so fast they were actually running on their stilts. I could barely walk on mine without falling over. Then we did the walls, climbing tall ladders. Milton and Sean moved their ladders forward while they were standing on them, by jumping. They were like circus acrobats.

My first paycheck was a happy day; I had earned $400. Because I was living with Sharon and Gib and still had no car, my personal expenses were small, and I was able to send $340 to my mom. I was so proud as I walked into Portland's halal market, which was the unofficial *hawala* money-transfer station. I handed over my cash to the guy behind the counter, he took an extra $6 for every hundred as a fee. Then he communicated by computer with the *hawala* kiosk in Mogadishu, where my mom went in and claimed the money.

She was so happy she bought a goat and slaughtered it, cooked a pot of rice, and threw a party for the neighbors. Macalin Basbaas came and enjoyed the meal. My mom said he prayed for me: "May God keep him safe and working hard."

Every day we batted different houses and buildings in different towns. Ten miles, twenty miles, and sometimes as far as eighty miles. We had to finish batting a whole house within the same day, so we moved fast. Lunch break was only thirty minutes. Milton and Sean ate doughnuts, sometimes burgers they brought with them. I always sought a clean place and prayed. They both would come look at me bowing my head and reciting the Koran.

"What are you doing?" Milton asked me.

During the prayer I am not supposed to speak, so I was quiet and answered when I finished. "I was praying."

Milton picked up his phone and called everyone else who worked at the company and even his old lady. He made fun of the whole thing. "This dude bows and says he's praying," he said with a laugh.

I had to tell them that I am Muslim, I have to pray five times a day. "They got Muslims in Africa?" Sean asked.

Of course they thought all Muslims look like Osama bin Laden.

After work, Milton and Sean would stop at a convenience store to buy beer and cigarettes. Often they would ask to borrow money from me until the next payday. I always gave them a few dollars when they asked, but they never paid me back. I wasn't sure if it would be polite to remind them on payday.

One day on the job my hard hat disappeared. Another day my staple gun, then my winter coat. When I asked what could have happened, Milton laughed and said, "That's what happens when you're new here." The boss said he couldn't do anything. I had to buy a new hard hat and a new staple gun from the shop. I had no idea who was stealing my stuff until one day I found my hard hat in the back of Milton's pickup truck. The same guys I'd been working with for months, and when I asked, they said nothing! It was humiliating, and it felt as if my American dream was shrinking.

I asked Joey to put me on a different batting squad, and I was told to work with a guy named Tom. He was respectful to me, rolling down his window when smoking weed. He had been to prison several times, due to drugs, and he said he wanted to stop. But he explained that he needed the weed to do his job. Tom wanted to go to college, and he asked me questions about my life back in Africa. I told him about the wars and the death and the escapes, and he shook his head in disbelief. "Dude!" he said. "I grew up with an abusive dad and I spent seven years in prison, but that's nothing compared to your shit."

Tom and I got along well. I felt it was safe to leave my things in his truck. He wanted to see the world outside the United States; he wanted to explore. He told me he liked watching *National Geographic* TV shows. He watched shows about the Maasai Mara and Serengeti national parks in Kenya and Tanzania. We talked about lions, hyenas, and wildebeests. I told him stories about my mom and dad facing lions in real life. I liked Tom, but I noticed the drugs he took to cope with work also seemed to cause his troubles.

There was always a radio on the work site, always blaring rock and roll, blues, or country music. The guys could name all the bands and artists, but they didn't know anything about American history. They couldn't name many presidents except the most recent ones or George Washington, and they didn't know about the Black Hawk Down incident, even though there were pictures on the Internet of dead American soldiers being dragged through the streets of Mogadishu. They had no idea where Somalia was.

Many of the guys on the batting squad had lost their licenses from drunk driving, so they all gave each other rides home. Milton gave Sean a ride, and Tom picked up two other people. I asked if someone could give me a ride home, and Milton said I would have to pay him gas money. None of the other guys gave him gas money, but he wanted twenty dollars a week from me. I told him I was happy to walk home, even though I was so tired and dirty after work.

I don't know if the guys on the batting squad were racist; I hadn't been in America long enough to know about that. But it did feel like something I understood very well: the tribalism of Somalia. I have heard Americans complain that Africans bring on their own problems with their tribal feuds, and there is some truth to that. But these Maine guys had a tribe too. Maybe they didn't call themselves Darod or Hawiye, but it was a tribe, and I definitely was not a member.

So I had to walk home, up Main Street, looking like some homeless guy in my filthy work clothes and covered in pink fiberglass threads. Fortunately, the people of Yarmouth got to know me and realized I was just a hardworking guy. When I got home, I took off my rough clothes, took a warm shower, dressed up nice, and walked back toward Main Street to relax at the Dunkin' Donuts. People waved and smiled. I started to feel like part of the community and not just an outsider like I felt at work.

The batting squad guys were getting excited for winter because it meant they did not have to worry about sweating so much on the job. The trees went bare, like skeletons. A cold wind came straight in from the sea, but the sky was bright blue. On my day off I walked across the meadow of dry grass behind the house. Natalya's horse was growing a winter coat. At the dinner table the weather news was on; there was a brutal and early winter storm coming to Maine, they said. A "northeaster." People were instructed to drive slow; schools were canceled. Everyone around the table had been preparing. There were shovels ready at the front door. Wood was thrown into the burning stove.

"We'll have to give you a ride to work tomorrow," said Gib. "It will be hard to walk in the storm." I went to bed at seven o'clock as usual and woke up at four, when it was still dark outside. Out the window of my room I saw it was snowing a lot—my first snow! I noticed the flakes falling silently, not like rain. The sky was glowing white and hazy.

I got dressed and went outside to help Gib shovel the walkways. Snow covered the cars and roofs. The roads were hardly recognizable. Trees were dancing in the storm; the only sound was limbs creaking under the snow, which kept falling and falling. My hands turned numb from the cold, even with gloves. As we drove to work, the car heater was still warming up and I was shivering, both hands buried in my lap. "This is what we call *winter,* Abdi," said Gib, smiling. "It may get even worse." All day at work I was freezing because there was not yet any heat in the buildings where we were installing the batts. I needed warmer clothes.

The winter went on. So much snow fell that I could hardly see our house, or out of our house; the snow was higher than the windows, and the paths we had shoveled became like the walls of a giant maze. We were running out of places to put all the snow. Dump trucks were taking snow from the store parking lots to the ocean. It felt good to come home from work in the evening for a warm shower and a tasty dinner. I turned up the heat, browsed Netflix, and watched lots of movies, one every night before bed. I watched movies I had seen back in Africa that inspired me with the American dream because watching again helped me understand many things. In Somalia once I watched *The Grey,* with Liam Neeson playing a guy battling wolves in Alaska after his plane crashes. I didn't really understand how terrible it could be in the wilderness during a snowstorm. Now I watched it again and it made sense.

Every night after a great movie I buried myself underneath a warm blanket and thought about my past life, the tough times, the near-death escapes. My heart warmed with the knowledge that I was far away from that pain, even as I worried for my family. But waking up in the morning for work, I had to face another freezing day on the batting squad, my own real-life version of *The Grey*. At least there were no wolves. I didn't mind the hard work, but I hated the cold.

One day the manager of the company called me into his office to tell me I was getting a raise to twelve dollars an hour. He put me on the night shift with a batting squad insulating a new school building on an island off the coast of Portland. Every evening we took our truck out to the island on a ferry, then worked all night as more and more snow fell. One of the crew members was Bob, a tiny guy who had piercings in his lower lip and tattoos on his neck. The other guys called him Mini because he was so small. His nickname reminded me of the militiamen in Somalia who had nicknames like "Long-Eared" and "One-Eyed," and I called him Bob. He seemed to like doing his job, but he cursed a lot, maybe to make up for his small size.

One time during our midnight break, Bob started a conversation with me. "Man, I am fucking scared for my wife," he said, explaining that he didn't like leaving her home alone all night. He said his town had a bad record of gun violence and thugs breaking into houses. He had lost a brother to a drug dealer who shot him twice in the head. "I got a fucking gun in my house so my wife can protect herself," he said. I asked him if he had ever seen anyone get shot and he said no, just animals when out hunting.

All of my co-workers liked to go hunting; they shot deer and turkeys and sometimes even moose and bears. They told stories about Americans getting accidentally killed by guns in the woods and how you needed to wear orange during deer season. They talked all the time about guns and what kinds of guns they liked best. I knew lots of guns too, but not the kind they took hunting. Of course I always saw lots of weapons in Hollywood movies but didn't really understand how much

Americans thought about shooting guns. It wasn't just hunting; all over the news that winter were stories of black Americans getting shot by police. There was so much talk of racism; I didn't know this existed in the United States. Every day was a new surprise.

I couldn't believe Americans were scared for their lives in their own homes until I heard stories like Bob's. I slept in my big white room peacefully, with no sounds of gunfire anywhere around or police kicking down my door for a bribe.

Then we had a gun incident at work. Jimmy, one of the older guys working at the company, was fired for smoking weed inside the office. I guess he couldn't wait until getting on the truck. His co-workers had a day full of fun talking about their friend getting fired as I listened in surprise. But the next morning Jimmy returned to the shop with a rifle in his hand, threatening to spray bullets on us. It was a Friday and payday, so all the guys had been in a good mood, talking about how they would spend their money over the weekend. But the happy day turned into a frantic game of hide-and-seek as we scattered behind stacks of insulation. The cops soon arrived and managed to get the gun from Jimmy before they arrested him. It was still so early in the morning most of Yarmouth was still asleep. Until then the only white Americans I had seen with guns were those handsome marines in Mogadishu, and they always pointed their weapons away from us. I had no idea Americans turned guns on each other like Somali militiamen, and this left me scared and confused.

Months passed and the winter finally ended. The warm weather felt so good, but I realized I had been in America almost a year and without much progress. I was trying so hard to fit in, but I had so much to learn. One day I left the stove on, I forgot you have to turn it off, it's not like a cookfire that burns out. Sharon and Gib were so patient and kind, but my pride made me embarrassed to make mistakes. Sometimes I went upstairs, lay in my bed, and remembered the good old days when thinking about America was heavenly. I was realizing nothing is easy, even in America.

Somalis are pretty reserved around strangers; until you know someone, it's considered best to listen respectfully and be quiet. But most Americans speak their minds right away. They are not afraid of starting a conversation. I struggled for months to gain such confidence.

I didn't want to admit this to myself, but I was also suffering from post-traumatic stress disorder. Since then I have learned that virtually all Somali refugees have some version of this. I would wake up at night in a sweat, having nightmares, which only made me more tired at work. When I wasn't working, I spent more and more time up in my room watching movies and surfing the Internet. I talked on the phone with Hassan a lot, and for some reason I found peace talking to him about life, even though he was still at the mercy of the brutal Kenyan police. He kept telling me that everything would work out fine. Hassan was preparing to marry his new sweetheart—another Somali refugee, a woman he had met in Little Mogadishu who was selling fruits and milk on the street. Together we planned his wedding over the phone. We had fun talking about the music and food he would arrange for the wedding.

I found myself missing all my African friends and our shared language and culture. I missed drinking Somali tea and sitting around on floor mats eating dinner with our hands, no forks, no spoons. I realized that as horrible as my life was in Africa, I was homesick.

I knew I could not reasonably go back to Kenya even for a visit, much less Somalia, but I longed to see more of America. I wanted to see the America from movies, where black people in sneakers play basketball on the side of the street. I heard that a group of immigrants played soccer every weekend in Portland, and I decided to join them.

Gib gave me a ride down to the pitch on Back Cove. I couldn't believe what I saw—Iraqis, Burundis, Rwandans, Somalis, Latin Americans, and other people, all playing soccer together. I heard Spanish, French, Swahili, Somali, Kinyarwanda, Arabic, and more. But together we all spoke English, our one common language. I had no idea all these people lived in Maine! About a third of the players were female, white American women who loved soccer. They played hard and scored goals, roaming the pitch as defenders, strikers, and even midfielders. I'd never seen anything like this either.

I joined up quickly and had an amazing day, even scoring a goal. We played rough, lots of tackling and tripping, stuff that would definitely draw penalties in a professional match. But at the end of the day it was handshakes and congratulations to the winners, so much fun. As much as I loved my family in Yarmouth, I decided I needed to be close to these people.

16

Respect

Through a friend of Sharon's I was introduced to Abdul, a young man who ran an agency in Portland that helped settle new Somali immigrants, most of whom suffered from trauma and emotional stress and spoke no English. Abdul took me to the main mosque in town, and I couldn't believe all the Somalis, most of whom had cars, jobs, and their own homes. Within a week I said warm good-byes to my new American family, quit my job on the batting squad, and moved into an apartment in Portland with Abdul and three other Somali guys. The second-floor apartment was in a complex of several nearly identical buildings, spread out on a winding road amid lots of trees, like a suburban street. Many of the apartments had Somali and other refugees, or really poor Americans, and were publicly subsidized. We paid the market rate because we all had green cards and could work. My plan was to get a job in Portland; until then I would pay my four-hundred-dollar monthly rent and utilities out of savings.

It sounded like a TV show: five Somali guys in a small Maine apartment. There was Abdul, the only one of us who had already become an American citizen. Yussuf and Awil worked at Walmart and the Shaw's grocery store; Mohamed was a taxi driver. The apartment had only two bedrooms and one bathroom, but we just spread out mattresses and slept all over the floor, taking turns in the bathroom. I was in charge of making breakfast, usually Somali sour pancakes called *anjara,* with peas and some cubed lamb or goat from the halal market. For lunch everyone was off at work; dinner was the Somali version of beans and rice known as *ambulo,* drizzled with sesame or olive oil and a little sugar. Okay, a lot of sugar. Of course we ate on the floor, with our hands, just like in Africa. We laughed so hard, wrestled, drove together to soccer games and the mosque, and maybe washed dishes once a week.

My roommates had all been in Maine over ten years, making me the new guy in town. But I was surprised how little American culture they had absorbed. I would play the latest hip-hop songs on my phone while I cooked, but they just listened to Arabic chants called *nasheeds.* No one except me had a passion for America. Abdul was the only one who had even bothered learning English, which he needed for his work. In their jobs stocking shelves at Walmart and Shaw's, Yussuf and Awil didn't really need to speak English. They knew where the cans went, how to open boxes, how to punch in and out of the time clock. When customers approached them with a question, they would scurry away—too embarrassed to confront an American and be caught with no English, like being naked. The same with Mohamed, who knew only enough English to collect fares and enter addresses into the GPS of his taxi.

I said to them, "Ten years in America, why don't you learn English? You could get better jobs! Cashiers make more than shelf stockers, but they need to speak English. And you could have fun on the weekend, going to movies and parties." But Mohamed, Awil, and Yussuf felt like they were just biding their time until they could return to Somalia. They checked the Somali news every day, hoping peace would come. In a decade none of them had ever been outside Maine, except to Boston to make a flight back to Somalia. They had all returned home at least twice for visits, and they talked about enjoying camel milk and camel meat, which you can't find in Maine. Mohamed's dad was the chief of a village in southern Somalia, and Mohamed hoped to inherit the crown when his dad stepped down. When he went back to Somalia, the villagers gave him a royal reception, literally showering him in camel milk. It must have been hard to come back to Portland and pick up passengers at the bus terminal. Of course his family in Somalia thinks he's rich.

All my roommates were supporting their families back home. None of them had a savings account; every penny they did not spend on their own small expenses went back to Somalia. There were always too many people to support and not enough money. Every week was the same: you got paid on Friday; you sent whatever money was left over from the last week to your mom, or your dad, or your uncle or brother in Somalia or Kenya. Life was one paycheck at a time, so different from my American friends who always talked about their future goals. They wanted to go to college, get a good job, save money to buy a house or travel, the usual things. For most Somalis in Maine, the only future goal besides going home was to have money left over at the end of the week so your family in Somalia could boil some beans and maize.

My roommates were members of either the Hawiye or the Darod clan, each of which has a huge number of people living in Maine. My Rahanweyn clan does not have much of a presence here in Maine, and often I felt disconnected. Every Somali I met asked me about my clan. When I told them Rahanweyn, they would ask me what I was doing in Maine; there are more Rahanweyn in Minnesota or Seattle, they said. But I told them I was not here to reunite with my tribe, I was here to be American. That sounded like a crime to them—to abandon your clan and become an American! To them you could not be Somali without having a clan.

In Somalia, al-Shabaab and even the more moderate imams always told us that everyone in America was a crusading Christian bent on converting Muslims and destroying Islam. So I was really surprised when I got to Maine and saw that nobody I met was interested in talking about Jesus or Christianity. Most Americans seemed like they would rather spend their Sundays outside, or reading the paper, or having brunch, or doing just about anything besides going to church. In Kenya there are so many more Christian churches; pastors even get onto the public buses and preach, waving the Bible and spreading the word. I never saw someone preaching on a bus in Maine or Boston. I learned that when a stranger was nice to me, it was enough to just say "thank you," not "God bless you."

Shannon, my American friend from Bangor whom I had met on the health project in Kenya, and her friend Tina told me they were spiritual but not religious. They lived with their boyfriends, even though their families had big houses. They preferred to live their own way. That individual liberty was such a new concept to me, to most Africans, and it was scary but exciting. It got me thinking that this is a great nation where you can be anyone, as long as you can assimilate and learn the language and customs. That was my task, and I worked at it every day. So many figures of speech to memorize! Someone asked me, "What is your apartment situation like?" I started describing the kitchen, the bathroom, the location. Then he said he meant who were my roommates, how much was the rent, and so on. The "situation."

I have always been fast to learn languages, but now I was finding that customs and culture were much harder to absorb, and in these cases my language skills often failed me. Discussions about American music, sports, TV shows, food, breeds of dogs, and species of birds just made me sit there like an idiot. Sometimes I felt all I could talk about were my own life stories. People appreciated hearing them, but I also wanted to feel like I belonged here and could talk about American things. So I vowed to keep learning.

I was often invited by my American friends to go hiking, skiing, and other fun weekend things, and I always accepted. On these trips we would split the cost of everything, gas, food, hotel rooms. This is an aspect of American culture very different from Somalia, where it is the custom that one person is honored to pay for the meal. One time my roommates and I had lunch together at the Babylon Iraqi restaurant. After the goat meat and rice I took out my debit card and asked everyone to do the same. "Let's split it," I said. But they were all angry and astonished I would suggest this thoughtless American custom. They insisted I pay for it all.

Likewise in our apartment when Somali guests came from Minnesota or Seattle, we would let them share our beds. Two people in one bed. Or I would sleep on the floor in the living room and let them take my bed. But when I visited my American friends in their houses, they asked me to sleep in the living room. They never shared their own bed! I found myself constantly juggling the customs of these two different worlds.

When I returned from the movies or hikes or other fun things to my apartment, I would recount my activities. My roommates asked if I had prayed during all the fun. When I said no, they yelled at me for becoming too American. "You have abandoned your faith for a hike in the woods!"

My roommates also thought outdoor activities were stupid.

"Why bother building a camp in the wilderness when you can sleep in your freshly made bed?"

"We came here from refugee camps. Camping is not fun!"

"We hiked hundreds of miles through the bush into Kenya, now we have cars we don't need to hike!"

Birthdays were another strange concept to my roommates. Everyone in our apartment except me was born on January 1. One time an American co-worker at Walmart brought Yussuf some cupcakes for his birthday, and it made him so angry. He felt like this American had crossed unwritten boundaries by involving him in an American custom. In Somalia no one cares about age. People are born and die. Period. When he got home, he threw the cupcakes in the trash. My roommates thought I was crazy for picking June 20 as my birthday, but why was that any worse than picking January 1? Of course my family in Yarmouth put a huge effort into celebrating my birthday every year, with a cake and candles and a big dinner. And my American friends on Facebook always left me warm birthday wishes. On June 20, I always felt like I was born an American.

The Somali community in Maine is run by sheikhs and imams, who lead the prayers at the mosques. In Portland, the Muslim Community Center is where everyone gathers to pray, especially on Friday. Sheikh Ahmed is one of the top leaders, and he also owns a halal market. One day he delivered a speech warning Somali women not to fall into the temptations of individual liberty that American women have. "Look, they sleep with their boyfriends who are not married to them!" he said. "And their parents are fine with it! *A'udhu billahi minash shaitanir rajim.*" I seek shelter in Allah from the rejected Satan!

The women sufficiently condemned, he switched to the men.

"We've got a problem in the Muslim community in Maine. So many of our young men are abandoning the culture. Some even live with white families! Some are dating white non-Muslim women; some are drinking alcohol. This is a huge problem. We ask for your support to do counseling for these young men for them to return to the word of Allah."

I have always considered myself blessed by amazing good luck, which makes it hard to understand how Sheikh Ahmed could have lived right downstairs from us. He would pound on our door at five every single morning, waking us up and demanding we go with him to the mosque for morning prayers. Every day was the same: as we rode with him in his car, he asked us to read the Koran on the way so we should arrive safely at the mosque. Portland is not known for roadside bombs or militia roadblocks, so these prayers seemed like overkill on the short drive, but Sheikh Ahmed wasn't taking any chances. He recited the Koran every time he stepped out his door. To him Somalia and the United States were the same when it came to death. You could die any day, anywhere, and you'd better read the Koran to be safe.

In the evening, Sheikh Ahmed often came up to our apartment, to make sure Satan was not hanging around. I would have to stop the hip-hop music because he might curse at me. He walked around our house like he was doing an inspection. One time I had two portraits sitting next to my bed, Obama and Schwarzenegger. Sheikh Ahmed recognized Obama of course and told me to remove his image. "It is not good for you," he said. "Who is this other man?"

"A famous actor," I said.

"Please throw him in the trash! Angels are not coming into this apartment!"

The next day he brought us five beautiful calligraphy verses to hang in our rooms and a prayer mat.

After Sheikh Ahmed found out about my white family in

Yarmouth, he would come to our apartment for hours of talk and questions.

"Do they let you practice your religion?"

"Do they eat halal meat?"

"How do you deal with the dog?"

"Do they ever ask you to convert?"

"Can we convert them to Islam?"

To him there was no middle ground, no mixing. "You must choose one or the other." It was just like the clans, I thought. Either Rahanweyn or American, Christian or Muslim. I got frustrated and walked away. Then I started ignoring his morning prayer calls. There are two types of people in the Somali community: those who go to the mosque (the good ones) and those who go to the clubs and drink alcohol (the bad ones). Even though I didn't go to clubs or drink alcohol, I managed to be lumped into the bad-guy category because of my love for American culture.

The sheikhs in Portland told people to do the same things they expected in Somalia: women should not go outside without their husbands, men should wear ankle-length clothes and a beard, and on and on. But here in the United States they couldn't force people, especially me. I had memorized the Koran; I knew and respected my religion. But still my roommates and I got into heated debates about the message the Koran sends. To them the message was clear: you must be a God-fearing person and stay away from anything that could distract you from the five daily prayers. At their jobs at Walmart and Shaw's, Yussuf and Awil asked their bosses for prayer breaks. And so every day, somewhere in the back of the building with all the other Somalis, they would throw a mat on the floor and pray to Allah behind the stacks of canned hams and flat-screen TVs.

I came to see that my roommates would never assimilate,

and they were not alone. Like the first Italians or Chinese or Slovaks who came to America, the first-generation Somalis, many of whom were already old when they arrived, were too set in their language, culture, and religion. It would be the next generation to call themselves American, and they were the ones giving their parents, and the sheikhs, so many headaches by dating before marriage or even going to nightclubs and drinking alcohol.

Meanwhile, an army of caseworkers, many of them working for Christian organizations, rallied to help refugees navigate this strange new country. There was an opening for an interpreter on the Catholic Charities Maine website. People were needed in hospitals and courts who could help Somalis talk to lawyers, doctors, and judges. I quickly applied and a day later got a call from Lucy in its language department. "Oh, your English is good," she said. I went for an interview, filled out the usual forms. A week later I was hired, but before I could start the job, I was sent to take a required interpretation course at Southern Maine Community College.

My classmates were all foreigners from Burundi, Rwanda, Iraq, and even Russia. We were taught the medical and legal terms, the dos and don'ts of being an interpreter. They said we must never interact with clients outside the job; that would be unprofessional. I learned about the U.S. health-care system, medical terminology, basic human biology, systems, and treatments.

My first job was at Community Dental, translating for Farhan, an elderly Somali man who had been in Portland for two years. Farhan had a bullet wound on his head from a gunfight in Somalia. I sat across from him, next to the dentist, translating what the doctor said as well as what Farhan said. In the next few weeks I got more and more assignments, traveling to Maine Medical Center, Mercy Hospital, the Department of Health and

Human Services, Opportunity Alliance, Portland high schools, job fairs, the courts, and many other places around southern Maine.

I soon realized it would be impossible to maintain a professional distance from the clients. Many times they just wanted to ask me about my tribe or my background, and I felt it would be rude not to converse with them. Also, they often had so many questions about the law or the medical treatment that had not been answered by the lawyers or doctors. This was cultural: Sometimes a doctor would tell a patient to eat things, like yogurt, that I knew Somalis had never heard of. Doctors would ask female patients how often they exercised. I dutifully translated, but I already knew the answer: Somali women do not go around jogging in their hijabs. Often when we left the medical building, clients would pepper me with questions: *What does this mean? What did that mean?* Sometimes they would complain that the doctor must be stupid, then ask me where they could get traditional Somali medicinal herbs.

I had become an expert on the Portland public bus system, but I knew I would need to drive a car someday, so I started taking a driver's education course. The class, at Yarmouth High School, was all teenagers. I couldn't believe the way they sat with their feet up on desks, talking over the teacher and throwing things at each other. You would surely be whipped in Somalia for such disrespect. I paid careful attention, but I did not understand basic things like traffic lights or signs, things the American students all took for granted. The teacher was kind and helped me after class. When I was finally ready to start driving, the first thing I did was smash Sharon's car into her garage. It took me three times to pass the test for my license, but finally I became a safe and responsible driver.

In November 2015, I had saved enough money to buy a used car, which allowed me to take even more jobs. Now my assignments doubled, and I was interpreting for court cases in both Lewiston and Portland. I was in a courtroom with a Somali couple getting a divorce and arguing over the custody of their kids. I stood between the judge and the couple, simultaneously translating. As the couple's arguments heated up, my voice rose to match their angry tones. I felt like I was getting paid to be an actor, and in that moment I knew that all those years watching Hollywood movies in Falis's video shack were finally paying off.

One day I went to interpret at a dental center in Bath, Maine, about forty minutes up the coast from Portland. The patient was an elderly Somali woman, and her caseworker was the most beautiful girl I had ever met. She was tall, like me, with an open face and eyes that seemed curious to know all about the world. Half of her hair was uncovered, and she was wearing jeans with a light *dirac* on top. She seemed so outgoing and confident that at first I could not imagine she was a Somali immigrant. Her name was Fatuma, and she said she lived in Lewiston.

The old lady kept asking me about my tribe. We started discussing clans, animals, and life in the bush. Fatuma was just sitting there listening, but she had not said a word. I asked her to join our conversation, but she admitted her Somali wasn't very good and she couldn't follow us.

"A Somali who can't speak Somali?" I asked.

"I grew up in Vermont," she said in American English with no accent.

"So you are American?"

She smiled proudly. "My family came here when I was six."

Fatuma went to college in Vermont and Maine, earning a degree in social work. At age twenty-six she was already co-owner of the New Mainers Public Health Initiative, and she also worked with a community service agency. She was more

American than Somali, and for that reason she was under pressure from her parents to be more of a typical Somali girl who stays in the house and knows about her tribe and her family's history. Fatuma had two cats and lived in her own apartment with some of her siblings; I had never seen a Somali with a pet. She even named her cats after her best friends from high school, such an American idea. When I told her that I had been in the United States for only two years, she did not believe me. All she had been seeing in her work were newly arrived Somalis struggling to adjust. They would only talk about their tribes, but when Fatuma and I started talking, it was about movies we had seen, food we liked, and places we had hiked. It was just a typical American conversation, except with a Somali girl. That was a first for me, and the time flew by. Then the dental appointment ended and we said good-bye. A few nights later she texted me: "I like you. You are awesome!"

We got together for dinner a few times and began to develop a great friendship. I told her my life story and how I was the kid in Mogadishu known to all as Abdi American. She laughed so hard at the idea that I was already an American way back then. Every time we got together, Fatuma came with her hair showing and wearing pants. I told her she looked great. Her friends were American citizens; some were even white. They would have what they called girls' nights, and they would talk about makeup, clothes, and new music.

We took walks along the beautiful beaches of Maine; we drove to Vermont, where she showed me her old neighborhood in Burlington. I took her to Yarmouth and introduced her to my American family. Fatuma cooked traditional Somali samosas for Sharon and Gib; everyone liked her.

Then it came time for me to meet her parents. Although

they had been in the United States for twenty years, Fatuma's parents had not assimilated at all. Her dad had been an engineer in Somalia with a government job before the wars, but in Lewiston he didn't work; he spent his time in the mosque. Her mom was the breadwinner; she owned a store that imported all kinds of housewares and clothes for Somali immigrants. She traveled often to China, buying goods for her store.

I felt butterflies in my stomach the day I walked up to their house. Fatuma's dad was waiting outside the door. It was snowing, and frozen white flakes were sticking to his long beard like confetti. He shook hands with me and asked, "Did you pray today?"

I told him I did. He threw out several test questions about Islam, Somali culture, and places back home. I gathered he was not impressed by my tribe, but I think he still respected me because he and his wife had lived in Mogadishu in the 1980s, so we all had Mogadishan accents. As soon as we walked inside, he took out his phone and asked me for my dad's number. He dialed my dad in Baidoa and talked for a few minutes. Then he hung up and called my mom in Mogadishu. Within an hour, all four of our parents had arranged our engagement.

Fatuma and I felt so betrayed. We both well understood that in Somali culture "engagement" is not some symbolic commitment; Somalis don't get engaged and marry two years later, like Americans. It's basically a wedding announcement. Like with my sister, Nima, an engagement means the wedding will happen as soon as the goats and camels can be rounded up for slaughter.

Fatuma and I certainly felt stirrings of that commitment, but neither of us was ready to get married anytime soon; we just wanted to greet her parents out of respect. Fortunately, Fatuma was not afraid to speak up to them. She told her dad to hang up the phone with my mom and that she wanted to talk to him and her mom in private. The three of them disappeared into the bedroom for several minutes. When they came out, her dad was frowning, and her mom seemed mad.

Fatuma's parents were about to move back to Somalia. Her dad had health problems that he felt were made worse by the cold weather, and they decided to move back to their home in Kismayo in southern Somalia, even though it was surrounded by al-Shabaab and not very safe. They had saved money and were hoping to start a fishing business. They tried to encourage Fatuma to come with them, but she refused. Her home was America. Now they were understandably worried about their daughter being left alone, even though she had nine siblings in Lewiston.

"How can we trust him with you?" her dad said to Fatuma, as if I weren't in the room. "We don't want this American thing where people sleep together without being married. We are respecting our culture and glorifying our religion."

Then he looked me in the eyes and asked, "What is your intention?"

"Fatuma and I have only known each other for a couple of weeks," I said. "When we know each other better, we will make our own decision. We don't need someone to make decisions for us."

This would have been unthinkable to say to Faisa's dad in Mogadishu, but I was finding my American voice. Of course it helped that Fatuma was on my side. We were able to stand together and say no to an arranged marriage.

After that meeting, Fatuma's parents called her constantly. They would ask where she was, what she was doing, making sure she was not spending too much time with me. Finally the day came in April 2017 when her parents were leaving for Somalia. I had been invited to their house to say good-bye the day before. Her dad took me to the mosque. We recited the midday prayers, then he called together a group of other elderly men. We all sat together in a corner. Fatuma's dad took out a Koranic book and opened it.

"Put your hand in the book," he said. I did.

"Now swear that you will not have sex with Fatuma until you get married."

I was so shocked I had no words. I was thirty-one years old! Would sheikhs be telling me how to live for the rest of my life? Was this what I came to America for? I wanted to run out of that mosque, run away from Fatuma's dad and his long beard and those other stern men in that corner, but my parents had always taught me to respect elders, it is part of Somali culture. Then I thought, what about respect for Fatuma and for her decisions? That would be American culture. I had never felt so stuck in the middle, so unsure of my values. To be honest, I was also scared. I wondered if Allah would hold me to this oath. Fatuma's dad pushed the Koran closer. His eyes were drilling holes in my own.

I thought of all my struggles in life. I had truly loved my parents, but so many times I disobeyed them to follow my dreams. If I had listened to them, by now I would be an imam in Mogadishu, or beating kids in my own madrassa, or most likely a dead Islamist soldier. Was it disrespectful to do what I needed to do, say what I needed to say, in pursuit of my American dream? In everything I did for myself, I never hurt anyone else.

I thought about Fatuma. She was the answer. She was as American as the California girls I had seen in countless Hollywood movies. She had gone to an American public high school and college, lived in her own apartment with cats, wore blue jeans, had no accent and no concern about someone's clan. But she was also proudly Somali and had dedicated her life to helping other Somali refugees. Even if we weren't ready for marriage, we had talked about it and decided that we would definitely want our children to grow up speaking both English and Somali. We wanted it all, which seemed pretty American.

Fatuma's dad closed the book on my hand. I shut my eyes and said, "I swear it."

Epilogue

When I woke up on November 9, 2016, I felt sure it was all a mistake. Maybe I was still asleep, dreaming. Soon I would really wake up and Donald Trump would go away. This was the same Trump whose book I had read with pleasure while hiding from police in Nairobi. Now I felt I needed to hide from him. I had not been so devastated by world events, and so afraid, since the Westgate Mall attack in Nairobi. The same knot in my stomach. The same vague fear that things beyond my control were conspiring to destroy my American dream.

My phone started ringing with friends and family. The first call was from Hassan, who had been watching the election in Kenya. "Abdi, stay strong," he said. I could feel his voice shaking. "I hope it ends well. I hope he does not do what he said."

Whatever Trump would do, his rhetoric on Muslims was enough to scare everyone I knew. I found some comfort talking to Hassan, but it also felt like the world had turned upside down. When I said good-bye to my brother more than two years earlier in Kenya, I told him, "I am going to the land of the free. I am done with fear."

But I was wrong. I never thought Hassan would be calling

me from Little Mogadishu to say, "Don't worry, everything in America is going to be okay."

Leo called from the BBC. "Hey, Abdi, I can't believe what is happening in the U.S. How are you feeling?"

"I feel fear," I told him. "I feel threatened. I am really scared now."

"Oh, this is not what I expected you would say to me in America, Abdi."

Friends all across the United States started calling, offering to help me or even shelter me if necessary. That made me feel better, but I stayed home. There were lots of Muslims in our complex, so I spent all day peeking through the windows of my apartment to see if police were out there cracking down on people. I had no idea if cops would actually start rounding up Muslims in America, but there was also the potential for vigilante gangs feeling empowered by the election. I played it safe and avoided going out that day. It was like Little Mogadishu all over again.

My roommates stayed home too. Abdul was also frightened, even though he was an American citizen and had voted on Tuesday. But Trump's election did not bother Awil, Mohamed, and Yussuf, who were hoping to move back to Somalia anyway. "I will save enough money to buy camels," said Mohamed. "Soon I will be a chief and run my town."

So being deported was no big deal for them. But like all Muslims in America, they worried about violence. And for them, the election was proof of America's evil ways. "I told you!" said Mohamed. "America is the enemy of Islam. Now look! They have elected Trump." I had no argument against him that day.

We got a text to go to the mosque for a community meeting that evening. We rode together, and after evening prayers the sheikhs called for calm but also caution. "Don't go to the rallies," Sheikh Ahmed warned. "Avoid going to restaurants, parks, soccer games. Don't even go to the drive-through window at Starbucks. They can read your name from the debit card." Compared with some other states, Mainers generally treated Muslims with civility—the mosques had no security—but now we had reason to feel unsafe: that summer during the presidential campaign, hate notes had been left on the door of a Muslim family in Westbrook, near Portland, and some people said they had been threatened on Facebook with hate crimes and deportations.

"Women must not go to groceries by themselves," said Sheikh Ahmed. "They must go with men. You must pray more. Come to the mosque regularly. We are in a non-Muslim country, and we need to pray to Allah to keep us safe here until we can go back to our country." I raised my hand and shouted "Amen!" with everyone else. The threat was real. I felt I needed the safety of the community and prayers.

Sheikh Ahmed looked down into my face without saying anything, but from his burning eyes I could see he was thinking, "I told you so!"

I knew I could always go back to Yarmouth and stay with Sharon and Gib for safety, but I felt this was a time that the Somali community needed my support. Few refugees spoke English, so my interpretation skills could be needed more than ever if there was trouble. So I stayed close, went to the mosque every evening, and listened to updates of events during the day.

About a week after his inauguration, the president signed an executive order barring citizens of seven countries, including Somalia, from coming to the United States. That included permanent residents with green cards, like me. I was advised by a lawyer not to leave the United States for any reason, because I might not get back in. It was a comfort to see Americans protesting against the ban, followed by court orders striking it down. But the damage was real and affected my own family just as I had feared. A few days after the executive order, Hassan received a final denial letter from the U.S. embassy in Nairobi. It said, "As the request to review the case again has been rejected, the applicant has exhausted all avenues to seek a new decision on his refugee application and the original decision remains final."

My brother had now been a refugee in Kenya for fifteen years. Throughout that time he went back and forth for interviews to get resettled in the United States. Now his dream of coming to America was gone forever.

Hassan is now a husband and a dad of twins, a boy and a girl. There is no denying his marriage to Nasra had a practical side: Hassan knew that a single man applying for resettlement in America has fewer chances than a married man because he is more likely to be a terrorist. And for Nasra, marrying a Somali with a brother in the United States was a form of security. Nasra's parents live in Mogadishu, three miles from our mom. Her parents got together with my mom and slaughtered four goats, ate rice, and drank camel milk at the wedding, even though the bride and groom were not there.

As a gift, I sent a thousand dollars for Hassan to get a twin bed and some cooking utensils, new clothes, and some jewelry for his wife. He went back to school after things calmed down in Little Mogadishu, and in March 2017 he got his undergraduate degree in community health. Sharon had paid all his tuition. But now Hassan is back on the streets of Little Mogadishu hawking socks and shoes, struggling to support his family. In Kenya refugees are not allowed to work, even refugees with English and a college degree.

One day Nasra and the twins got sick. Hassan can't afford a clinic in Nairobi, so he did what our parents would do in Somalia: he read the Koran and made them drink holy water. Even though his children were both born in Nairobi, they do not have the right to be Kenyan citizens. Hassan is currently applying for their refugee papers.

Meanwhile in Mogadishu, my other nieces and nephews are growing up in the same civil war that has raged in one form or another for more than a quarter century. Somalia has changed little since I left. Al-Shabaab is active, and the African Union troops are still fighting them. Mogadishu has been reduced to rubble more than ten times. In October 2017, two truck bombs exploded in Zobe Square, the place where my brother used to hang out with his friends, killing more than 500 people, including two guys I had played soccer with.

My sister Nima's children are growing up in the usual Somali way. They go to the madrassa and get beaten so they will learn the Koran. The girls have undergone genital mutilation. When they come back to their two-room hut of corrugated-metal sheets at night, my mom tells them the same stories that she told us about the nomadic life in the bush. Chasing the dik-diks, jumping over thornbushes, singing around the campfires, and praying for rain.

The other day they sent me a picture of everyone. I could not tell my mom from my sister; they both look the same age. Nima has five kids. All her labors were in the house with no professional medical care; each was more complicated than the last, and her sixth child died inside her before being born. She underwent surgery; they said it was fifty-fifty she would live. She survived but remains sick and weak, and she stays inside the hut all day.

Omar, Nima's husband, no longer receives money from his cousin in America. Apparently, his demands grew too large after raising a family, and the cousin cut him off. He is jobless, wandering the streets of Mogadishu by day and returning home in the evening empty-handed. On May 8, 2017, his younger brother was killed in an al-Shabaab attack when they were walking together on the street. The terrorists were targeting a government official with a roadside bomb, but Omar and his brother happened to be there. Omar was slightly injured and is recovering. When I spoke to him on the phone, he said, "*Inshallah* I will be fine!"

Thanks to me, his kids don't have to beg for food. I do my best to keep food on their table and clothes on their backs, sending four hundred dollars every month. I know how hard it is to watch your own dad reduced to doing nothing in life. I trust at least they will not starve to death like my baby sister Sadia, but a new drought in Somalia has driven up the price of scarce food, and I can send only so much money.

My dad is in Baidoa with three kids from his second wife. He calls to ask for money. Sometimes I can't help him; it is hard to support everyone. But the drought has touched Baidoa hard, it is very dry and hot there. People and animals are in pain and dying fast. How can I let my dad go hungry? So I send him what money I can to keep him alive. I tell him to bring his family to Mogadishu and stay close to my mom so they can eat together to survive. But the road to Mogadishu is under the control of al-Shabaab, and they kill people leaving Baidoa. He is stuck.

Macalin Basbaas is an old man now and can barely walk, but he takes small steps to our house to say hello to my mom. He often visits at the end of the month when he knows I send money to her. She gives him food and sometimes buys him clothes. And several times I have sent him money directly. This may seem hard to understand after all the cruelty he showed me, but it would stress my mom to see him in misery, so I have helped. I also realize that without him I would never have memorized the Koran; those verses do comfort me every day. Macalin Basbaas probably does not remember cursing me when I danced at my sister's wedding. Back then I was the stupid man, the wasted student, not like my friend Mukhtar, his devoted assistant who died in jihad. Macalin Basbaas respects me now.

Siciid, my father's friend and our truck driver, died of natural causes. Falis, who introduced me to American culture in her video shack, also escaped Somalia. The last I heard, she was living in Nairobi, but I am no longer in touch with her.

In early 2017, I joined a group chat on WhatsApp with Faisa, who is living in the Dolo Ado refugee camp in Ethiopia. She recognized my voice and sent me a private message: "Is this Abdi American?" In no time we were speaking on the phone. When I told her I was in the United States, she could not believe it. We talked about our memories of good times on the beach in Mogadishu, before al-Shabaab came and ruined it. Our first stolen kiss, under the mango trees and the chattering monkeys by the river in Afgooye. How life had changed for us. Faisa is married now and so could not speak long to me.

I knew she had met a man of her own tribe a few years back. This was the guy in Sweden; they had connected online. He took the dangerous route out of Somalia through Kenya and Sudan and then across the Sahara Desert. He got arrested in Libya for a few months by gangs. His family bailed him out, and eventually he crossed the sea into Italy, and from there to Sweden, where his uncle lives. He has applied for asylum and is living in a crowded apartment with other refugees. He gets an allowance of sixty-five dollars a month from the government of Sweden. He can't drive, work, or travel. The government has not yet accepted his asylum, but the pictures he sent to Faisa got her excited about Europe. With the hope that this man will one day become a Swedish citizen, she accepted his marriage proposal. Their wedding, which her husband could not attend, was held at the Dolo Ado refugee camp. Several goats were slaughtered. Faisa said she danced. That made me happy.

Muna is still in Little Mogadishu, still looking for Mr. Right on Facebook. She is "dating" several men in the United States, one in Seattle, another in Minnesota, a third in Atlanta. She tells me she is getting close to the guy in Atlanta, who drives a truck. He is older and has another wife but has promised Muna that he will bring her over to the United States. He insists he can marry two wives at the same time in the United States under Somali culture, not the American system. I tell her that is not really possible and she will have no married rights in America. Muna doesn't bother to flirt with me. We are just friends and can share our stories and dreams.

My mom is getting old. She can't see or hear well, and she has no way to get eyeglasses or hearing aids. But she can still run fast and jump high; brave Madinah is still strong. She dreams of a Somalia without violence so that she can go back to her nomad life. I dream of bringing her to America, just for a visit, so at least she can experience a different life. I would love her to see snow and fall foliage, and let her taste the sweet drinks at Starbucks. I would take her to some farms in America where they have cows she could touch and smell, even if they're big and fat, not like the skinny long-horned cows my mom and her family had. Then I would let her go back and spend her final days in her beloved bush, gathering the fragrant herbs of the desert, bathing under the Isha Baidoa waterfall, and calling out to camels and goats. People can still actually live that way in the twenty-first century.

In Somalia, at least the politics have become a bit brighter. Along with the U.S. elections in 2016 came a presidential election in my country. The winner was a Somali American from

Buffalo, New York. His government is still only provisional and is not in control of the whole country, but it is a start. Half of the people in the current Somali government are from the United States. Some of them can't even speak proper Somali; they grew up here. So the "brain drain" is reversing course; Somalis who came to America as refugees are returning as leaders.

In the four years since I arrived in America, I have been on radio and television, in newspapers, and to conferences. I was a keynote speaker at the University of Maine. I talk often to high-school students around the state. I have traveled as far as Nashville to speak at Vanderbilt University. Every time I tell my story, I am reminded how lucky I am to be here. Abdi Iftin, a child of war in Mogadishu, with no more formal education than Macalin Basbaas's madrassa, speaking at famous universities! Once I wanted to be like Arnold Schwarzenegger; now my idols are those students I meet. I have enrolled at the University of Southern Maine and plan eventually to study law. Someday I hope to stand for president of Somalia.

No one from my Rahanweyn clan is yet able to run for Somali president. They are still considered lower class and unfit for the top job under the power-sharing system set up after independence in 1960. But the Rahanweyn are many, and politics can change. Someday I would like to be Somalia's first Rahanweyn president, but I want to run as a Somali American, not a Rahanweyn, promising peace and justice for all Somalis regardless of clan.

I want to land at Mogadishu Airport one day with a heart full of love and ambition for my people. Somalis overseas send back $1.4 billion every year to their home country, according to a 2016 World Bank report, through remittances to family members. This is more than all foreign government aid. But I think we could do more. What if we could spend that money to start schools in Somalia, teaching more than just the Koran? What if we built roads, sanitation systems, hospitals, apartment buildings? Islamic extremism is currently the greatest roadblock. Al-Shabaab prefers madrassas and child soldiers to clinics and colleges. And because they thrive on chaos, they love Trump and other politicians around the world who shake their swords at Islam.

But radical Muslims do not represent Islam. Nor do they represent the hopes and dreams of the Somali people. You can pray to Allah five times a day and still hold hands at the movies, this I know. I know it is possible to savor camel milk and democracy, to chase dik-diks across the bush and stop at red lights, to proudly name your nomadic ancestors and dance to hip-hop at your own wedding. These are not contradictions or abominations but reflections of our universal humanity and, yes, our shrinking world. How else to explain an African boy's love of *Terminator* movies, or African drumming classes being taught in American high schools?

My passion for America was ignited by Arnold Schwarzenegger. Hiding from militia fighters in Falis's video shack in Mogadishu, watching the Terminator dispatch his enemies from the seat of a motorcycle, I had no idea that my hero was not even born in America. Like me, he had a dream to call himself American since he was a child suffering abuse—in his case beatings from a strict dad. Like me, he had Hollywood movie heroes, including the athlete Johnny Weissmuller (also a poor immigrant!) of Tarzan fame. He taught himself English and made sure he was always ready when good luck came his way. And of course, no one had any clue he would one day become governor of California. Now I can see so many ways this poor boy from war-torn Austria was like the poor boy from violent Mogadishu. When Arnold was born, right after World War II, many people thought the countries of Europe were incapable of democracy; the same is said today about African nations. It took time and the support of America, but finally many of those European nations, including Germany itself, became beacons of freedom and tolerance. I hope that holds, but more important I hope that my own example reminds people of what is possible. No one gets to choose when or where to be born, but what happens after that is what you can imagine.

Acknowledgments

I could not have written this book without the tireless support, prayers, and encouragement of my family: my mother, Madinah Ibrahim Moalim; my father, Nur Iftin; my brother, Hassan Nor Iftin; and my sister, Nima Nor Iftin, have all shared stories from my childhood and their own. While these stories were already a part of my life, my parents and siblings filled in countless details important to researching the book over many hours of phone conversations between Maine, Kenya, and Somalia. Often these stories were painful for them to recall, and I applaud their bravery in revisiting ugly memories. While shocking to Westerners, my family's continuing struggle to survive will be sadly familiar to millions of other Somalis—to those like me, who got out, and to those like my family, who remain behind.

I also want to graciously thank the team that came to my rescue when I was living in Mogadishu as a young man hunted by radical Islamists and other armed factions: Paul Salopek, Cori Princell, Dick Gordon, Ben Bellows, and Sharon McDonnell and her family made a dream team that set up a fund to support my family and my journey out of Somalia to Kenya and finally to the United States.

In Nairobi, special thanks to Pamela Gordon, who took risks to help me, and to my friends Yonis and Farah, for standing with me together and texting each other when we became prey for the police.

I am grateful to have a wonderful literary agent, Zoë Pagnamenta, who mentored this book and my writing so diligently, and the fantastic team at Knopf, including Andrew Miller, Zakiya Harris, and Bette Alexander. Thanks to Max Alexander for the passion and guidance he brought to this book. I am lucky to live in the same state as Max, and the work we did together on this book was remarkable. Thank you, Max, for being such a good and supportive friend.

Very special thanks to Sharon McDonnell and her husband, Gib Parrish, for their generosity in allowing me to become a member of their family and to write this book in their house in Yarmouth, Maine. I would not have been able to complete it without their moral and material support. Thanks to Becky Steele and her husband, Douglas McCown, for standing up for me and other Maine Somalis after candidate Trump implied that we were criminals. Thanks to Kirk and Camille, who volunteered their time and ideas.

Finally, thanks to Nicole Bellows, Margaret Caudill, Leo Hornak, and the BBC, *This American Life* and Ira Glass for following and documenting my story in Kenya and America. I also want to thank Elizabeth Harvey, Yussuf, Abdul, Mohamed, Awil, Jihan, Hannah Read, Maya Tepler, Gil Morino, Meg, Rick, Nene Riley, Shannon Sayer, and Natalya and Morgan McDonnell.